ORDNANCE SURVEY MEMOIRS OF IRELAND

Volume Nineteen

PARISHES OF COUNTY ANTRIM VI
1830, 1833, 1835–8

Published 1993.
The Institute of Irish Studies,
The Queen's University of Belfast,
Belfast.
In association with
The Royal Irish Academy,
Dawson Street,
Dublin.

Reprinted 2021 by Ulster Historical Foundation

Grateful acknowledgement is made to the Economic and Social Research Council and the Department of Education for Northern Ireland for their financial assistance at different stages of this publication programme.

Copyright 1993.

All rights reserved. No part of this publication may be reproduced, stored in a retrieval system or transmitted, in any form or by any means, electronic, mechanical, photocopying, recording or otherwise, without the prior permission of the publisher.

Paperback ISBN 13: 978-0-85389-458-2
Hardback ISBN 13: 978-0-85389-457-5

Printed in Ireland by SPRINT-print Ltd.

Ordnance Survey Memoirs of Ireland
VOLUME NINETEEN

Parishes of County Antrim VI
1830, 1833, 1835–8

South-West Antrim

Edited by Angélique Day and Patrick McWilliams.

The Institute of Irish Studies
in association with
The Royal Irish Academy

EDITORIAL BOARD

Angélique Day (General Editor)
Patrick S. McWilliams (Executive Editor)
Nóirín Dobson (Assistant Editor)
Dr B.M. Walker (Publishing Director)
Professor R.H. Buchanan (Chairman)

CONTENTS

	Page
Introduction	ix
Brief history of the Irish Ordnance Survey and Memoirs	ix
Definition of terms used	x
Note on Memoirs of County Antrim	x

Parishes in County Antrim

Ballyscullion	1
Connor	16
Cranfield	32
Drummaul	33
Duneane	94
Shilvodan	127

List of selected maps and drawings

County Antrim, with parish boundaries	vi
County Antrim, 1837, by Samuel Lewis	viii
Coat of arms from Shane's Castle	67
Edenduffcarrick from Shane's Castle	68
Leather vessel from Ballycloghan townland	110
Forts from Lisnevenagh townland	136

List of O.S. maps, 1830s

Kells and Connor	17
Randalstown	34
Shane's Castle and neighbourhood	49
Toome	95

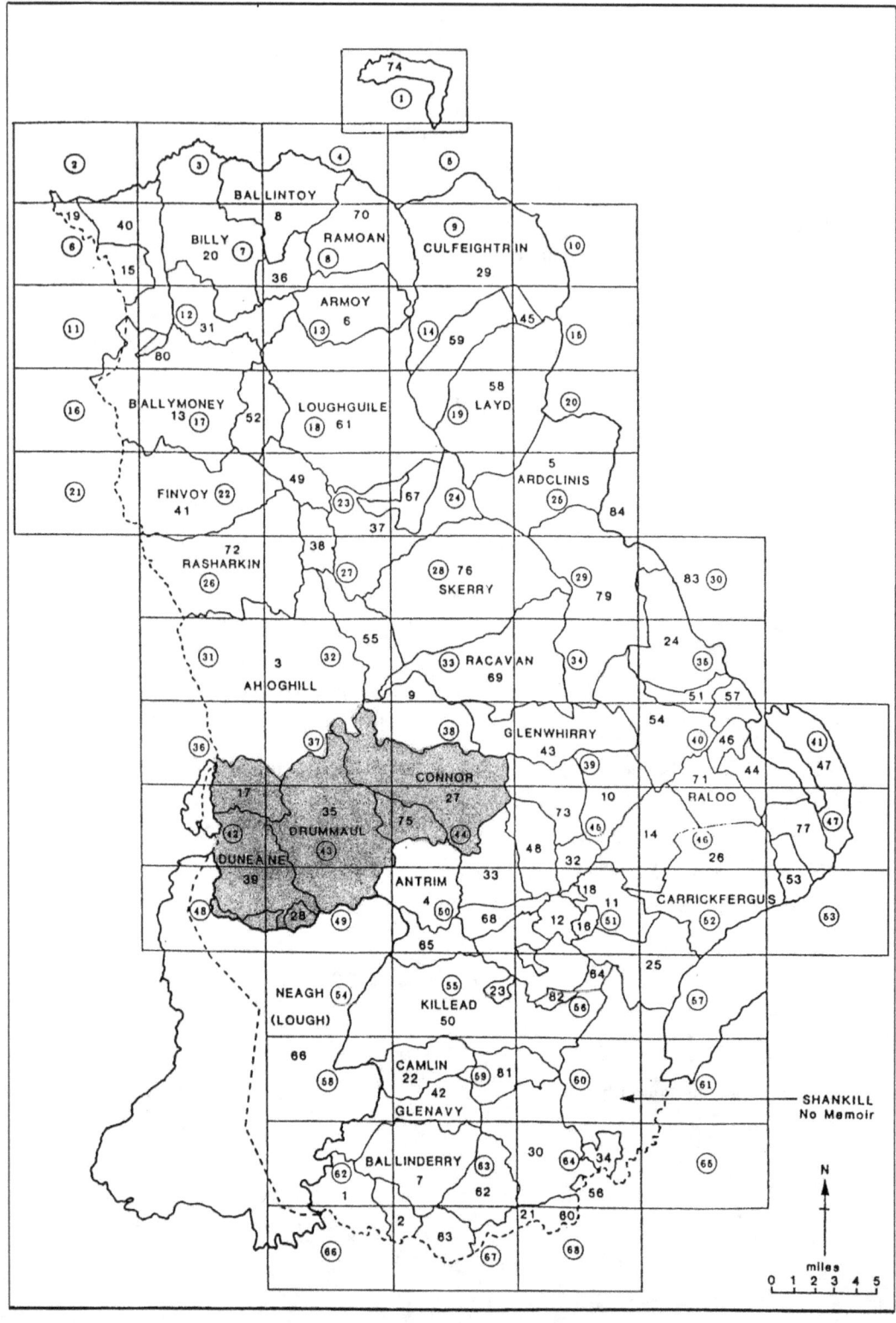

ACKNOWLEDGEMENTS

During the course of the transcription and publication project many have advised and encouraged us in this gigantic task. Thanks must first be given to the Royal Irish Academy, particularly former librarian Mrs Brigid Dolan and her staff, for making the original manuscripts available to us. We are also indebted to Siobhán O'Rafferty for her continuing help in deciphering indistinct passages of manuscript.

For permission to copy sections of the first 6" O.S. maps, we are grateful to Mr Roger Dixon, Irish and Local Studies Librarian, Belfast Central Library.

We should like to acknowledge the following individuals for their special contributions. Dr Brian Trainor led the way with his edition of the Antrim Memoir and provided vital help on the steering committee. Dr Ann Hamlin also provided valuable support, especially during the most trying stages of the project. Professor R.H. Buchanan's unfailing encouragment has been instrumental in the development of the project to the present. Without Dr Kieran Devine the initial stages of the transcription and the computerising work would never have been completed successfully: the project owes a great deal to his constant help and advice. Dr Kay Muhr's continuing contribution to the work of the transcription project is deeply appreciated. Mr W.C. Kerr's interest and expertise have been invaluable. Professor Anne Crookshank and Dr Edward McParland were most generous with practical help and advice concerning the drawings amongst the Memoir manuscripts. We would like to thank the Director of the Ordnance Survey, Dublin and the keepers of the fire-proof store, among them Leonard Hines. Finally, all students of the nineteenth century Ordnance Survey of Ireland owe a great deal to the pioneering work of Professor J.H. Andrews, and his kind help in the first days of the project is gratefully recorded.

The essential task of inputting the texts from audio tapes was done by Miss Eileen Kingan, Mrs Christine Robertson, Miss Eilis Smyth, Miss Lynn Murray, and, most importantly, Miss Maureen Carr.

We are grateful to the Linen Hall Library for lending us their copies of the first edition 6" Ordnance Survey Maps: also to Ms Maura Pringle of QUB Cartography Department for the index maps showing the parish boundaries. For providing financial assistance at crucial times for the maintenance of the project, we would like to take this opportunity of thanking the trustees of the Esme Mitchell trust and The Public Record Office of Northern Ireland.

Left:

Map of parishes of Country Antrim. The area described in this volume, the parishes of south-west Antrim, has been shaded to highlight its location. The square grids represent the 1830's 6" Ordnance Survey maps. The encircled numbers relate to the map numbers as presented in the bound volumes of maps for the county. The parishes have been numbered in all cases and named in full where possible, except those in the following list: Aghagallon 1, Aghalee 2, Ballyclug 9, Ballycor 10, Ballylinny 11, Ballynure 14, Ballyrashane 15, Grange of Ballyscullion 17, Ballywillin 19, Blaris and Lisburn 21 & 60, Grange of Carmavy 23, Carncastle 24, Cranfield 28, Derryaghy 30, Derrykeighan 31, Grange of Doagh 32, Donegore 33, Drumbeg 34, Grange of Drumtullagh 36, Dunaghy 37, Grange of Dundermot 38, Dunluce 40, Glynn 44, Inver 46, Island Magee 47, Kilbride 48, Killagan 49, Grnage of Killyglen 51, Kilraghts 52, Kilroot 53, Kilwaughter 54, Kirkinriola 55, Lambeg 56, Larne 57, Granges of Layd and Inispollan 59 & 45, Magheragall 62, Magheramesk 63, Grange of Muckamore 65, Newtown Crommelin 67, Grange of Nilteen 68, Rashee 73, Rathlin Island 74, Grange of Shilvodan 75, Templecorran 77, Templepatrick 78, Tickmacrevan 79, Tullyrusk 81, Umgall 82.

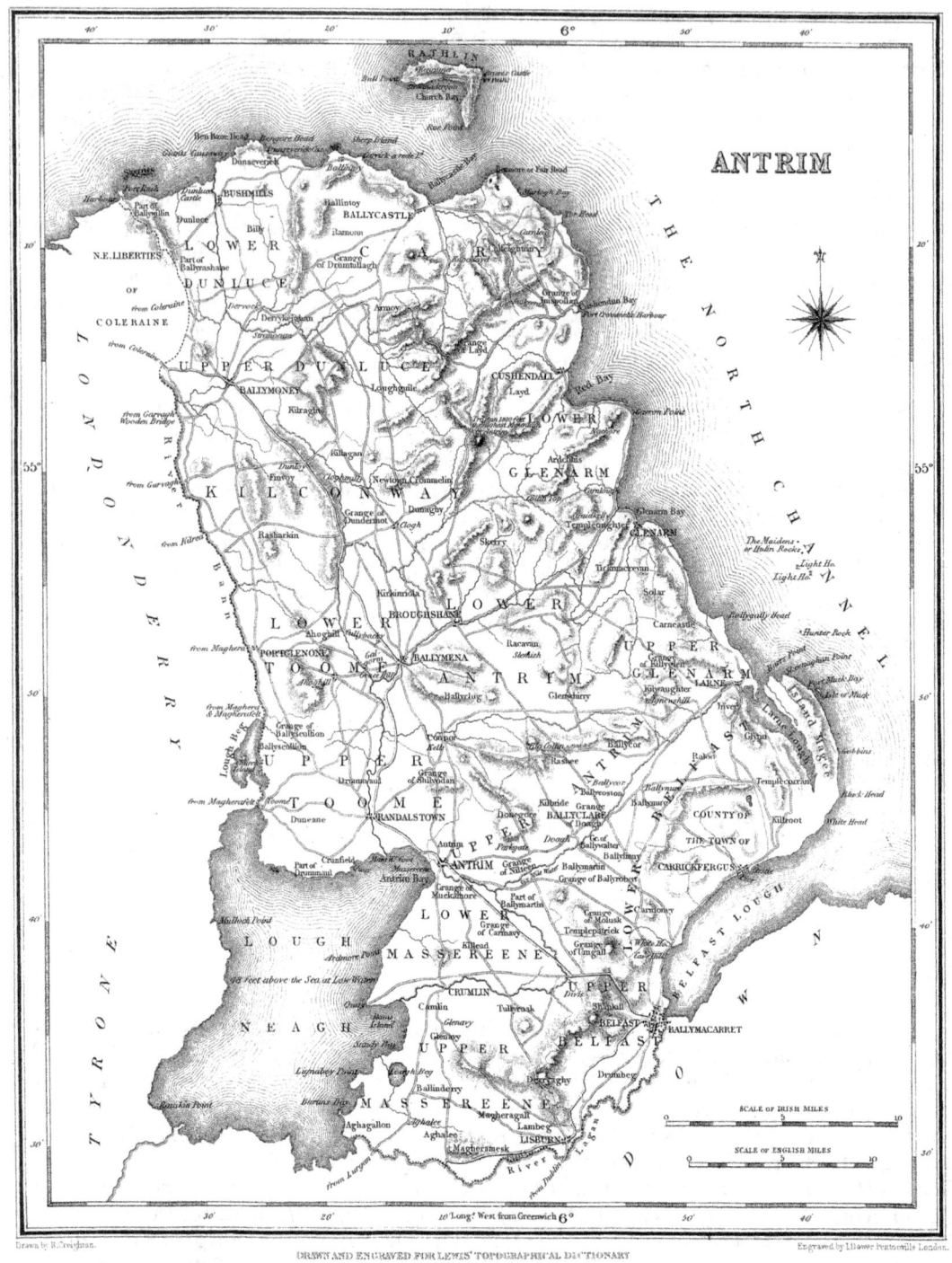

Map of County Antrim, from Samuel Lewis' *Atlas of the counties of Ireland* (London, 1837)

INTRODUCTION AND GUIDE TO THE PUBLICATION OF THE ORDNANCE SURVEY MEMOIRS

The following text of the Ordnance Survey Memoirs was first transcribed by a team working in the Institute of Irish Studies at The Queen's University of Belfast, on a computerised index of the material. For this publication programme the text has been further edited: spellings have been modernised in most cases, although where the original spelling was thought to be of any interest it has been retained and is indicated by angle brackets in the text. Variant spellings for townland and lesser place-names have been preserved, although parish and major place-names have been standardised and the original spelling given in angle brackets. Names of prominent people, for instance landlords, have been standardised where possible, but original spellings of names in lists of informants, emigration tables and on tombstones have been retained. We have not altered the Memoir writers' anglicisation of names and words in Irish.

Punctuation has been modernised and is the responsibility of the editors. Editorial additions are indicated by square brackets: a question mark before and after a word indicates a queried reading and tentatively inserted information respectively. Original drawings are referred to in the text, and some have been reproduced. Manuscript page references have been omitted from this series. Because of the huge variation in size of Memoirs for different counties, the following editorial policy has been adopted: where there are numerous duplicating and overlapping accounts, the most complete and finished account, normally the Memoir proper, has been presented, with additional unique information from other accounts like the Fair Sheets entered into a separate section, clearly titled and identified; where the Memoir material is less, nothing has been omitted. To achieve standard volume size, parishes have been associated on the basis of propinquity.

There are considerable differences in the volume of information recorded for different areas: counties Antrim and Londonderry are exceptionally well covered, while the other counties do not have quite the same detail. This series is the first systematic publication of the parish Memoirs, although individual parishes have been published by pioneering local history societies. The entire transcriptions of the Memoirs made in the course of the indexing project can be consulted in the Public Record Office of Northern Ireland and the library at the Queen's University of Belfast. The manuscripts of the Ordnance Survey Memoirs are in the Royal Irish Academy, Dublin.

Brief history of the Irish Ordnance Survey in the nineteenth century and the writing of the Ordnance Survey Memoirs

In 1824 a House of Commons committee recommended a townland survey of Ireland with maps at the scale of 6", to facilitate a uniform valuation for local taxation. The Duke of Wellington, then prime minister, authorised this, the first Ordnance Survey of Ireland. The survey was directed by Colonel Thomas Colby, who had under his command officers of the Royal Engineers and three companies of sappers and miners. In addition to this, civil assistants were recruited to help with sketching, drawing and engraving of maps, and eventually, in the 1830s, the writing of the Memoirs.

The Memoirs were written descriptions intended to accompany the maps, containing information which could not be fitted on to them. Colonel Colby always considered additional information to be necessary to clarify place-names and other distinctive features of each parish; this was to be written up in reports by the officers. Much information about parishes resulted from research into place-names and was used in the writing of the Memoirs. The term "Memoir" comes from the abbreviation of the word "Aide-Memoire". It was also used in the 18th century to describe topographical descriptions accompanying maps.

In 1833 Colby's assistant, Lieutenant Thomas Larcom, developed the scope of the officers' reports by stipulating the headings or "Heads of Inquiry" under which information was to be reported, and including topics of social as well as economic interest. By this time civil assistants were writing some of the Memoirs under the supervision of the officers, as well as collecting information in the Fair Sheets.

The first "Memoirs" are officers' reports covering Antrim in 1830, and work continued on the Antrim parishes right through the decade, with special activity in 1838 and 1839. Counties Down and Tyrone were written up from 1833 to 1837, with both officers and civil assistants working on Memoirs. In Londonderry and Fermanagh research and writing started in 1834. Armagh was worked on in 1835, 1837 and 1838. Much labour was expended in the Londonderry parishes. The plans to publish the Memoirs commenced with the parish of Templemore, containing the city and liberties of Derry, which came out in 1837 after a great deal of expense and effort.

Between 1839 and 1840 the Memoir scheme collapsed. Sir Robert Peel's government could not countenance the expenditure of money and time on such an exercise; despite a parliamentary commission favouring the continuation of the writing of the Memoirs, the scheme was halted before the southern half of the country was covered. The manuscripts remained unpublished and most were removed to the Royal Irish Academy, Dublin from the Ordnance Survey, Phoenix Park. Other records of the Ordnance Survey, including some residual material from the Memoir scheme, have recently been transferred to the National Archives, Bishop Street, Dublin.

The Memoirs are a uniquely detailed source for the history of the northern half of Ireland immediately before the Great Famine. They document the landscape and situation, buildings and antiquities, land-holdings and population, employment and livelihood of the parishes. They act as a nineteenth century Domesday book and are essential to the understanding of the cultural heritage of our communities. It is planned to produce a volume of evaluative essays to put the material in its full context, with information on other sources and on the writers of the Memoirs.

Definition of descriptive terms

Memoir (sometimes Statistical Memoir): an account of a parish written according to the prescribed form outlined in the instructions known as "Heads of Inquiry", and normally divided into three sections: Natural Features and History, Modern and Ancient Topography, Social and Productive Economy.

Fair Sheets: "information gathered for the Memoirs", an original title describing paragraphs of information following no particular order, often with marginal headings, signed and dated by the civil assistant responsible.

Statistical Remarks/Accounts: both titles are employed by the Engineer officers in their descriptions of the parish with marginal headings, often similar in layout to the Memoir.

Office Copies: these are copies of early drafts, generally officers' accounts and must have been made for office purposes.

Ordnance Survey Memoirs for County Antrim

This volume, containing the Memoirs for 2 granges and 4 parishes in south-west Antrim, is the sixth publication for the county and the nineteenth in the present series. It describes the scenery and life of this rural area, encompassing the ancient ecclesiastical foundation of Connor which gives name to the diocese, the bleaching district of Kells through to Randalstown and its hinterland down to the northern shores of Lough Neagh.

The amount of material for each of the parishes varies considerably, mainly in proportion to the extent of each, the parish of Cranfield comprising a few notes, while the parishes of Drummaul and Duneane are documented by very comprehensive accounts, including a brief early officer's report. The main Memoir writer for these parishes was James Boyle, a senior civil assistant, who was probably a small landowner in the mid-Antrim area, which may account for his candid remarks about the shortcomings of Lord O'Neill, the most extensive landlord in the area. His somewhat cumbersome style contrasts with his assistant, John Bleakly's more contracted style in the Fair Sheets. Boyle was responsible for the Antrim Memoir which was written in the same year as Drummaul, 1838, and which provides an interesting comparison.

The scope of the material is broad, covering aspects of economic and social life as well as history and antiquity. The accounts for both Ballyscullion and Duneane mention the decline of the domestic linen industry and its effect on local spinners and weavers, and describes the introduction of mill-spun yarn which kept hand-loom weaving and the local manufacture of union and calico as an important source of household income.

Among the different subjects covered by the heading Topography are a fine description of Shane's Castle, Dunraymond Cottage, a shooting lodge in the cottage orné style, and an account of the ancient bell of St. Patrick and its shrine, one of Ireland's finest examples of early metalwork, now in the National Museum, Dublin.

The Social Economy sections provide some of the most detailed descriptions of traditional life in this area. Bleakly's Fair Sheets for Ballyscullion contain interesting examples of the opening and closing prayers of the local temperance society at Grange Millquarter. Boyle records wake games in his account of Duneane; he also gives an eyewitness description of the rare occurrence of a moving bog at Magheralane in 1835.

To assist readers some of the material, particularly the Fair Sheets, has been rearranged to conform more closely with the Heads of Inquiry. Material relating to the parish of Cranfield has been transferred from the Duneane account and information for the parish of Rattass is included in the grange of Shilvodan.

Drawings in the Memoir papers are listed below and are cross-referenced in the text; some are illustrated. A drawing from the Drummaul Memoir appears to have been transferred, probably in the 1890s, to the volumes of bound antiquities sketches in the Royal Irish Academy catalogued as the 12T series. The manuscript material is to be found in Boxes 4, 5, 8, 9, 10 and 16 of the Royal Irish Academy's collection of Ordnance Survey Memoirs, and section references are given beside each parish below in their printed order.

Grange of Ballyscullion:	Box	4	IV 3, 4 and 1, 2 and 6.
Connor:	Box	8	II 4, 1, 2, 3.
Cranfield:	Box	8	III 1; also parts of Box 10 IV 6 and Box 5.
Drummaul:	Box	9	VI 4, 3, 1, 2, 5.
Duneane:	Box	10	IV 5, 4, 1, 4a, 3, 2, 6.
Grange of Shilvodan:	Box	16	I 4, 1 and 2, 3; also parts of Box 5.

Drawings

Ballyscullion (section 2):

Water wheel of Grange Park corn mill by J. Bleakly.

Drummaul (sections 1, 2 and 3):

Basalt column near Shane's Castle [by G.W. Hemans].

Marginal drawing of quern at Craigmore; plan of Roman Catholic chapel.

The Rock, Barnish townland, outline sketch of stones.

Plan of Three Island Cottage [all by J. Bleakly].

Map of Randalstown showing ancient borough boundary.

Ruins of Shane's Castle, front view looking from the west.

Inscription on doorway of vault at Shane's Castle.

Giant's grave, townland of Barnish, ground plan with dimensions.

Giant's grave, townland of Barnish.

Dunmore Fort in Shane's Castle demesne, scaled plan.

Ancient fortification in Shane's Castle demesne, scaled plan.

Fort in Shane's Castle park, scaled plan.

Forts in Shane's Castle Park, 8 scaled plans.

Forts with townland names, recording instances of fort types in each.

Arms sculpted in stone near Shane's Castle [illustrated].

Edenduffcarrick, the Black Face of Stone, at Shane's Castle, sketch showing face [illustrated].

Baptismal font at the Three Islands, view and section with dimensions.

Flint spears, flint arrow, brazen hatchet and stone hatchet, full size.

Ornamented quern, views and sections with dimensions [all by James Boyle].

Duneane (sections 1 and 3):

Wall of ancient Duneane church (small). Door of Duneane church (small).

Gable of Duneane church (small); cove in Ballyclaghan, plan and section with dimension.

Fragments of Toome Castle, with dimensions.

Cove in Mullaghgawn, plan with dimensions; cove in Moneynick, plan with dimensions; helmet from Derryhollagh bog.

Brazen dish object found in Derryhollagh bog, with section and dimensions.

Fragment of rim of decorated pottery crock from Derryhollagh, with side view and dimensions.

Leather drinking vessel, side views and bottom [illustrated].

Map showing relative position of standing stones [all by J. Stokes].

Flint arrowhead.

Brass hatchet.

Cave in Mullaghgawn, plan with dimensions.

Cave in Moneynick, plan with dimensions.

Cave in Ballycloghan, plan with dimensions.

Ancient meader from Ballycloghan townland.

Helmet found in Derryhollagh.

Brass hatchet found in Aghacarnahan.

Cave in Mullaghgawn, plan with dimensions [all by J. Bleakly].

Shilvodan (section 1):

5 forts, plans and sections, in townland of Eskylane; 4 forts, plans and sections, in townland of Tavnaghmore.

7 forts, plans and sections, in townland of Lisnevenagh [illustrated].

Brazen instruments: decorated pin brooch, pins, spearhead and axehead [all by James Boyle].

Grange of Ballyscullion <Ballyscullin>, County Antrim

Statistical Report by Lieutenant C.H. Mallock, August to October 1830

NATURAL STATE AND NATURAL FEATURES

Name and Situation

Grange of Ballyscullion, universally known throughout this part of the country as the grange. The spelling above is correct according to the authorities I could obtain, but adjoining the grange is a parish called Ballyscullion, thus spelt according to authorities obtained by Lieutenant Dalton. [Insert marginal note: See remark under the head of Divisions].

It is situated on the north west side of the half barony of Upper Toome, on the south east border of the county of Antrim, about 23 miles north west to west of Belfast and about 5 south west by west of Ballymena.

Boundaries, Extent and Divisions

It is bounded on the north by the parish of Ahoghill, on the south by the parishes of Duneane and Drummaul, on the west by the parish of Ballyscullion, on the east by the parish of Drummaul. It extends from the south about 3 miles, from the east to the west about 3 miles. It contains 4,263 acres. It is divided into 9 townlands, almost the whole of which are the property of the Massereene family. There appears to be much doubt if the grange ought properly to be called the grange of Duneane, or that of Ballyscullion. I have taken the name as given by the Boundary Department. The inhabitants, such as are Catholics, frequent the chapels in Duneane and are attended by the Duneane priest. The Presbyterians have a meeting house within the grange. They do not appear to be any way connected with Ballyscullion parish.

Surface and Soil

The ground rises gradually from the west, where its level is about 100 feet, to the east where the highest part is about 450 feet. There are not any very marked features. The hills throughout are generally low and round-topped and, as in the parish of Duneane, covered with large blocks of stone with stunted underwood and furze growing up between the stones. The general appearance is that of a thriving district, which is not so much owing to the fertility of the soil, it not being remarkably good, as to the leases under which the farms are held, which are almost all perpetuities.

Produce, Turbary and Minerals

The land is well cultivated, and produces wheat, oats, flax and barley. Oats and potatoes are the most productive crops. [Insert marginal note: See woods]. Turbary is abundant and of a good quality. Not any limestone: the nearest point from which it is obtained is from county Derry mountains. Not any minerals: the only stone in the parish appears to be greenstone.

MODERN TOPOGRAPHY

Towns and Villages

Not any town: the only place that can be called a village is situated in the townland of Taylorstown. Here there are 1 or 2 public houses and a Presbyterian meeting house.

Manufactories

In the grange, in common with the surrounding district, weaving of linen was a constant source of profitable employment to every member of a farmer's family, when their labour was not required on the farm. The employment is still continued, but the profit is now very trifling. On the banks of the Bann is a small brickyard. Bricks made there [are] not in much repute.

Roads

The principal roads through the grange are those leading to Toome, Ballymena and Portglenone <Portlenonge>. These roads are all pretty good. Besides the roads above mentioned, there are many throughout the grange, affording a ready communication from every part.

NATURAL FEATURES

Rivers

For about a quarter of a mile the north west corner of the grange is bounded by the River Bann. There are not any streams of consequence within the grange.

Bogs

The east portion, for about a quarter to half a mile from the boundary, is almost all bog. There is also some bog immediately adjoining the western boundary. These bogs afford a sufficient supply of fuel for the inhabitants. I think from the position of the ground there would be little difficulty in draining the whole of them, but the inhabitants generally, or the immediate proprietors, would not be very thankful for having it done, as it is of more value as fuel than it would be if reclaimed.

Woods

There are not any, but there are several orchards, all of which appear to be young. The trees look thriving, but there was little produce when I had an opportunity of seeing them.

SOCIAL ECONOMY

Population

The inhabitants are either Presbyterians or Catholics, and appear generally in comfortable circumstances. The nearest markets which they frequent are those of Portglenone, about 6 miles distant, Ballymena, about 5, and Randalstown <Randlestown>, about 5. To the latter almost all the grain is carried and the greater portion of the other produce. There is not a single resident gentleman within the grange.

ANCIENT TOPOGRAPHY

Antiquities

A few old forts <forths> are the only antiquities, and of these none are remarkable [signed] C.H. Mallock, Royal Artillery, Mohill, August 12th 1830.

SOCIAL ECONOMY

General Remarks

During the last few years the linen trade has been gradually declining. Most of the hands that were formerly employed as linen weavers are now employed on cotton. The land in the grange is all held in perpetuity under the Massereene family by a few individuals, and let again by them in small farms on leases of 3 lives, or a term of years. Rents average from 15s to 25s per acre. [Signed] C.H. Mallock, Lieutenant Royal Artillery, Antrim, October 27th 1830.

Memoir by James Boyle, April 1836, with additions from Draft Memoir, May 1835

NATURAL FEATURES

Hills

The surface of this grange extends over a small portion of the hilly ridge extending along the west of this county from the parish of Finvoy near its northern end to Lough Neagh at its southern end. The ground rises from the western side of the grange, from an average level of about 100 feet to that of 450 feet along its eastern side, on the summits of the ridge. The descent westward is broken by innumerable little oval hills, on the summits of which the basalt makes its appearance, and they are in general abrupt, particularly on their eastern side. The principal points are Taylorstown, 483 feet, Highland hill, 425 feet, and Gills' Tow, 413 feet above the level of the sea.

Lakes

A portion of Lough Beg, containing 4 acres 2 roods 32 perches, is included in the boundary of this grange, at the north west corner of which it is situated. Its elevation in summer above the level of the sea is about 46 feet, but it rises from 5 and a half to 7 feet in winter and, by its requiring a long time to subside, it retards the cultivation of the ground along its shore. Its deposit is immaterial. Its extreme depth in this grange is 20 feet.

Rivers

The River Bann flows for 726 yards along the western boundary of this grange. It issues from the southern extremity of Lough Beg and is 20 feet in depth and 106 yards broad in its course along this grange. It is navigable for vessels of 60 tons, but is not usefully situated for the purposes of machinery or drainage, owing to its trifling fall. It is subject to floods in winter and inundates the almost level country along its banks. It makes little or no deposit, but prevents the cultivation of the ground. Its bed is of a tough whitish clay, its banks almost on a level with the surface even in summer and the scenery along them cheerless and dreary. There is a ferry (the property of Lord Ferrard) across it in this grange. It forms an important means of communication between the neighbouring towns of the counties of Antrim and Londonderry. Its breadth 170 yards. A further description of this ferry will be found under the head of Communications.

Grange of Ballyscullion

The grange is amply supplied with spring water and water from rivulets for domestic uses, and several of the little streams flowing down are converted to the purposes of machinery and irrigation.

Bogs

A very extensive tract of bog extends along the eastern boundary of this grange, at an average elevation of about 430 feet above the sea. It extends into the adjoining parish of Drummaul, in which, under the head of Bogs, a description of it will be found. It is commonly known by the name of Groggan Island bog.

There are several small tracts of bog in the grange. The largest of these is near its western side. Fir and oak timber occur in them all. Their subsoil near the shore is whitish clay; in the interior of the grange it is bluish clay. But there is nothing in these bogs worthy of notice: in general they seem to have been the beds of small lakes or pools.

Woods

It is within memory since there was a good deal of the natural wood which covered the grange in existence, and within a century much of it has been standing. It has been principally oak, but all that now remains is brushwood, principally holly, hazel and oak, which abound in almost every townland. There are a few yews which do not, however, seem indigenous to the grange. [Insert addition: The summits of the hills are for the most part covered with a stunted underwood and furze growing up between the rocks. There are about 8 or 10 old yew trees scattered throughout the grange. These are very seldom to be met with in other parts of Antrim].

Many years ago, probably nearly 2 centuries ago, this grange was celebrated for its being the manufactory from whence the neighbouring towns were supplied with wooden houses, and those in the town of Antrim, which are built of and floored with oak planks, are said to have been constructed here.

Climate

The seasons in more interior parts of this grange are rather earlier than in its western districts and the crops ripen from a week to a fortnight earlier than in Drummaul. Along the western side the climate is rather moist and damp.

MODERN TOPOGRAPHY

Towns

There is neither town nor village in the grange. [Insert addition: The only place that can be called a village is situated in the townland of Taylorstown. Here are a Presbyterian meeting house and 2 public houses].

Public Buildings

The public buildings consist of a Presbyterian meeting house, situated in the townland of Taylorstown and on a road leading from Toome to Ballymena. It is a simple and substantial building 58 feet long and 22 feet wide, and well fitted up, and containing a gallery, and accommodation for about 550 persons. It was erected in 1833 at the cost of about 500 pounds, which was raised by subscription. [Insert addition: It was built in 1833 by the Grange congregation at the cost of 240 pounds already; will cost as much more before finished. It contains accommodation for 110 persons].

The Quaker meeting [house] is an uninteresting thatched building 30 feet long and 17 feet wide, and containing accommodation for 110 persons. It is situated in the townland of Mill Quarter and near the western side of the grange. It was erected in 1704 at the expense of Mr Walter Clark, who would not reveal the expense.

Gentlemen's Seats

There is not a gentleman residing in the grange. Lakeview is a prettily situated and modern residence in the townland of Taylorstown. It is inhabited by a Mr Canning, a respectable farmer.

Machinery

The machinery of the grange consists of 2 corn mills: one is situated in the townland [of] Mill Quarter and is propelled by an undershot water wheel 14 feet in diameter and 3 feet 4 inches broad [insert addition: fall of water 11 feet]. The second is in the townland of Grange Park and is propelled by an undershot water wheel 14 feet 8 inches in diameter and 3 feet broad [insert addition: fall of water 3 feet].

There is a small brickyard on the banks of Bann, in the townland of Culnafay.

Communications

This parish possesses every facility of communication with the neighbouring country, by means of the numerous roads traversing it in every direction, all of which are kept in repair by the baronies through which they pass. The principal road is that from Belfast to Portglenone, which traverses the centre of the parish for 4 miles from south to north. Its direction is poor and it is kept in tolerable repair. Its average breadth is 24 feet. This road is intersected near its southern end by the road from Toome to Ballymena, of which there is 1 mile in the grange. Its average breadth is 23 feet. It is unavoidably hilly, but is in pretty good order.

The by-roads are pretty good and are sufficiently numerous. All these roads are repaired with broken whinstone, which is abundant.

The ferry on the Bann, on the road from Bellaghy to Ballymena, is at the north west corner of this grange. Its direction is diagonal to the course of the stream and its extreme length between the landing places 170 yards. It is supplied with 2 boats: a small one for conveying passengers and a larger one for carts, cattle etc. The latter is a large flat-bottom float, with a falling gangway at either end forming an inclined plane to the landing place. A chain passing through 2 uprights in this boat, and made fast at each end of the ferry, is pulled by 2 men and the boat merely shot across. The charges are for each person 1d, for a man and horse 3d, for a cart 6d. It is the property of Lord Ferrard, who lets it at an annual rent of 18 pounds.

General Appearance and Scenery

The appearance of the lower districts of this grange are bleak, dreary and desolate, owing to the numerous patches of bog scattered over its surface, the partial cultivation of the ground and the almost total absence of plantings, which is not at all relieved by the untidy and generally comfortless appearance of the houses of the peasantry. Towards the east of the grange its appearance improves considerably. Cultivation and farming are making rapid strides, houses are particularly neat, cleanly and nicely whitened, and the prospect from the higher grounds is very extensive and beautiful. The very diversified surface of the grange render it admirably adapted for planting, particularly in its most uncultivated parts.

SOCIAL ECONOMY

Early Improvements

The western side of the grange of Ballyscullion is inhabited by a race who seem to be the descendants either of the aborigines of the country or of the earliest settlers in it, while the higher but eastern district is occupied almost exclusively by the descendants of the Scottish settlers of the 17th century. Among the former the names of McErlane, Ritchie and Kenedy, particularly the first, are prevalent, while among the latter, those of McDowel (pronounced here Madole) and Glover are very common. The difference between the 2 races is still very striking in almost every respect, the Irish being uncivilised, turbulent and riotous, poor in their circumstances, slovenly in their persons and habitations, and not very industrious; while the Scots are industrious and orderly, comfortable in their stations and remarkably neat in their habitations.

The differences between them, though still remarkable, is diminishing, and has diminished materially within memory, and it may therefore be inferred that the settlement of the Scots here was the earliest cause of improvement. They seem, in occupying the higher ground, to have chosen the most fertile, and that the original inhabitants retreated gradually among the woods and swamps in the lower districts, which are still far behind in cultivation, there being much wasteland in the grange and it being a comparatively short time since it was cleared of the natural woods which covered its surface.

The subsequent causes of improvement have been the fusion of useful and religious knowledge by the more active clergy of the present day and the increased facility of acquiring instruction, by the establishment of schools under societies which, by contributing to their support, enable the teachers to afford instruction at a low rate and place it within the reach of almost all.

Weaving

The manufacture of calico has been carried on very generally in this grange for many years and has afforded employment and support to the adult male and female population, children of 13 or 14 years of age being able to weave that article. The wages for weaving calico have latterly become very low and linen is now taking its place, but this is almost only the case on the eastern districts of the grange, where their cottages are of a better description, many, indeed most of those in the western side of the grange, being unfit for the manufacture of linen. "Union" (a fabric composed of cotton and linen yarn) is also manufactured here and the material of both it and linen are supplied by manufacturers, who give out the mill-spun yarn to be woven and pay the weaver according to the quality of his work. This has been an advantageous circumstance for the people and there are individuals residing in the grange who employ from 100 to 400 weavers.

Farming

From its having been so long a manufacturing district, farming has been, until within a very few years, almost wholly neglected, the people deriving almost their sole support by weaving. The consequence is that, except in the townland of Taylorstown (at the eastern side of the grange), the state of husbandry is very backward and a large portion of the grange remains uncultivated. There is little or no irreclaimable land in it, and it might be easily rendered capable of supporting an industrious population one-third greater than its present: but, except in the townland just mentioned, there exists a degree of apathy, negligence and apparent indolence in the people. Of course there are some few exceptions, in an occasional neat farmhouse, but these only tend to make the others look worse than they are.

Influence of Landlord

The people have been sadly neglected and the want of a resident gentleman, who could, by his station influence or example, control or improve them, or a landlord who would pay attention to their comfort or character, is sadly felt, as here there is no such thing, except the proprietor of Taylorstown, Samuel Thompson of Muckamore Abbey (near the town of Antrim) Esquire, who has set an example to landlords by the improvements which he has caused among his tenantry.

Among others may be mentioned the encouragement of the growth of green crops, by giving 7 premiums annually of from 10 to 40 barrels of lime each, according to their quality, for the best 7 half-roods of turnips, to enable the tenant to have a sufficient stock of winter feeding for his cattle; and that no tenant may be prevented from sowing turnips in consequence of not having a sufficient quantity of manure both for them and potatoes, a loan of lime to all who will plant potatoes on it and reserve the manure for turnips is offered. Seed for vetches is also given by Mr Samuel Thompson. Lime, which is very distant and dear, is laid down by him and the houses roughcast and whitened at his expense. The consequence is that in almost any district, but particularly in this, the townland of Taylorstown presents a most striking appearance of neatness, comfort and general improvement. It should have been mentioned that Mr Thompson offers as an encouragement for the bringing in of wasteland half the quantity of lime necessary, gratis.

These have been the more recent causes of improvement and it is to be hoped that their increased intercourse with strangers, and the example set them by their neighbours, may cause a more progressive improvement in the inhabitants of the more remote districts of the grange.

Obstructions to Improvement

The want of a resident gentleman or magistrate and the neglected state of the people by their landlords, having almost neither precept nor example nor assistance of any kind, and the retired and out-of-the-way situation of the western districts of the grange, where the people have little or no intercourse with strangers, are serious disadvantages which must tend to retard their civilisation and improvement.

Local Government

There are neither magistrates, police, manor courts nor petty sessions held in the grange of Ballyscullion. The nearest manor courts or petty sessions are those held in Toome, the former once a month and the latter on every alternate Tuesday. A good deal of illicit distillation is carried on here along the western districts of the grange, but not near so much as formerly. Riots, quarrels and assaults are frequent among the people in the west of the grange, but any outrages are base, arising from private quarrels. A few are occasionally imprisoned for these offences. There are few, if any, insurances.

Dispensary

There is no dispensary in the grange, but patients from it are admissible to that in Randalstown. It has materially increased the comforts of the poor man and improved the health of the people, as it in many instances affords assistance which, from the poverty of the people, could not otherwise be procured. Fever and rheumatism, arising from the want of sufficient nutritious food, the increased moisture of the climate, the insufficient state of their houses to withstand the weather, their slovenliness and absence from lime, are the principal diseases; but no separate list of those occurring here is preserved. For further details relevant to the funds of this dispensary, see parish of Drummaul.

Poor

This is one of the few northern districts in which a legal enactment to secure a provision for the aged, helpless and infirm is much wanting. As there is [no] support for them except in the charity of their neighbours and as there are few rich, very many poor and such an equality as to circumstances, much cannot be expected from them.

Schools

Schools are doing much good in this grange and their effects are beginning to be perceptible among the rising generation. Their introduction here is of modern date and, so far as the people are able, they avail themselves of the benefits of education; but very many are still unable to pay the trifling sum necessary.

Religion

The grange of Ballyscullion is episcopally united to the parish of that name, but pays no tithes. The few Protestants in it worship at the church in Duneane. The Presbyterians support their clergyman in the usual manner and worship at their meeting house in this parish. The Roman Catholics worship at one of the Roman Catholic chapels in the adjoining parish of Duneane. By the revised census of 1834 there are in this grange 512 Episcopalians, 1,536 Roman Catholics, 1,321 Presbyterians and 82 other Dissenters, who are chiefly Quakers.

Employment

As has before been stated, the great majority of the male and a portion of the adult female population of the grange are engaged in the manufacture of either linen, union or calico; but most of these also farm, holding from 2 to 5 acres. There are a few weavers who hold no land, and there [are] also some cottiers who are employed as agricultural labourers, but their numbers are few, there being little employment for them. Along the western and northern districts of the grange they are in general [crossed out: very] poor, but as they approach its western side, they improve. There are few of the class that is generally understood by "farmers" and there [is] much equality as to circumstances.

Houses

Towards the west their houses are in general small, comfortless, badly roofed and anything but neat-looking, built of stone, thatched and having the usual accompaniment of a manure heap. They are dirty and damp, seldom consisting of more than 2 apartments and frequently of only one. They are usually in clusters of from 3 to 6, built without attention as to their position with regard to each other. But they are improving in their habitations and those lately built are pretty comfortable and neat. The farmers' houses are large and substantial. In the townland of Taylorstown the houses are equal in cleanliness and neatness of appearance to those of any other district, being annually whitened, well roofed and kept in good order; but for this purpose they receive lime gratis from their landlord, while in the other districts they are unable to procure it, from its distance and expense, and this certainly is some excuse for the appearance of their houses.

Habits of the People

In their habits considerable difference exists, the Scottish being rather industrious and peaceable and well disposed, and more neat in their system of farming, and still retaining much of the custom and dialect of their forefathers; while the others are careless, turbulent and quarrelsome, slovenly in their persons and habitations, and not very civil or obliging. They are quite different in many parts in their manner and are free from the dialect of the others. Ribbonism also exists here. They drink an immensity of whiskey and attend wakes for amusement.

Their food consists, throughout the grange, chiefly of potatoes and milk, some freshwater fish, salt herrings and a little meal; but scarcely any animal food (except among the farmers) is consumed. Along the western districts their dress through the week is bad; indeed, this is the case throughout the grange, but particularly so in these districts, where they are slovenly in their persons; and even at fairs and on Sundays their appearance is inferior, as their clothes, though warm and comfortable, are not so good or neatly put on. In these districts also, the women do not always wear bonnets, which is not the case in the others. Turf, which is very abundant, is their fuel.

Among the Roman Catholics marriages take place at an earlier age than among the Presbyterians, but there are no remarkable instances on that head, nor on that of longevity. It is said that their age is decreasing in length owing to the early age at which the children are now put to work and their food not being so nutritious as formerly. The usual number in a family is 6.

Grange of Ballyscullion

Amusements

Cock-fighting and dancing are still their favourite amusements, particularly in the west of the grange. The former is kept for a few days in Easter week and other times, but not so much so as formerly. Going to wakes and fairs is still, with some of them, a source of amusement. The Ribbonmen have occasionally celebrated Patrick's Day by walking in procession, but they have no patrons' days. There are no ancient customs nor traditions except those relating to enchantments, fairies etc. There is nothing peculiar in their appearance, except that those in the eastern side of the grange are rather uncouth looking.

Emigration

From 12 to 15 persons have annually emigrated to the British settlements in America during the last 2 years, previous to which time many more used to go annually; but the want of encouragement has given check to emigration. Very few return. A few go annually to the Scottish harvests and return when they are over. This custom also is decreasing, from a similar cause.

Remarkable Events

There are not any remarkable events upon record, nor has this grange given birth to any remarkable person.

Table of Schools

[Table contains the following headings: name, situation and description, when established, income and expenditure, physical, intellectual and moral education, number of pupils subdivided by age, sex and religion, name and religion of master or mistress].

Name [blank], in a suitable house originally built partly by the Kildare Place Society and partly by subscription, in the townland of Taylorstown, placed under the Board of National Education in 1834; income: the board pays the teacher an annual gratuity of 8 pounds, from pupils 16 pounds; intellectual education: Greek and Latin, Homer, Horace, spelling, reading, writing, arithmetic, book-keeping, mensuration, books of the National Board; moral education: Sunday school, all versions of Scriptures at stated hours and catechisms on Saturdays; number of pupils: males, 16 under 10 years of age, 9 from 10 to 15, 5 over 15, total 30; females, 13 under 10 years of age, 12 from 10 to 15, total 25; total number of pupils 55, 3 Protestants, 32 Presbyterians, 20 Roman Catholics; master James McDonnell, Roman Catholic.

Name [blank], in an excellent and suitable house built for the purpose partly by the London Hibernian Society and partly by subscription, in the townland of Mill Quarter; established 1828; income: the Society pay the teacher an annual gratuity of 7 pounds, from pupils 12 pounds; intellectual education: spelling, reading, writing and arithmetic, books of the London Hibernian Society; moral education: Sunday school, visits from Protestant clergy, Authorised Version of Scriptures daily and church and Presbyterian catechism on Saturdays; number of pupils: males, 8 under 10 years of age, 5 from 10 to 15, 2 over 15, total 15; females, 13 under 10 years of age, 7 from 10 to 15, total 20; total number of pupils 35, 12 Protestants, 7 Presbyterians, 16 Roman Catholics; master Thomas Scullion, Roman Catholic.

[Totals]: income from public societies or benevolent individuals 15 pounds, from pupils 28 pounds; number of pupils: males, 24 under 10 years of age, 14 from 10 to 15, 7 over 15, total 45; females, 26 under 10 years of age, 19 from 10 to 15, total 45; total number of pupils 90, 15 Protestants, 39 Presbyterians, 36 Roman Catholics.

Fair Sheets by J. Bleakly, March and April 1837

NATURAL FEATURES

Bogs

The flow bog near the Bann in the grange is about 20 feet deep in the deepest part and about 10 feet in the edge; was never cut away. The imbedded timber consists of oak chiefly. The largest is 2 feet in diameter, found near the edge and points eastward.

There is a by-road at present making through the above bog, but not finished. It is 16 feet clear of drains and fences, by presentment. From John Harris, farmer. 24th March 1837.

The small bog below Mr Harris' house in Millquarter townland was about 20 feet deep, but has been all cut away twice and is now cutting the third time. It is nearly 10 feet deep at present. Chiefly fir is the imbedded timber and at present presents the appearance of pinnacles about 2 feet above the surface. The largest stick found in this bog made the mill axles <axils> for Ballymatoskerty corn mill. From John and William Harris and William McMullan.

The flow bog of Ballyscullion is about 20 feet

deep. Oak 4 feet in diameter found 2 years ago, top eastward.

The road leading through the above bog is 21 feet clear of drains and fences, by presentment, and in very bad repair; a by-road. From John Smyrell, farmer, Ballyscullion.

MODERN TOPOGRAPHY AND SOCIAL ECONOMY

Grange

The grange is situated east of the River Bann and near Lough Beg. It contains 3,351 inhabitants, viz. of the Established Church 512, Presbyterians 1,221, Roman Catholics 1,536 and of other denominations 82. There are 3 places of worship in the grange, viz. a Presbyterian meeting house, a Baptist meeting house and a Quakers' meeting house.

Presbyterian Meeting House

The Presbyterian meeting house is situated in the townland of Taylorstown, on the road leading from Toome to Ballymena <Ballymenagh>. The meeting house is not quite finished. It is 54 by 40 feet outside and contains 51 single pews. Each pew would contain 7 persons. There are 10 oblong windows on each side 2-storey high, and 2 Gothic windows on each end; 1 door on the end, no gallery. Meeting house was commenced in 1833 by subscription and cost about 376 pounds. The congregation consists of about 300 families, average at 5 persons to each family, who come from Duneane parish, Ballyscullion, Drummaul and a few from Ahoghill <Aoghil>.

The average collection for the poor on each Sunday amounts to 5s. The following are the persons who gave towards its erection, who are not members of it: Lord Ferrard gave 5 pounds, Marquis of Donegall 5 pounds, Lord O'Neill 5 pounds, General O'Neill 5 pounds, the Earl of Belfast 5 pounds, Samuel Thompson Esquire of Muckamore Abbey 5 pounds, Sharman Crawford Esquire gave 13 pounds, Reverend John Brown 5 pounds, John Shiel Esquire 2 pounds, county Derry, and the rest by subscription of the congregation. This is the third meeting house which was built on the site of the old one, on the same ground. 23rd March 1837.

The Presbyterian meeting house contains 51 single pews, each 7 by 2 feet 7 inches, total dimensions inside 50 by 36 feet inside.

Original Clergy

About 20 years ago the grange and Duneane were a union of parishes. The following are the original ministers as far back as can be ascertained, from the oldest inhabitants: 2nd was the Reverend [blank] O'Brian; 3rd was the Reverend Robert Scott; and in 1824 the Reverend Robert Rusk, who still continues and whose income is 100 pounds per annum, viz. 50 pounds regium donum and 50 pounds stipend. His residence is near the meeting house in the townland, in a low thatched house. The trees round the meeting house yard were planted about 20 years ago, chiefly fir. From the Revd Robert Rusk, minister, and William Reaney.

Baptist Meeting House

The Baptist meeting house is situated a little above the Presbyterian meeting house, in the same townland. The house is not yet finished, nothing but the walls and roof. It is 24 by 18 feet inside and of stone, slated, with 6 oblong windows no longer than the windows of a common farmhouse, and cost about 50 pounds, chiefly by subscription of the congregation, except 21 pounds viz. 16 pounds from Dublin and 5 pounds from Belfast. There is no regular minister. The members speak themselves and are about 20 in number. This is the first Baptist meeting house which has ever been erected in this part of the country. It is about 30 years since the Baptist congregation commenced in this parish and held their meetings through the houses in the neighbourhood. From the Reverend Robert Rusk, Presbyterian minister, and William Reaney, a member.

Origin of Baptists at Grange

July 27th 1809, the Reverend George Grey, Baptist minister, who was educated under the superintendence of Robert Holden Esquire of Edinburgh, a Baptist, came to the old Presbyterian meeting house of Grange and preached a sermon, and established a Baptist congregation in the grange.

Corn Mill

The corn mill at Millquarter is of stone, thatched and only in middling repair. Single-geared; the machinery is contained in 1 house. The water wheel is 15 feet in diameter and 3 feet broad across the buckets. The fall of water is 8 feet, but idle in spring and summer from want of water.

Quakers' Meeting House

The Quakers' meeting house is situated a short distance from the mill in Millquarter and is 31 by

Grange of Ballyscullion

18 and a half feet inside, and contains 12 single pews, or rather seats as there are no boarded backs to them, each 14 by 2 and a half feet. No gallery except a platform without seats and in bad repair: no pulpit. The meeting house was built about 130 years ago, of stone, thatched, at the [expense] of Mr Walter Clarke, a Quaker. 3 square windows each 4 by 3 feet. The gallery occupies 11 by 18 and a half feet. The wall in front is 5 feet high and built in 1836 at the expense of the congregation, and cost 5 pounds 5s.

There is no minister. The congregation consists of only 3 members, who meet on every Sunday and Thursday from 11 till 1 o'clock. The yard contains 3 roods of ground, meadow which was originally for the use of the congregation's horses, but now the produce of hay goes to defray the expense, and was granted also by Walter Clarke. This congregation is considerably decreased. From Mr Thomas Chapman and Isaac and Samuel Clarke, members.

Quakers' Graveyard

Near Harris' corn store at Millquarter the Quakers have a small burial graveyard, the mould of which is supposed to have been [?] sifted, from its fineness, and without a single stone or lump in the whole. There are no gravestones in this yard. It was granted by the person who gave the meeting house yard.

Original Quaker Settlers

The Clarkes were the first Quaker settlers in the grange, and came from England with the Massereene family about the year 1655. Their first meeting, before the meeting house was built, was held in the house of Gabriel Clarke, a Quaker, near the meeting house. From Mr Thomas Chapman, Quaker.

Orange and Mason Lodges

There are 2 Mason lodges in the grange and 2 Orange lodges in the grange. One of the Mason lodges admits into it members of all denominations and the other, held in Aghavery, will take none but Protestants and Presbyterians. From Thomas McLoughlin.

Grange House

Grange House was built by Thomas Courtney Esquire upwards of 100 years ago. It is 2-storey high, slated and situated on the road leading from the Cross Keys to Portglenone, in the townland of Culnafoy. Joseph Courtney Esquire was the last proprietor, but has let it to a farmer named Patt Devlin. The planting consists of fir chiefly, about 6 acres English measurement, about 12 years planted. House in bad repair. 28th March 1837.

2-storey House in Millquarter

[The] 2-storey house in Millquarter is about 50 years built and occupied by Mr John Harris. Was rebuilt about 24 years ago by him, but is not in good repair at present. From John Harris, proprietor.

Lowburn House

Lowburn House was 3-storey high, and was standing about 10 years ago, but at present only a part is standing, which is occupied by Dr McDowell who has established a medical repository. George Charleton Esquire was the original proprietor, now deceased <diseased>. The house is situated near the Cross Keys in the townland of Ardnaglass. From Dr McDowell.

Rock Lodge

The 2-storey house near the Quakers' meeting house is called Rock Lodge and is occupied by a Quaker called Thomas Chapman. From Thomas Chapman, 1st April 1837.

Lakeview House

Lakeview, which is the residence of Philip Cannon Esquire, who came to it 1835: it was erected about 47 years ago by Pooly Shuldhane Esquire. The Reverend Samuel Shenton Heatley resided in it for some short time. The ornamental ground consists of about 3 acres Irish plantation measure, chiefly fir, and oldest planted about the time the house was built and the latest about 27 years ago. The house is slated, 2-storey high, in very good repair. The improvements are a new range of excellent office houses, slated, built by Mr Cannon within the last 2 years. From Philip Cannon Esquire, proprietor, and Edward Duffin, carpenter.

Slated House in Ardnaglass

The 2-storey house which appears so very conspicuous on the hill in the townland of Ardnaglass is slated, and occupied by Mr James Dobbin. From James Dobbin, proprietor. 31st March 1837.

Dispute about Right of Boundary

About 22 years ago a dispute took place about right of bog boundary in Gillistown, between

Viscount Ferrard, Captain Henderson of Castledawson, county Derry, John Sheil Esquire of Black Rock, county Derry, and Charters Reaney, farmer. Each claimed a part and Lord Ferrard claimed 2 parts. Each held land adjoining the bog and consequently claimed a part of the bog. Viscount Ferrard gained 2 parts by law and John Sheil Esquire gained one-third. Also a dispute between Viscount Ferrard, John Sheil Esquire and Nesbitt Downing Esquire, about a patch of bog in the townland of Aghavary, about 12 years ago. Messrs Sheil and Downing won it by law.

The above flow bog is about 20 feet deep. The imbedded timber consists of oak and fir. One oak about 3 feet in diameter is the largest, and pointed towards the east. The fir about 2 and a half feet in diameter, indiscriminately. From Joseph Hemerston and James Dobbin, farmers.

Roads

The leading road from Millquarter or Cross Keys to Ahoghill is 21 feet clear of drains and fences, and in middling repair, by presentment of grand jury, about 4 miles, by William and George Templeton. Information obtained from Lawrence McKenna, James Reaney and Patrick McErlain.

The leading road from Grange Presbyterian meeting house to Portglenone is 21 feet clear of drains or fences and in bad repair, and very hilly, chiefly near the old graveyard called Templemoyle in the townland of Taylorstown. Mr Holmes of Kilrea started a machine from Kilrea to Belfast, which is said to have ceased to run about 2 months ago on account of the road being so bad. This road is kept in repair by presentment. Also the road leading from Toome to Ballymena by the Cross Keys is 21 feet clear of drains and fences and in middling repair, by presentment. From Patt McErlaine and Lawrence McKowen.

ANCIENT TOPOGRAPHY

Ancient Graveyard

The old graveyard called Templemoyle is situated in the townland of Kilvillis, on the farm of Lawrence McKowen. Tradition says St Bridget intended to build a church here, but could not succeed in raising it higher than the foundation, on account of the workmen becoming drunk on beer distilled from heather, which had no froth on it until St Bridget ordered them to take some froth from the mouth of a boar which was to pass that way and cast it into the vessel which contained the beer, and which caused it ever after to contain a froth. When St Patrick heard of the conduct of St Bridget, in allowing the workmen to get drunk, he ordered her to wander about till she could find 2 blackbirds perched on a deer's horns, and which she found at Duneane church, and there she was desired to build a church, which now stands without a steeple, a "moyled temple."

Duneane signifies in the Irish language Dughen or Deahen or "2 birds perched on a deer's horns." The foundation of the old church is in the centre of the graveyard and is 75 by 25 feet in the clear. The oldest gravestone visible is dated 1749, name McClenaghan. From Lawrence McKowen. 29th March 1837.

MODERN TOPOGRAPHY AND SOCIAL ECONOMY

Licensed Shops and Illicit Distillation

There are 8 licensed grocers' shops and 6 publicans in the grange.

Illicit distillation was practised to a considerable extent in the lower part of the grange and in Ballyscullion until this year, which, from the scarcity of fire, it cannot be carried on to so great an extent. From Mr Thomas Chapman and Samuel Clark, farmers.

Grain Stores

The new grain stores at Millquarter are slated and 2-storey high, built by Mr Joseph Harris in 1835. From the proprietor Joseph Harris.

Public Characters

Peggy Frizell, a public character, is an idiot <idiott>, 35 years of age, resides chiefly at the Millquarter in grange, where she was born. She is a pauper.

Kate McCann is also an idiot about 60 years of age, and resides in Millquarter where she was born. Her sinews are completely contracted, which prevents her from ever moving. Her features are all disfigured. She was born so. From the Reverend William Boyes. 30th March 1837.

Corn Mill

The Grange Park corn mill is double-geared <geered> and is worked by 1 water wheel which is 14 feet in diameter and 2 feet 8 inches across the paddles. [Marginal drawing of water wheel]. The machinery is contained in 1 house 2-storey high, slated and in bad repair. Idle during the summer from want of water. The reason why this mill is in such bad repair is owing to the failure of Joseph

Courtney Esquire of Grange, as there is no regular owner at present for the mill. From Hugh Carmichael, miller.

Temperance Society

Grange Millquarter Temperance Society was established on the 16th May 1834, through the instrumentality of the Reverend Samuel Shenton Heateley and Mr Thomas Chapman, and held in the Millquarter schoolhouse. At its first meeting there were 16 names enrolled and has increased to 53 at the last meeting. The committee consists of a chairman, a secretary and 6 of a committee. The members at present meet in the house of James Reaney of Grange Park.

The first meeting was opened with prayer by the chairman, the Reverend Samuel Shenton Heatley, minister of Randalstown <Randlstown>, and followed by a short address delivered by Mr Martin, as a deputation from the parent society, in a very impressive speech. The Reverend Mr Smith of Craigmore succeeded him in enforcing the great object they had in view, to promote temperance. The Reverend William Boyes, minister of Duneane, succeeded him and addressed the meeting in a very eloquent and impressive speech, and made some excellent observations in favour of the society. The meeting concluded with praying. Resolution: "We whose names are herewith subscribed resolve to abstain from the use of ardent spirits and to promote temperance"; here follows the names. The meetings are held on the first Monday of each month. From the Reverend William Boyes, minister, and James Reany, member. 27th March 1837.

Opening Prayer for Grange Temperance Society

"Almighty God, who searchest all hearts and understandest all the imaginations of the thoughts, we beseech thee to pardon our utter unworthiness, and to suffer us now to approach thee through the new and living way which thou hast mercifully revealed, even thy son our Lord and Saviour Jesus Christ. We have begun, O Lord, to do a great work, and we look to thee only to give it effect. We cast all our care upon thee, for thou carest for us. We trust in thee with all our hearts and we pray thee to direct our paths. Guard us against trusting to ourselves and teach us to feel that if this work be of man, it will come to nought, but 'if it be of thee, it can never be overthrown.'

Grant that this and every other temperance society may be an instrument in thy hand for promoting thy glory and the good of man, of bringing many into the path of holiness, and of preparing the way of the Lord. Give wisdom to our deliberations, strength to our resolutions, success to our designs and a holy union and faithful perseverance in our object. Make us consistent in our lives and enable us, while we set ourselves to oppose drunkenness, to forsake also every other sin. Enable us to bear with patience the reproach and opposition of others. Be thou pleased to convince and convert them and give us wisdom in making to answer those that oppose themselves. Enable us to be temperate in all things, to live soberly, righteously and godly, and make us watchful against every sinful compliance, however moderate or trifling, which would invite us into the path that ends in drunkenness and sin.

We thank thee for the advocates and friends that have raised up in the cause of temperance, and for the fruit thou hast given to our labours, and we pray thee that thy spirit may guide and comfort them and us, and all who are engaged in it. Grant that all may have such a sense of the sin and evil of intemperance, that they may shun the customs and companions which lead to it, and keep us ever mindful that thy word declares not only the murderer but the drunkard shall not inherit the Kingdom of God. Bless all who are in any way striving faithfully for the increase of holiness, and for the spirit and temporal good of others, and succeed their labours. Bless them and us by thy spirit through Jesus Christ Our Lord, amen."

Concluding Prayer of Temperance Society

"Almighty and most merciful Father, who art the giver of every good and perfect gift, we, thine unworthy servants, humbly beseech thee to enable us to draw near to thee in prayer, with holy desires, with meek sincerity and with fervent devotion. Remove from our hearts every thought which would distract or unfit us for this solemn duty, and suffer us not to draw near to thee with our lips while our hearts are far from thee. Let thy spirit help our infirmities, for we know not what we should pray for as we ought. We desire to offer unto thee our most humble and hearty thanks that it has pleased thee to put into our hearts to follow the example of those who are striving in thy strength, to check the destroying flood of intemperance.

We praise thee for the success which thou hast given to our weak efforts, especially for those whom thou hast by strength reclaimed or preserved from drunkenness. Lord increase our faith and let these thy favours encourage us, in thy strength, to persevere and to rest our hopes for this society, and for all our earthly concerns, on thine arm alone. Remove, we beseech, every obstruction to the progress of truth, raise up everywhere powerful and devoted agents in this work, and spread abroad over this neighbourhood and nation the blessings of temperance, peace and godliness. Deliver us from the sin of wasting or abusing thy gifts by converting the fruits of the land into instruments of drunkenness. Give to all people just views of the grievous sin of intemperance, of the source from which it springs and the means by which it may be checked.

We implore thy mercy on behalf of those who are in any degree given to it. Thine arm is mighty to save. O be pleased to pardon them, and by thy converting grace, to turn them from the broad road that leads to eternal destruction of body and soul. Whatever good thy hast mercifully put into our hearts this evening, be pleased to establish, strengthen and settle within us, and keep it ever in our minds that of ourselves we can do nothing that is good, but that with thee all things are possible.

O let thy blessing rest upon us and our undertaking, and upon all who are engaged in it, and grant that our way may be made prosperous and that we may have great success. Let thy spirit rest upon us and go forth with us, to keep us unspotted from the world, and let it evermore guide, sanctify and strengthen us, and fill us with all joy and peace in believing. We ask all in the name etc., amen." From James Reany.

Moravian Settlement

About 8 years ago Mr Patrick McCort pulled down an old Moravian meeting house, which was thatched, a quarter mile from the Presbyterian meeting house on the road leading to Portglenone, in Taylorstown. A Moravian settlement was about to be established in Grange and was commenced, but did not succeed. From the Reverend Mr McCort, priest [insert alternative: curate] of Moneyglass chapel.

Houses in Taylorstown

There is a degree of neatness in all the houses on the property of Samuel Thompson Esquire of Muckamore Abbey. In Taylorstown all the houses are white outside and very neat inside. The lime is given free, and if poor, a workman is paid to put it on by the proprietor Mr Thompson, who also gives the tenants forest trees and quicks of all sorts. From John Glover and Patrick McCort, farmers.

Longevity

An old woman named Jane Mills, 120 years of age, died from accidental burning at the Cross Keys in Kilvillis about 10 weeks ago in [blank]. From Michael McErlaine. 4th April 1837.

Reading Society

There is a meeting held in the Taylorstown South national schoolhouse, chiefly for the improvement of the teachers of the Sunday school in this neighbourhood. 4 years established, through the instrumentality of John Lee, Joseph Glover and David Baily. Commences with singing and prayer and concludes with the same, by some of the members, which are chiefly teachers of the Sunday school. Chiefly held during the winter season and from 5 till 8 o'clock p.m. A chapter is appointed and 8 days given to meditate upon it and each member make observations on it. There are 12 teachers of the Sunday school in attendance at present. The meetings are conducted on the catechetical system. Information obtained from John Lee, David Baily and John Glover, teachers of the Sunday school.

Roman Catholic Chapel

The Roman Catholic Chapel in Ballyscullion is 40 by 20 feet inside, slated, and cost about 50 pounds by subscription, in 1831. No pews, 4 square windows and 2 doors, viz. 1 on each end, oblong.

Migration from Ballyscullion Townland

List of persons who migrate annually from Ballyscullion. [Table lists name, age, townland, religion, port. All Roman Catholics, to Glasgow].

Hugh McKee, 40, Archy McKee, 36, Patt McKee, 38, John McKee, 18, Henry Toole, 20, James Scullion, 22, Reynold McKee, 30, Hugh Lafferty, 27, Joseph McCue, 36, Michael Feeney, 34, Hugh Hardy, 30.

Migration

List of persons who migrate annually from the grange of Ballyscullion.

Thomas Gunner, 30, Ardnaglass, Roman Catholic, to Glasgow. Robert Gordon, 25, Aghavary, Roman Catholic, to Glasgow. Charles McFalls, 30, Aghavary, Roman Catholic, to Glasgow.

Grange of Ballyscullion

Bernard McKowen, 35, Ardnaglass, Roman Catholic, to [?] Kilsea. Thomas Gunner, 28, Ardnaglass, Roman Catholic, to [?] Kilsea. 5th April 1837.

Emigration in 1835 and 1836

List of persons who have emigrated from the grange of Ballyscullion during the year 1835. [Table gives name, age, townland, religion, port].

Rose McKowen, 25, from Ardnaglass, Roman Catholic, to Philadelphia.

List of persons who have emigrated from the grange during the year 1836.

Ellen Reaney, 18, Gillistown, Presbyterian, to New York.

John Clarke, 36, Gillistown, Presbyterian, to New York.

Catherine McKowen, 32, Kilvillis, Roman Catholic, to New York.

John Clarke, 9, Kilvillis, Roman Catholic, to New York.

Robert Johnstone, 22, Millquarter, Established Church, to Glasgow.

Thomas Bovel, 28, Millquarter, Established Church, to Glasgow.

William Bovel, 35, Millquarter, Established Church, to Glasgow.

John Devlin, 20, Culnafay, Roman Catholic, to New York.

John Linsay, 23, James Linsay, 28, Taylorstown, Seceders, to New York.

James Graham, 20, Taylorstown, Baptist, to New York.

Margaret Linsay, 25, Taylorstown, Presbyterian, to New York.

Josh McDowell, 24, Taylorstown, Presbyterian, to New York, returned.

Jane McDowell, 31, Gillistown, Presbyterian, to New York, returned.

Andrew Murphy, 25, Taylorstown, Presbyterian, to New York.

James McDowel, 30, Gillistown, Presbyterian, to New York.

Arthur Devlin, 23, Taylorstown, Roman Catholic, to New Orleans.

Ellen Reaney, 36, Gillistown, Presbyterian, to New York.

Catherine McKown, 26, Killyloss, Roman Catholic, to New York.

John Clarke, 10, Killyloss, Presbyterian, to New York.

William Bovil, 30, Millquarter, Established Church, to Glasgow.

Thomas Bovil, 25, Ardnaglass, Established Church, to Glasgow.

John Bovil, 28, Ardnaglass, Established Church, to Glasgow.

Sampson McAllen, 50, Rachael McAllen 19, from Millquarter, Established Church, to Glasgow.

Elisa Bovil, 20, John Bovil Junior, 3, died, Rachael Bovil Junior, 1, Millquarter, Established Church, to Glasgow.

Andrew Murphy, 25, Grange Park, Presbyterian, to New York.

Day Schools

Grange Mill school is held in the room of a private house fitted up for the purpose near the mill. The schoolroom is 19 by 12 feet inside, thatched and is the property of the master; established in 1835. Income of the mistress from the London Hibernian Society 4 pounds 12s per annum and 1d per week from each pupil. Books published by the London Hibernian Society, with plain needlework and knitting is taught to the girls. Males under 10 years of age 17, above 10 years of age 2, total males 19; females under 10 years of age 15, above 10, or from 10 to 15, 15; total 49 viz. 19 males and 30 females, Established Church 19, Presbyterians 11, Roman Catholics 16, Quakers 3. Margaret Duff in Established Church. Visited by the Reverend William Boyes, curate.

Sunday Schools

Grange Millquarter Sunday school, held in the day schoolhouse; established in 1829 and superintended by the schoolmaster chiefly. The Presbyterian and Established Church ministers occasionally visit the school; only 1 male teacher. 100 children attend, viz. 60 boys and 40 girls, 10 Presbyterian and 90 Roman Catholics; 70 are exclusively Sunday school scholars. Sunday School Society for Ireland give books free, carriage excepted. From the schoolmaster Thomas Scullion.

On every Christmas Day the children of the 2 Sunday schools held in Taylorstown, viz. north and south, with their teachers, meet in the Seceding meeting house at Craigmore for the purpose of being examined by the Reverend Hugh Smith, who also delivers an address on the occasion. The teachers of one Sunday school examine the children of another, and the minister examines the whole. Premiums of books are given to the children. Established in 1831. NB The teachers are those who have been educated themselves at

Sunday schools. Information obtained from John Lee, David Baily.

With respect to Sunday schools, Miss Coates, the superintendent of the Lakeview Sunday school, holds them in the highest estimation, as institutions calculated in every point of view to promote the most salutary effects, both for time and eternity, by their communicating the greatest benefit which, helped by divine grace, man can confer on man. For when the word of God is made the exclusive object of study, and the teachers endeavour to explain and impress on the minds of the children the importance of those truths which they read, shall we not hope that the Lord will not allow his word to return unto him void, but that it shall accomplish the thing whereunto he sends it. Thus, through their instrumentality the Bible and the Bible's God shall find admission into many a neglected cottage and many a loving heart. The sabbath will be no longer profaned, but appropriated to its intended object, the acquisition of religious knowledge and the enjoyment of devotional feeling.

Notwithstanding the existence of many daily schools in this neighbourhood, the children in general are ignorant as to the principles of Christianity, a consequence always to be found when the Sunday school system is not properly brought into operation. The parent, but particularly the children, appear warmly attached to this institution, insomuch that the most severe weather does not deter them from attending, whenever they have an opportunity. But one instance has come under the personal observation of Miss Coates, when through the agency of sabbath schools' instruction, it pleased the Lord to apply his word with power unto salvation to the heart of a dear child lately gone to glory. During her illness she gave the most satisfactory evidence that she formed one of Christ's fold. Her name was Maria Gilmour.

Lakeview Sunday School

The Lakeview Sunday school contains 17 Roman Catholics, 19 Presbyterians, 2 of the Established Church and 2 Seceders. This school concludes with prayer only, by one of the superintendents, generally Mr Cannon. Information obtained from Miss Coates, Mr Cannon, and Mrs Cannon and Miss Cannon.

Table of Schools

[Table contains the following headings: name, situation and description, when established, income and expenditure, physical intellectual and moral education, number of pupils subdivided by age, sex and religion, name and religion of master or mistress].

Lakeview female school, held in a house fitted up for the purpose, attached to Mr Cannon's dwelling house in the townland of Taylorstown; the house is 16 and a half by 13 feet inside and is in good repair; established in May 1836; income of the mistress 8 pounds; intellectual education: books published by the London Hibernian Society with *Thompson's Arithmetic*, with plain and fancy needlework; moral education: visited by the clergy of the Established Church, the Authorised Version of Scripture is taught; number of pupils: 10 under 10 years of age, 31 from 10 to 15, total 41, all female, 3 Protestants, 13 Presbyterians, 13 Roman Catholics, 12 other denominations; mistress Catherine Rankin, Presbyterian.

Lakeview evening class, private, held in Mrs Cannon's house for 5 days in each week, from 5 to 6 o'clock p.m.; established in February 1837; income: taught by Mrs Cannon; intellectual education: Freeman's Card is only taught; moral education: not visited by any [clergy]; number of pupils: males, 8 under 10 years of age, a total of 8; females, 2 under 10 years of age, total 2; total number of pupils 10, all Roman Catholics; taught by Mrs Cannon of the Established Church. Report for March 1837.

Taylorstown South national school, on the road leading from Ballymena to Toome, in an old house, thatched, 21 feet by 16 feet inside; established 1830; income: from National Board 8 pounds, from pupils 17 pounds; physical education: none; intellectual education: books published by the National Board; moral education: not visited by any of the clergy; number of pupils: males, 7 under 10 years of age, 18 from 10 to 15, 3 over 15, total 28; females, 5 under 10 years of age, 5 from 10 to 15, total 10; total number of pupils 38, 1 Protestant, 34 Presbyterians, 3 other denominations; master John Harbeson, Established Church.

[Crossed out: Taylorstown North], held in the farm of William McDowell in Taylorstown North; established 1826; income from pupils 8 pounds per annum; physical education: none; intellectual education: books published by London Hibernian Society; moral education: visited by the clergy of the Presbyterian Church, Authorised Version of Scriptures is taught; number of pupils: males, 8 under 10 years of age, 7 from 10 to 15, 5 over 15, total 20; females, 14 under 10 years of age, 5 from 10 to 15, 1 over 15, total 20; total number of pupils 40, 7 Protestants, 25 Presbyterians, 4 Roman

Grange of Ballyscullion

Catholics, 4 other denominations; master William John McDowell, Presbyterian.

Grange Mill, held in the room of a private house near the mill, 19 feet by 12 feet inside, established 1835; income: from London Hibernian Society 4 pounds 12s, 18 pounds from pupils; physical education: none; intellectual education: books published by the London Hibernian Society, with plain needlework and knitting; moral education: visited by the clergy of the Established Church; number of pupils: males, 17 under 10 years of age, 2 from 10 to 15, total 19; females, 15 under 10 years of age, 15 from 10 to 15, total 30; total number of pupils 49, 19 Protestants, 11 Presbyterians, 16 Roman Catholics, 3 other denominations, Quakers; mistress Margaret Duffin, Established Church. Report for April 1837.

Sunday Schools

[Table contains the following headings: name, situation and description, when established, superintendent, number of teachers and scholars, hours of attendance, societies with which connected, observations].

Lakeview Sunday school, held in the day schoolhouse; established May 1836; superintendent Mrs Cannon; 4 female teachers, total 4; number of scholars: 2 Established Church, 19 Presbyterians, 17 Roman Catholics, 2 other denominations, 14 males, 26 females, total 40; hours of attendance from 4 to 6 o'clock p.m. during the summer and from 2.30 to 3.30 p.m. during the winter season; societies with which connected: the Sunday School Society for Ireland give books free, carriage excepted; observations: concludes with prayer only, by the superintendent.

Taylorstown North, held in the Presbyterian meeting house, established 1829; superintendent Reverend Robert Rusk, Presbyterian minister, and Sampson McDowell, farmer; 4 male and 1 female teacher, total 5; number of scholars: 5 Established Church, 72 Presbyterians, 10 other denominations, 43 males, 44 females, total 87, 50 exclusively Sunday school scholars; hours of attendance from 7 to 10 o'clock a.m. and from 5 to 7 p.m. during the summer; societies with which connected: the Sunday School Society give books free, carriage excepted; observations: commences with singing and prayer and concludes with the same.

Taylorstown South, held in the day schoolhouse, established 1829; superintendent David Bailey; 11 male and 1 female teacher, total 12; number of scholars: 6 Established Church, 131 Presbyterians, 6 Roman Catholics, 17 other denominations, 70 males, 90 females, total 160, 30 exclusively Sunday school scholars; hours of attendance from 8 to 10 o'clock a.m.; societies with which connected: Sunday School Society gives books free, carriage excepted; observations: commences with singing and prayers and concludes with the same. Report for April 1837.

Parish of Connor, County Antrim

Statistical Account by Lieutenant J. Chaytor, February 1833

NATURAL STATE

Name and Situation

It is a man's name i.e. Connor's parish, or parish of Connor, probably the name of the original founder.

It is situated in the barony of Lower Antrim, diocese of Down and Connor and county of Antrim.

Boundaries, Extent and Divisions

It is bounded on the north by the parishes of Ahoghill, Ballyclug and Glenwhirry, on the east by those of Rashee, Kilbride and Donegore, on the south by the parishes of Antrim and grange of Shilvodan, and on the west by the parish of Drummaul. Its average breadth from north to south is about 3 and a half and from east to west about 7 and a half British statute miles. It contains 17,135 statute acres. It is divided into 28 townlands. The principal proprietors are Lords Mountcashell and Ferrard, Mr Clarke, Mr O'Hara, Mr Reaford and Mr Millar, of whom the latter only resides in the parish. It is let in small farms from 10 to 50 acres, some in perpetuity, but the greater part on lease of 21 years, average rent from 5s to 1 pound 10s per acre.

NATURAL FEATURES AND NATURAL HISTORY

Surface and Soil

The south eastern part, comprising about a third of the parish, is mountainous, on which there is little cultivation, being principally rough pasture and turf bog. The soil of the high ground, on which there are some patches of cultivation, is of a light gravelly or sandy nature, hence the name Sandy Braes, by which a part of this district is generally known. In the vicinity of the villages of Kells and Connor, and from that west and north west, it is for the most part a productive and well-cultivated soil, though this comprises several portions of valuable turf bog.

Produce and Turbary

The principal produce is potatoes, wheat, oats, barley and flax. Many of the peasantry derive a support from digging turf during the summer months and selling them in the winter. There is abundance of excellent turbary in various parts of the parish. Such farmers as are possessed of lands in the vicinity of turf bog have for the most part a privilege of turbary in proportion to the size of their farm. Such as are not thus situated pay at the rate of 1 pound to 5 pounds per acre according to quality. Several of the adjacent parishes having little turf bog, the inhabitants are obliged to have recourse to this, which is the great means of rendering it so valuable. 1 rood of good quality is sufficient to produce as much turf as will keep up a moderate fire for 1 year.

Geology

There is very little variety in the geology of this parish. Basalt and porphyry are the only kinds of rocks worthy of notice. The former appears in various parts. In a corner of Mr Millar's bleach green, townland of Tawnybreak, there is a good quarry. Porphyry abounds in the townlands of Carnearny and Tardree. In the latter place there is an extensive quarry. It is highly prized by builders. A great quantity of it has been conveyed to Belfast for the erection of the new bridge.

MODERN TOPOGRAPHY AND PRODUCTIVE ECONOMY

Villages

There are 2 villages, Connor and Kells. The former, which is the larger, is situated about a quarter of a mile east south east of the latter. It contains 52 houses and 289 inhabitants. In it is situated the Presbyterian meeting house. The church and glebe are in its immediate vicinity. Kells (including the townland) contains 113 houses and 575 inhabitants. These villages hold 4 fairs each annually, chiefly black cattle. Most of the inhabitants are small farmers. The road from Ballymena to Parkgate and Doagh passes through them.

Manufactures

Linen is the only manufacture of the country. Most of the peasantry are weavers and the greater part of the farmers and their families turn their attention to the manufacture of this article during the winter months. Ballymena holds a weekly market to which they carry it for sale. There are several extensive bleach greens, with beetling

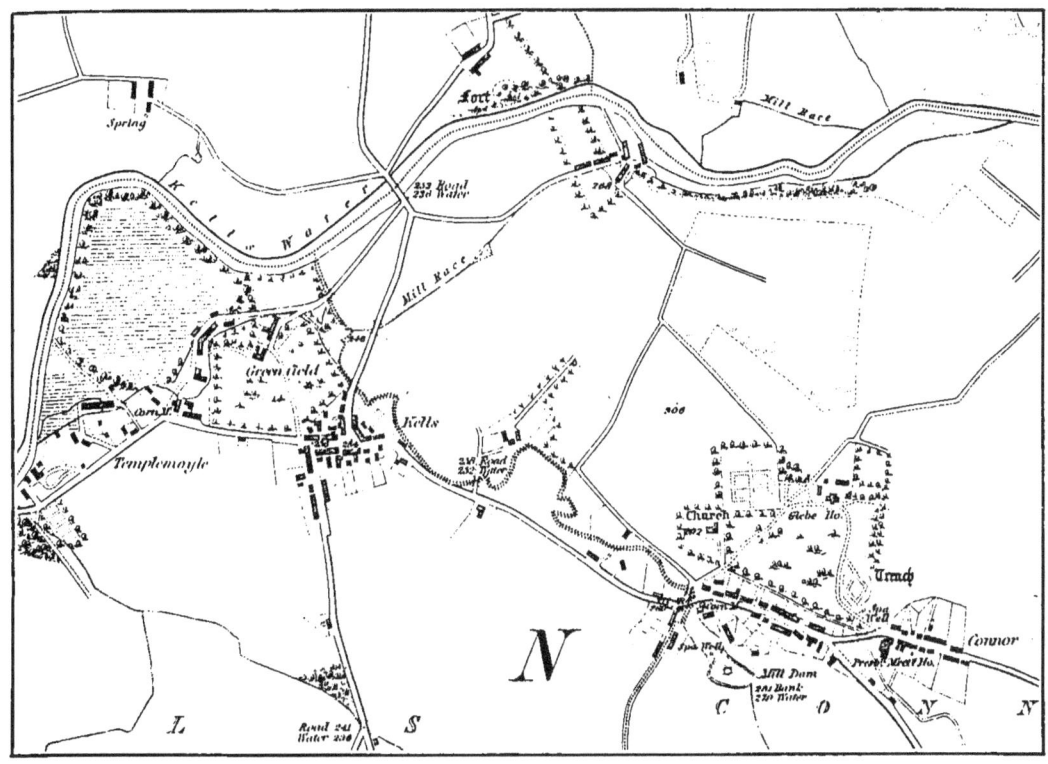

Map of Kells and Connor from the first 6" O.S. maps, 1830s

machinery, along the bank of the Kells water. There are 2 flax mills. Kells and Connor each have a corn mill.

Roads

This parish is well intersected with roads. They diverge from the villages of Kells and Connor to those of Doagh and Parkgate, and to the towns of Antrim, Ballymena and Larne. The mail coach road from Ballymena to Randalstown passes through the western extremity near the River Main for about a mile. East of the former and nearly parallel passes the road from Ballymena to Antrim. These are the principal roads in the parish. They are hilly but for the most part in good repair.

NATURAL FEATURES

Rivers

The Glenwhirry river takes its rise between the parishes of Glenwhirry, Ballycor and Rashee. It bounds the parish on the north for a distance of 2 miles, at which place it enters and passes through the parish of Connor, and at the distance of about 6 miles it joins the River Main. In its course through the parish it supplies 15 different houses of machinery, 13 of which are bleach mills or beetling engines. It bears a west south westerly course, its average breadth is 50 to 100 feet. Trout is the only kind of fish in this river. From the villages of Connor and Kells to its junction with the River Main it is called the Kells water.

The Braid river, after passing the town of Ballymena, bounds the parish on the north for 1 and a quarter miles, when it meets the River Main. From the junction of the two, the Main becomes considerable and bounds the parish on the west for 3 and a half miles, in which distance there are but 9 feet fall. Its average breadth is about 70 or 80 feet. It abounds with salmon and trout. The only fishery on the river is that near Lough Neagh, the property of Lord O'Neill. Its course is nearly south.

Woods

There is no ancient wood. In the townlands of Ross, Tawnybreak, Kells and Kildrum there is considerable quantity of scattered planting, principally fir. This, with the exception of a few trees about farmhouses, comprise all the wood in the parish.

Social Economy

Population

By the census of 1831 the population amounted to 7,848, of which 25 families are Protestants, 1,000 Presbyterians and the remainder Roman Catholics. They are generally speaking a peaceable and industrious people. They speak the English language. Their dialect bears a strong similarity to that of the Scotch. There are no independent gentry. Those who comprise the better class follow the manufacture and bleaching of linen.

The church is small. It has a small tower but no spire. It was erected in 1815. The present incumbent is the Reverend Mr Hobson, who resides in the Glebe, who receives the vicarial, and Lord Ferrard the rectorial tithes. The inhabitants of the adjoining grange of Shilvodan also pay tithes to the incumbent of Connor. The meeting house is spacious and in good repair. It was erected in the year 1815. It is rated a first-class congregation of the Synod of Ulster, regium donum 100 pounds. The officiating clergymen are the Reverend Messrs Henry and Hamilton, who reside in the parish. There being no chapel, the Roman Catholics go to worship at Crebilly in the adjoining parish of Ballyclug. Some bury in Templemoyle. The churchyard is the chief burial ground in the parish.

Ancient Topography and History

Antiquities

The Reverend Mr Hobson says that a cathedral called St Saviour <Zavier> was founded by King James I in the year 1610, no trace of which at present remains. It was situated at right angles with and near the site of the present church.

There is the remains of an ancient building in the townland of Kells, situated a short distance west of the village. It is said to have been an abbey. It is called Templemoyle or Templemoil, which is also the ancient name of the townland of Kells, the English translation of which is "a church without a steeple." There is but 1 gable and a small portion of a side wall standing, immediately adjoining which there is a vault and a small burial ground.

There is also the remains of an ancient building situated near the Glebe House. Several old silver coins have been found about the walls. By some it is said to have been a monastery, and after the Reformation was converted into a cathedral for the diocese of Connor. Some say it was the bishop's palace and others assert that it was a fortification. It is now commonly called the Trench. The present occupant, the Reverend Mr Hobson, has levelled the rubbish and soil of the interior, in which he has planted various ornamental shrubs. Templemoyle and the Trench are both so very ancient that no authentic or satisfactory date of their origin or use can be obtained.

There are 23 Danish forts interspersed through the various parts of the parish.

Land Divisions

Down and Connor were each in themselves a distinct diocese until the year 1438, when they were united and given to one bishop by King Henry VI. It is now called the united diocese of Down and Connor.

Karte is a district of country embracing the whole of the adjoining parish of Ballyclug and 7 townlands of the parish of Connor, viz. Ballee, Ballycowan, Crumkill, Kilgad, Tawnybreak, Tullaghgarley and Slatt. Laughlin O'Hara (a branch of a family of that name who were chieftains of considerable note in the county Sligo) joined the forces of Henry II on the first invasion of Ireland in 1136, from whom he obtained a grant of the manor of Karte, since which time it has remained in the possession of the O'Hara family. In 1607 James I made a further grant to Cahil O'Hara, the then proprietor, and it remained thus without change until Oliver Cromwell invaded Ireland, when he made a grant of Killgad and Tawnybreak (with other lands not part of Karte) to one of his officers, of which Mr Millar of Ross is now the proprietor. The grant was confirmed by parliament on the restoration of Charles II and there has not been any change since. It holds a court, of which Michael Harrison Esquire is seneschal. In some records it is called "the tuogh of Kearte in the Lower Clandeboy, in the province of Ulster and county of Antrim."

Clandeboy or Clannabuoy was a district, part in county Antrim, part in county Down. It went by the name of Upper and Lower. Lord Dufferin took the name of Dufferin and of Clanabuoy from the district. Clanabuoy signifies the "yellow clan." [Signed] John Chaytor, Lieutenant Royal Engineers, 10 February 1833.

Memoir by James Boyle, November 1835

Natural Features

Hills

The portion of this parish north of the Kells water occupies the southern extremity of the feature extending southward from Slemish mountain, in the more northern parish of Racavan. The highest point in this feature in this parish is at its eastern extremity, where it is 481 feet above the sea. From this it declines rather rapidly to the Kells river on the south, the average elevation of which in this parish is 287 feet above the sea. Its fall to the Main river, at the west of the parish, is more gentle and gradual. The south east portion of the parish, including about a third of its entire extent, is mostly of a mountainous character. There is a gradual ascent southward from the Kells river, until it attains an elevation of 1,043 feet above the sea at Carnearny mountain near the southern extremity of the parish. From Carnearny a ridge extends in a north easterly direction along the eastern side of the parish.

The principal points in this ridge are Carnearny, 1,043 feet, Tardree, 798 feet, Standing Stone, 787 feet and Ballygowan, 633 feet above the level of the sea. The general aspect of these mountains is bleak and uninteresting, there being nothing striking in the features and the country sadly deficient in planting or hedgerows. The western portion of the parish is low and undulating.

Lakes

There are no lakes in this parish.

Rivers

The Main river, which takes its rise in the parish of Killagan at an elevation of 298 feet above the sea, after flowing south for 12 miles and descending to an elevation of 116 feet above the sea, enters on the western boundary of this parish and, after flowing along it in a southerly direction for 3 miles, descends to a level of 101 feet, being an average fall of 1 foot in 1,056 feet. It finally, after an entire course of 25 miles, discharges itself into Lough Neagh, 1 and three-quarter miles south of the town of Randalstown, through which it passes. Its average ordinary breadth is 50 feet and depth variable, from 1 and a half to 4 feet. It flows through an almost level country which it frequently inundates, and in wet weather the adjacent country is under a broad sheet of water which naturally, though slowly, subsides. These inundations and the trifling deposits it makes are seldom injurious. Its bed is soft, its banks very low and the scenery along them dull and cheerless. It is not usefully situated for machinery, though it is for drainage and irrigation.

The Kells river, which takes its rise in the mountains in the parishes of Glenwhirry, Ballycor <Ballycorr> and Rashee at an elevation of 1,200 feet above the sea, after flowing west for 6 miles and descending to a level of 474 feet, enters on the northern boundary of this parish, along which it flows for 2 miles. It then enters and passes through the parish of Connor and, after an entire and westerly course of 14 miles, it discharges itself into the River Main at the western side of the parish and at an elevation of 101 feet above the level of the sea. Its average fall is 1 foot in 67 feet, its average breadth 70 feet and its depth varies from 1 and a half to 4 and a half feet. Its bottom or bed is uneven and its course interrupted by numerous rapids and shallows. Its bed is gravelly and stony, and its banks for the most part high. It is subject to frequent and sudden floods, which rise very rapidly and subside equally so. They are very violent while they last and some of them, particularly that on the 7th of November 1834, have done considerable injury.

The flood alluded to has destroyed the bridge at Kells by carrying away 3 piers and arches. It likewise swept the soil off some fertile holmes and threw up stones and gravel on others, carrying away ditches. The injury done by this flood was very serious. In moderate floods it rather enriches the meadows it inundates. Its deposits are usually gravel and therefore injurious. It is very valuably situated for machinery, as in its course through this parish it furnishes 15 mills of various descriptions with water power. Its banks are mostly high and the scenery along them is in general pleasing, as they are most diversified and only require a little planting. From the villages of Connor and Kells to its junction with the Main river this river is called the Kells river. Above that, it is called the Glenwhirry river.

The River Braid, which takes its rise in the parish of Tickmacrevan, flows for 1 and a quarter miles along the northern boundary of this parish. Its height on entering it, above the level of the sea, is 123 feet, and on quitting it is 111 feet, being a fall of 1 foot in 660 feet. It discharges itself into the Main river at the west side of the parish. Its average breadth is 56 feet and depth 3 feet. Its bed is soft and gravelly, its banks low and it frequently overflows them, particularly in winter, when the adjacent country is under a broad sheet of water. It seldom does harm or makes any deposits by its inundations. It is usefully situated for machinery and irrigation.

This parish is amply supplied with spring water and water from streams and rivulets for domestic uses. There is a strongly impregnated chalybeate spring in the lawn of the vicar at Connor. It is considered very powerful and is used for the strengthening the constitution. Whiskey, when mixed with it, turns black, and it is also said to injure and discolour the teeth.

Bogs

The most extensive tracts of bog in this parish are those in the mountains. Macadoo bog at the western side of the parish is very extensive. Its elevation above the sea is about 200 feet and above the Main water 100 feet. It is exceedingly deep and has not yet been cut to the bottom. One layer of fir stumps is found in this bog, but the trunks are mostly carried off. They appear broken at the same height and close to the root.

In Kilgad townland is a bog of about 60 acres. It is 410 feet above the sea and 90 above the Kells water. Fir stumps or blocks are found standing in it near the surface. There are few trunks in it. They appear to have been broken at the same height and to have been of considerable size. The depth of this bog varies from 4 to 10 feet. The subsoil of the bogs in this parish is a whitish clay.

In Tullynamullan townland, near the south west side of the parish, is a small tract of bog which is nearly cut out. There is 1 little insulated hill rising about 6 feet above it. It is of a whitish clay and is thickly studded with oak stumps or blocks which are broken off just at the surface of the clay. They average about 18 inches in diameter on the top of the stump. There are also a few oak trunks imbedded in this little island. An old whitethorn tree grows on its summit. It is accounted a "very gentle place" by the country people, who say they frequently see and hear the fairies and their music on it, and no one would be so impious as to cut it down.

In almost all the bogs in this parish, particularly in that in the townland of Ballee, the subsoil is thickly studded with oak blocks which are broken off near the stump and just at the surface of the clay. Many of the trunks also lie imbedded in the clay. They do not preserve any particular direction but lie indiscriminately. It may be observed that there are no branches attached to the sticks, nor are there any branches lying in the bog. This bog is very deep and slightly convex, and there is a good deal [of] fir timber lying indiscriminately in it.

Woods

The only ancient wood in this parish is that found in the bogs and the small patches of hazel and holly brushwood on the more rocky parts and along the banks of the Kells river.

Climate

The climate of the mountainous part of this parish has improved much within memory. The crops in the mountains now ripen much about the same time as those in the low grounds. This improvement in the climate is owing to the increased cultivation of the mountains. The south wind is the most prevalent and the south west that most followed by rain, the vapours about the lake and the Bann being wafted over to this parish by these winds and condensed on approaching the mountains. The crops ripen about the same time as in Kirkinriola.

MODERN TOPOGRAPHY

Village of Kells

There are no towns in this parish. There are 2 villages, Kells and Connor, near the centre of the parish and within a quarter of a mile of each other.

The village of Kells is situated in the townland of the same name. It is 134 miles north of Dublin, 24 miles north west of Belfast and 6 and a half miles north of Antrim. There is a running post who conveys the mail directly from the latter town to Kells. The situation of Kells is rather agreeable, the neighbouring country being well cultivated and there being some planting near the village. The Kells water also flows near its western side.

Kells consists of a little square with 4 outlets formed by the roads which intersect it. It contains 16 2-storey and 43 1-storey houses. They are all small, those in the square being neat, cleanly and comfortable, while the rest are filthy, untidy and comfortless. The inhabitants are of the humbler class, except those living in the square who are mostly dealers and seem rather comfortable in their circumstances. They are industrious, quiet and peaceable (see Table of Trades and Occupations).

There are no public buildings in Kells. The ruins of an old abbey stand a little west of the town and it is probable this abbey determined its site. The gable and side walls only remain. There is no architectural or other ornament about them. Nothing is known as to the origin of Kells, but it is said to have at one time, though very distant, [been] a place of considerable importance. There are 3 police (constabulary) stationed in Kells. The only gentlemen's families living in Kells are those of

Parish of Connor

the Reverend Mr Henry, Presbyterian minister, and Miss Brown.

Fairs are held here (custom free) on the 8th January, 1st March, 10th June and 12th September. Cattle of all kinds are sold in them, but not in any great numbers. Cows and pigs are principally sold, and some of the latter are bought up by dealers for exportation. Kells is neither increasing nor improving.

Village of Connor

The village of Connor is situated a quarter of a mile east south east of that of Kells. It consists of 1 straggling street about 300 yards long, which contains 52 1-storey houses of a bad description and very dirty, comfortless and irregular, being in bad order and badly thatched. Connor, it is said, was at one time a place of considerable importance and consequence, and extended to a standing stone about 1 mile west of the village. It is said to have been the residence of a bishop and the site of an abbey, a monastery, a cathedral and a castle. An octagonal stone building, about 9 feet high and somewhat like a fort, still remains. It is filled with rich earth to the depth of 6 feet and is paved at the bottom. There are several chiselled stones about it, such as may have been the mullions of windows. The summit of it is now converted into a flower garden by the vicar. Where the church now stands, there were formerly the ruins of an abbey, which were demolished by persons looking for money.

Public Buildings: Connor

The public buildings consist of: the church, which stands near the north side of the village. It is rather a neat building and has a simple square tower at its western extremity. Its dimensions are 60 feet long and 30 feet broad, and it contains accommodation for 200 persons. This church was rebuilt in 1814 and is in excellent order. Roman Catholics do not, or are not allowed to, bury in the churchyard. There are some tombstones bearing the dates of 1656 in it.

The Presbyterian meeting house, which stands at the east side of the village, was erected by subscription in 1815 and cost 1,600 pounds. It is a simple and substantial building 100 feet long and 40 feet broad, and contains accommodation for 1,100 persons. It is well finished and fitted up inside.

The appearance of Connor is uninteresting, irregular and straggling. The street is dirty and the houses mean. The people are all of the poorer class and engaged in agriculture. There are 3 petty grocery and spirit shops. It is neither increasing nor improving but rather declining.

Cattle fairs are held in it on the 1st February, 1st May, 2nd August and 28th October. Some horses and a tolerable number of cows and pigs and some sheep are sold in these fairs. Some cows and pigs are bought by dealers for exportation. There are no customs.

Public Buildings in the Parish

The public buildings in the parish consist of the Covenanters' meeting house in the townland of Carnaghts. It is a plain building, substantial and in good order and is prettily situated under the high bank and on the edge of the Kells river. Its dimensions are 60 feet by 30 and it accommodates 600 persons. It was erected by subscription in 1806 and cost 400 pounds.

Gentlemen's Seats

The Glebe, the residence of the Reverend John Hobson, the vicar, is situated in the townland of and near the village of Connor. It was built by the Board of First Fruits in 1820 and has been recently enlarged by the present occupant. It is a nice residence, modern and 2-storey, and there is some thriving fir planting about it.

Ross Lodge, the residence of Captain Millar, in the townland of Ross.

Fort Hill, the residence of Mrs Taylor, prettily situated on an eminence in the townland of Ballycowan.

Greenfield, contiguous to the village of Kells, the residence of [blank] Maxwell Esquire.

Kildrum, in the townland of the same name, the residence of Jesse Millar Esquire.

Templemoyle, in the townland and near the village of Kells, the residence of William Millar Esquire.

These are all modern and comfortable 2-storey residences. There is a good deal of planting, chiefly fir, about them, and though there is not anything worthy of description in their architecture or style of building, they are nevertheless suited for the residence of a gentleman's family.

Bleach Greens and Mills

There are 5 bleach greens in this parish. One of these is in Kells townland and extends over 19 acres 2 roods. The second is partly in the townlands of Tawnybrack, Ross and Kilgad, and extends over 51 acres 1 rood 13 perches. The third is in the townland of Cross and extends over 4 acres 2 roods. The fourth is in the townland of Kildrum and extends over 2 acres. The fifth is in the townland of Crevillyvalley and extends over 8 acres 1 rood.

The machinery of 1 beetling and wash mill in Kells townland is propelled by 1 breast water wheel 16 feet in diameter and 4 feet broad; the second mill with breast water wheel 16 feet in diameter and 4 feet broad; the third mill by 2 wheels, one 16 feet in diameter and 4 feet broad, the second 18 feet in diameter by 5 feet broad.

Kildrum townland: 2 wheels: 1st, 18 feet by 3 feet, breast water; 2nd, 15 feet by 2 feet 6 inches, breast water; 1 beetling mill, 17 feet by 2 feet 6 inches, breast water; beetling and wash mill (2 wheels): 1st, 18 feet by 3 feet 6 inches, breast water; 2nd, 15 feet by 4 feet, breast water.

Crevillyvalley townland: beetling and wash mill (3 wheels): 1st, 18 feet by 3 feet 8 inches, breast water; 2nd, 18 feet by 3 feet 6 inches, breast water; 3rd, 14 feet by 2 feet, breast water; beetling mill, 16 feet by 5 feet 6 inches, breast water.

Kells townland: beetling, calendering and washing mill (2 wheels): 1st, 16 feet by 4 feet, breast water; 2nd, 18 feet by 5 feet, breast water; beetling mill (2 wheels): 1st, 14 feet by 3 feet 4 inches, breast water; 2nd, 14 feet 8 inches by 4 feet, breast water; beetling and washing mill, 16 feet by 4 feet, breast water; beetling and washing mill, 16 feet by 4 feet, breast water; tuck mill, 13 feet by 1 foot 6 inches, breast water.

Tawnybrack: beetling mill, 18 feet by 7 feet, breast water; beetling mill (2 wheels): 1st, 18 by 3 feet 6 inches, breast water; 2nd, 18 feet by 3 feet 8 inches, breast water; beetling mill (2 wheels): 1st, 16 feet by 4 feet, breast water; 2nd, 16 feet by 4 feet, breast water.

Kilgad: beetling mill (2 wheels): 1st, 20 feet by 3 feet 6 inches, breast water; 2nd, 18 feet by 3 feet 6 inches, breast water; beetling and washing [insert addition: and rubbing] mill (3 wheels): 1st, 14 feet by 2 feet 6 inches, breast water; 2nd, 16 feet by 2 feet 4 inches, breast water; 3rd, 14 feet by 2 feet 6 inches, breast water.

Lisnawhiggal townland: beetling and washing mill, 12 feet 6 inches by 3 feet, breast water; beetling mill, 17 feet by 4 feet, breast water.

Corn mills: Kells townland, 15 feet by 6 feet 6 inches, breast water; Connor townland, 13 feet 6 inches by 2 feet 4 inches, breast water.

Flax mills: Maxwell's Walls townland, 14 feet by 2 feet, breast water; Kildrum townland, 12 feet by 2 feet 2 inches, breast water.

[Insert addition: All these mills, with the exception of the corn mill in Connor and the flax mill in Maxwells Walls, are driven by the Kells river].

There is no obstruction, legal or otherwise, to the erection of machinery.

Roads

This parish is amply supplied with roads which traverse it in every direction. The principal are: the mail coach road from Ballymena to Belfast through Randalstown, which traverses the western side of the parish for 4 miles. Its average breadth is 25 feet. This road is very hilly and not in good repair. It is, however, about to be avoided by a new line of mail coach road from Belfast to Coleraine which will leave out the town of Randalstown. This road is kept in repair by the county at large.

The main road from Ballymena to Belfast (and that travelled by the stage-coaches) traverses the western side of the parish, nearly parallel to the latter, for 5 miles. This road is almost level and averages 27 feet broad, but it is very heavy and soft, particularly in winter. It is judiciously laid out, but injudiciously made in some places. It passes for some distance through a soft and very extensive bog and here it is in a bad state, being lower than the bog, hollow in the centre, with very little metalling on it, and not properly drained. The consequence is, it is in one or two spots almost impassable and the coach has more than once stuck in it. It might be made a very fine road by raising it in the centre and putting on a sufficient coat of metalling.

The main road from Ballymena to Parkgate through Kells and Connor passes for 5 and a quarter miles through the parish. It is a good hard road, rather hilly and 23 feet broad.

The main road from Ballymena to Doagh through Kells and Connor passes through the parish for 6 miles. This is a tolerable road but rather hilly. It is 23 feet broad.

The main road from Kells to Larne passes for 2 and three-quarter miles through this parish. It is a pretty good road and tolerably laid out. Its average breadth is 22 feet.

These roads are kept in repair at the expense of the barony.

Bridges

The principal bridges are: that over the Kells water, on the road from Ballymena to Antrim. It is a plain substantial structure 130 feet long and 22 feet wide, and consists of 7 semicircular arches.

The bridge over the River Main on the road from Ballymena to Toome consists of 9 small semicircular arches and is 22 feet wide and 80 feet long.

The bridge over the Kells water near the village of Kells was, except one arch in the centre and another at one end, carried away by a dreadful flood in the river on the 7th of November 1834 and has not since been rebuilt. The communication at this point is therefore cut off and conveyances have to go a considerable distance round. The proposed estimate for rebuilding it is 1,000 pounds.

General Appearance and Scenery

Except along the banks of the Kells water, the scenery and appearance of this country is dull, tame and monotonous, there being neither hedgerows nor planting, except about the few gentlemen's seats, to relieve the eye. Except towards the north of the parish, the ground is but little diversified, though it rises to a considerable height at the south east side of the parish. Still, there is not anything striking or interesting in the features of the ground.

SOCIAL ECONOMY

Early Improvements

The inhabitants of this parish are almost exclusively the descendants of the Scots who came over in the 16th and 17th centuries. It would seem from their names that they came from Argyllshire, as the names of Campbell and Stuart are among the most prevalent. There are also several highly respectable families of Millars, who have extensive bleach greens in this parish. Bones is a name also to be met with, though not very frequently. The other names are evidently Scottish and many of the people seem to inherit the abodes of their forefathers.

It would be difficult to say where the earliest improvements commenced in this parish, as vestiges and remains of monastic and other public buildings are still to be found in the villages of Kells and Connor, and it would seem from these, as also from their conspicuous figure in ancient history, that improvements and civilisation had commenced here at a period long prior to that of any other part of the county.

It is said that St Patrick converted the inhabitants of this parish to Christianity about the middle of the 5th century and that this was the first parish in the diocese, and that the diocese took its name from the town of Connor, which is said then to have extended off from its present situation to a stone on the roadside 1 mile east of it. It bears all the marks of a place of antiquity and former importance, but at present its inhabitants are among the poorest in the parish. They are chiefly weavers and possess small farms of 1 to 4 acres, sowing a little flax and manufacturing it themselves. Besides this, they are considerably engaged in the manufacture of linen from the mill-spun yarn which has lately been introduced into this country. It is given to the weavers by the proprietors, some of whom in this manner afford employment to from 400 to 1,500 weavers.

They pay them good wages for their work and thus save them the expenses and fluctuations of price consequent on a public market. There has not for many years been any system which has tended more towards the amelioration of the farmer and manufacturer than the introduction into this country of machinery for spinning linen yarn. The yarn, and consequently the linen, can be produced at a price much lower than that made from hand-spun yarn. This country can therefore compete with others in a foreign market and, the demand for linen being increased, a greater quantity of flax is now sown than ever was before. No crop has ever paid so well: that of the present year (1835) paying from 16 pounds to 20 pounds per acre. All classes have therefore benefitted by it and the country is in as prosperous a state as it has been for years.

The introduction came at a time when it was much wanted, as the linen trade, the main and only support of the country, was then at a very low ebb. The prices for farm produce were low and the manufacturer had never given his attention to farming. The people of this parish are very much of the same grade as to circumstances and rank in life. They are not affluent but are comparatively [comfortable ?] in their circumstances. The several extensive linen bleachers give constant employment to many and thus contribute much to their support, as also to preserving a degree of regularity and good conduct, which is often wanting where there is a large manufacturing population and but few resident gentry.

Obstructions to improvement: none.

Local Government

There is 1 magistrate, Captain Millar of Ross Lodge, who is respected and influential, and possesses the confidence and esteem of all parties. His residence is rather conveniently situated.

There are 3 constabulary in Kells. There are no manor courts: petty sessions are held in Ballymena. No outrages of any kind have been committed even within a distant period. There formerly was a little illicit distillation. It never was very extensively carried on here, but has totally ceased from causes similar to those of other places. There are few or no fire or life insurances.

Dispensary

A dispensary was established here in the year 1831. It was supported partly by a voluntary annual subscription of 30 pounds, to which the county add a similar sum. No regular list of cases, except for this year (1835), has been preserved. It is, however, universally believed to have added greatly to the comfort of the poor man, by affording medicine and advice where, in many instances, both of which must have been otherwise wanting. By inculcating cleanliness and ventilation, and affording prompt assistance in contagious diseases, their spreading must be prevented, and sickness and disease consequently much lessened. Nothing of this kind is at present prevalent in this parish (see Establishments for Mental and Bodily Diseases).

Schools

It is generally considered that schools have contributed as much, if not more, to the improvement of the morals of the people of this parish than anything else. The schools are sufficiently numerous and of a tolerable description. There is, at most of them, considerable attention paid to their moral education and there are few in the parish who cannot read and many can write. They are anxious to have their children instructed but do not possess much taste for information. The introduction of Sunday schools is also general and their results have been beneficial.

Poor

There is no regular provision for the poor of this parish, except the usual collections on Sundays. The people, particularly the lower class, are charitable and never withhold their assistance (which consists usually of a "gowpen", 2 handfuls, of meal, or 2 gowpens of potatoes) from the beggar at their door. There is, however, little street or out-of-door begging. This is owing principally to a custom annually practised at Connor meeting house, namely an annual sermon is preached and a collection made, at the commencement of winter, for the purpose of buying blankets and clothes and distributing them among the poor householders. Another sermon is preached and a collection made in spring for the purpose of buying a hogshead of flax seed, which is also distributed among the poor householders. The great object of this is to check begging and also to prevent it. No strollers are assisted and the claims of those applying for assistance are strictly scrutinized before they receive it. It may be remarked that the Presbyterians of this congregation do not extend their charity beyond the members of their own sect.

Religion

The inhabitants of this parish are almost all Presbyterians (either of the Synod of Ulster or Covenanters). The proportion is 1 Episcopalian, 36 Presbyterians and 3 and a half Roman Catholics. The rector has a glebe house and 28 acres of glebe land attached to it. He has also the tithes of this parish (70 pounds per annum) and also of the parish of Killagan. The grange of Killyglen is also attached to this parish. The Presbyterian minister is superseded but still retains (as is the custom) the regium donum. His assistant and successor, during the life of the former, only receives the stipend. The Covenanter clergyman, who resides in Ballymena, is supported by his stipend, but accepts no regium donum. The priest is supported by his flock in the usual variety of ways.

Habits of the People

The inhabitants of this parish are industrious, honest and peaceable. They are, however, rather fond of whiskey and not at all attentive to neatness and cleanliness. They are principally engaged in the manufacture of linen, which affords them constant employment and good wages. Most of them possess a little land, generally from 1 to 4 acres, but more frequently 2. They are civil and obliging in their manners and hospitable and charitable in their disposition, but still they are stiff and obstinate in their prejudices, particularly against episcopacy, though not so much so as formerly, and not very open to conviction.

They are comparatively comfortable in their circumstances, though not so much as in Kirkinriola, but more so than in Ballyclug parish. They, like their Scottish forefathers, are canny and cautious in their dealings and in expressing their opinion. They were almost to a man engaged in the rebellion of 1798. This, however, may not be wondered at, as most of the rich and respectable persons in the neighbourhood and some of their ministers were deeply concerned in it.

However, since that time, their politics have changed and they now seem indifferent and careless on the subject.

Houses and Diet

Their houses are usually in clusters of from 3 to 5. Those of the lower class are all built of stone, 1-storey, thatched and consist of 2 or 3 apartments, but chiefly the former. They are substantially built and roofed, and if kept neatly would be very comfortable. Little regard, however, seems paid to neatness and few of them want a manure heap before the door. There are generally a few trees about each cluster of houses. Their furniture is of a tolerable description as is also their bedding.

Milk, meal and potatoes constitute their principal food. Salt herrings are much used, but except at Christmas or Easter they seldom indulge in animal food. They then treat themselves to a little salt meat such as bacon. The use of tea and baker's bread has become more common of late. There is not so much meal used as formerly and much more corn is brought to market. There are several substantial farmers in this parish who live well and have good 2-storey residences, about some of which there is all the appearance of neatness and comfort.

Dress and Customs

The lower and indeed all classes dress well in this parish and very little inferior to those in Kirkinriola, and they make an interesting and respectable appearance at fairs and markets and on Sundays, when they are regular in their attendance at worship. They do not marry remarkably early. They are rather long-lived and many attain the age of 80. The usual number in a family is 6.

There are no such things as patrons or patrons' days known among them, nor are there any local customs nor games. They are not very fond of amusement. Dancing is their only one, but they do not indulge in it so often as formerly. At Easter they assemble in a field and both sexes join in what is called the round ring, which has been elsewhere described. They have not any traditions among them, nor is there anything peculiar in their habits, manners or appearance.

Emigration and Migration

From 12 to 15 individuals annually emigrate in spring to Canada. They are generally of the working class and do not return. Emigration has of late years declined considerably. They are beginning to find themselves more comfortable at home and the accounts from abroad are less encouraging.

Few, if any, go to the Scots or English harvests. The people are engaged in manufacturing at home, where they can obtain good wages, and they reprobate the idea of going from home for work.

Remarkable Events

There is no record in this parish of its having been the scene of any remarkable event, nor having given birth to any remarkable person. During the rebellion of 1798 the centre arch of the bridge over the Kells water near the village was blown up and destroyed by the rebels, to retard the pursuit of the king's troops. This arch was afterwards rebuilt and was the only one left standing by the flood which destroyed the bridge in November 1834.

Establishments for the Indigent

[Table contains the following headings: name, object, management, number relieved, funds, annual expenses of management, relief afforded, when founded].

7 schools wholly or partly supported by subscription, object: the removal of ignorance; management: sundry societies; numbers relieved: 393 pupils receiving instruction; funds: from societies annually 15 pounds, from Lord Ferrard 15 pounds; when founded: at sundry times.

Clothing fund, object: prevention of mendicity by clothing indigent householders; management: the clothes are distributed by the elders of the congregation; numbers relieved: from 50 to 60 annually receive some articles of clothing; funds from private individuals: a fund averaging 17 pounds 10s collected at a sermon and laid out in clothing; relief afforded: from 50 to 60 annually receive some article of clothing; when founded: 1790.

Flax fund, object: assisting poor householders by keeping them in their houses; management: a hogshead of flax is purchased and distributed in small quantities among poor householders; number relieved: fluctuates; funds from private individuals: at an annual sermon for the purpose 3 pounds is collected; relief afforded: a small quantity of flax is annually given to each poor householder; when founded: 1790.

[Total funds]: from public bodies 15 pounds, from private individuals 35 pounds 10s.

Establishments for Mental and Bodily Diseases

Dispensary, management: a secretary and treasurer; number relieved: in the year 1835, 21; funds:

from the treasury of the county 35 pounds, from private individuals 35 pounds; annual expense of management: house rent 6 pounds, to the surgeon 40 pounds; total expenditure 67 pounds; when founded: 1831.

School Statistics

[Table contains the following headings: name, situation and description, when established, income and expenditure, physical, intellectual and moral education, number of pupils subdivided by age, sex and religion, name and religious persuasion of master or mistress].

Under the Kildare Place Society, in a part of the session house of the Presbyterian meeting house in the village of Connor, established 1826, income: from Lord Ferrard annually 5 pounds, from pupils 13 pounds; intellectual education: books of the Kildare Place Society and a library of 60 volumes from same society; moral education: Sunday School, occasional visits from the clergy, Shorter Catechism and Scriptures daily; number of pupils: males, 31 under 10 years of age, 14 from 10 to 15, 4 above 15, 49 total males; females, 13 under 10 years of age, 8 from 10 to 15, 21 total females; total number of pupils 70, all Presbyterians; master James Madol, Presbyterian.

Under the Kildare Place Society, in a house built for the purpose by subscription in the townland of Tawnybrack, when established: unknown; income from pupils 15 pounds; intellectual education: books of the Kildare Place Society; moral education: Sunday school, occasional visits from the clergy, Shorter Catechism and Scriptures daily; number of pupils: males, 15 under 10 years of age, 13 from 10 to 15, 1 above 15, 29 total males; females, 6 under 10, 5 from 10 to 15, 11 total females; total number of pupils 40, 8 Protestants, 30 Presbyterians, 2 Roman Catholics; master Robert McKee, Covenanter.

Under the Kildare Place Society, in a very good house built for the purpose by subscription in the townland of Tullygarley, established 1827; income from pupils 24 pounds; intellectual education: books of the Kildare Place Society and a library of 60 volumes; moral education: Sunday school, occasional visits from the clergy, Shorter Catechism and Scriptures daily; number of pupils: males, 2 under 10 years of age, 35 from 10 to 15, 3 above 15, 40 total males; females, 2 under 10 years of age, 18 from 10 to 15, 20 total females; total number of pupils 60, 58 Presbyterians, 2 Roman Catholics; master James Nichol, Presbyterian.

Under the Kildare Place Society, in a house built by subscription for the purpose in the townland of Abalteen, established 1820; income from pupils 15 pounds; intellectual education: books of the Kildare Place Society; moral education: Sunday School, occasional visits from the clergy, Shorter Catechism and Scriptures daily; number of pupils: males, 4 under 10 years of age, 16 from 10 to 15, 20 total males; females: 8 under 10 years of age, 12 from 10 to 15, [sic] 30 total females; total number of pupils 40, all Presbyterians; master John [?] Mears, Protestant.

Under the Synod of Ulster Education Board, in a house built by subscription for the purpose in the townland of Kells, established more than 50 years; income from pupils 25 pounds; intellectual education: books of the Kildare Place Society, *Jackson's Book-keeping*; moral education: Scriptures, Authorised Version, and Shorter Catechism daily; number of pupils: males, 19 under 10 years of age, 17 from 10 to 15, 1 above 15, 37 total males; females, 8 under 10 years of age, 11 from 10 to 15, 19 total females; total number of pupils 55, 53 Presbyterians, 2 Roman Catholics; master Christopher Fea, Presbyterian.

[Subtotals]: annual income from benevolent individuals 5 pounds, from pupils 92 pounds; number of pupils: males, 71 under 10 years of age, 95 from 10 to 15, 9 above 15, 175 total males; females, 37 under 10 years of age, 54 from 10 to 15, 91 total females; total number of pupils 265, 8 Protestants, 251 Presbyterians, 6 Roman Catholics.

Under the Board of National Education, in a house built for the purpose by subscription in the townland of Tawnybrack, established 1810; income: from the Board of National Education annually 10 pounds, from pupils 15 pounds; intellectual education: books of the Board of National Education; moral education: Sunday School, occasional visits from the minister, Authorised Version of Scriptures; number of pupils: males, 13 under 10 years of age, 10 from 10 to 15, 2 above 15, 25 total males; females, 4 under 10 years of age, 7 from 10 to 15, 4 above 15, 15 total females; total number of pupils 40, 3 Protestants, 27 Presbyterians, 10 Roman Catholics; master John Magee, Roman Catholic.

Under the Synod of Ulster Education Board, in a house built by subscription for the purpose in the townland of Maxwell's Walls, established 1810; income: by a grant from Lord Ferrard, which with money and house and garden amounts to 15 pounds annually, 15 pounds from pupils;

Parish of Connor

intellectual education: books of the Kildare Place Society, reading, writing and arithmetic; moral education: Sunday school, visits from the minister, Scriptures and Shorter Catechism; number of pupils: males, 30 under 10 years of age, 20 from 10 to 15, 5 above 15, 55 total males; females, 23 under 10 years of age, 8 from 10 to 15, 2 above 15, 33 total females; total number of pupils 88, 6 Protestants, 81 Presbyterians, 1 Roman Catholic; master [blank], Presbyterian.

In a house built by subscription for the purpose in the townland of Tardree, established 1810; income from pupils 13 pounds; intellectual education: *Manson* and the *Universal spelling and reading book*, writing and arithmetic; moral education: Authorised Version of the Scriptures and Shorter Catechism daily; number of pupils: males, 11 under 10 years of age, 7 from 10 to 15, 18 total males; females, 8 under 10 years of age, 6 from 10 to 15, 14 total females; total number of pupils 32, 3 Protestants, 27 Presbyterians, 2 Roman Catholics; master [blank], Presbyterian.

[Overall totals]: income from benevolent individuals 30 pounds, from pupils 135 pounds; number of pupils: males, 115 under 10 years of age, 132 from 10 to 15, 16 above 15, 273 total males; females, 76 under 10 years of age, 75 from 10 to 15, 2 above 15, 153 total females; total number of pupils 425, 3 Protestants, 27 Presbyterians, 2 Roman Catholics.

Table of Schools

[Table contains the following headings: name of townland where held, name and religion of master or mistress, free or pay school, annual income of master or mistress, description and cost of schoolhouse, number of pupils subdivided by religion, sex and the Protestant and Roman Catholic returns, societies with which connected].

Maxwell's Walls, master Archibald Wilson, Presbyterian; pay school, annual income 20 guineas and pay of scholars; schoolhouse stone and lime, cost 40 pounds; number of pupils by the Protestant return: 80 Presbyterians, 44 males, 36 females; by the Roman Catholic return: 23 Presbyterians, 2 Roman Catholics, 17 males, 8 females; connected with Kildare Place Society, Lord Ferrard gives 20 guineas to master.

Barnies, master John McDonnel, Presbyterian; pay school, annual income 9 pounds; schoolhouse stone and lime, cost 20 pounds; number of pupils by the Protestant return: 36 Presbyterians, 24 males, 12 females; by the Roman Catholic return: 36 Presbyterians, 24 males, 12 females; associations none.

Connor, master William Shannon, Presbyterian; pay school, annual income 14 pounds; schoolhouse a barn; number of pupils by the Protestant return: 30 Presbyterians, 18 males, 12 females; associations none.

Greenfield, master Alexander Stephenson, Presbyterian; pay school, annual income 14 pounds; schoolhouse stone and lime, cost 25 pounds; number of pupils by the Protestant return: 1 Established Church, 28 Presbyterians, 1 Roman Catholic, 14 males, 16 females; by the Roman Catholic return: 1 Established Church, 28 Presbyterians, 1 Roman Catholic, 15 males, 15 females; associations none.

Kells, master Christopher Fry, Presbyterian; pay school, annual income 24 pounds; schoolhouse stone and lime, cost 40 pounds; number of pupils by the Protestant return: 58 Presbyterians, 2 Roman Catholics, 40 males, 20 females; by the Roman Catholic return: 23 Presbyterians, 2 other denominations, 2 Roman Catholics, 15 males, 12 females; associations none.

Carnaught, master Hugh Hill, Presbyterian; pay school, annual income 16 pounds; schoolhouse stone and lime, cost 30 pounds; number of pupils by the Protestant return: 28 Presbyterians, 4 Roman Catholics, 23 males, 9 females; associations none.

Crumkill, master James McClelland, Presbyterian; pay school, annual income 20 pounds; schoolhouse stone and lime, cost 30 pounds; number of pupils by the Protestant return: 38 Presbyterians, 2 Roman Catholics, 20 males, 20 females; associations none.

Tullygarty, master James Darragh, Presbyterian; pay school, annual income 7 pounds; schoolhouse stone and lime, cost 20 pounds; number of pupils by the Protestant return: 56 Presbyterians, 1 Roman Catholic, 36 males, 21 females; associations none.

Applebee, master Joseph Fenton, Presbyterian; pay school, annual income 15 pounds; schoolhouse stone and lime, cost 30 pounds; number of pupils by the Protestant return: 42 Presbyterians, 5 Roman Catholics, 31 males, 16 females; associations none.

Flush, master John Henry, Roman Catholic; pay school, annual income 20 pounds; schoolhouse stone and lime, cost 15 pounds; number of pupils by the Protestant return: 46 Presbyterians, 4 Roman Catholics, 28 males, 22 females; associations none.

Fannybrack, master James Moore, a Moravian; pay school, annual income 25 pounds and pay of scholars; schoolhouse stone and lime, cost 105 pounds; number of pupils by the Protestant return: 44 Presbyterians, 8 Roman Catholics, 30 males, 22 females; connected with Kildare Place Society, J.W. Miller Esq. built the schoolhouse.

Escalane, master Hugh Haney, Roman Catholic; pay school, annual income 12 pounds; schoolhouse stone and lime, cost 17 pounds; number of pupils by the Protestant return: 14 Presbyterians, 8 Roman Catholics, 13 males, 9 females; by the Roman Catholic return: 16 Presbyterians, 18 Roman Catholics, 22 males, 12 females; associations none.

Tamlaghtmore, master James Ward, Roman Catholic; pay school, annual income 10 pounds; schoolhouse stone and lime, cost 20 pounds; number of pupils by the Protestant return: 17 Presbyterians, 2 other denominations, 16 Roman Catholics, 18 males, 17 females; by the Roman Catholic return: 17 Presbyterians, 2 other denominations, 16 Roman Catholics, 18 males, 17 females; associations none.

Glenwhirry, master William Millen, Presbyterian; pay school, annual income 20 pounds; schoolhouse stone and lime, cost 30 pounds; number of pupils by the Roman Catholic return: 62 Presbyterians, 35 males, 27 females; Kildare Place Society made a grant towards the schoolhouse.

Glenwhirry, master Charles Rogers, Presbyterian; pay school, income not stated; schoolhouse a hired room; number of pupils by the Roman Catholic return: 22 Presbyterians, all males; associations none.

Draft Memoir by J.R. Ward, 1835

NATURAL FEATURES

Hills

The south eastern portion of this parish, comprising about a third of the whole, is of a mountainous character, ascending gradually southward from the Kells river to Carnearny mountain, which is the principal point [insert addition: and 787 feet above Kells]. It is situated on the south south west of the parish. The eastern part of it is much more broken and steep than the western. It may be termed a promontory of the mountain district which runs along the east of the country. It is 1,043 feet above the sea and 995 feet above Lough Neagh. South of the Kells river the country is broken and undulated, but falling gradually to the south west. Kilgad, the highest point, situated near the western boundary, is 450 feet above the sea.

Lakes and Rivers

Lakes none.

The Main water forms part of the west boundary for 3 miles.

The Kells water runs through the centre of the parish, flowing westerly for [blank] miles. Its average breadth is 90 feet but is shallow. It is a continuation of the Glenwhirry river. It is usefully situated both for drainage and water power. The floods benefit the meadows, but this is at the expense of the cultivated ground. The banks are well cultivated and present to the beholder rather a pretty appearance, but planting is much wanted to beautify them. NB For further particulars, see Glenwhirry parish.

There are numerous smaller streams or burns which are useful in draining and some are capable of turning small wheels for flax mills. The parish is likewise well supplied with springs. There is a mineral well strongly impregnated with iron situated near the Trench in Connor.

Bogs

There is at the western part of the parish a bog of considerable magnitude called the Macadoo bog. It is very deep, so much so that the depth of it has not been ascertained. The wood found in it is principally fir. [Insert marginal note: This bog is in Mr Hannyngton's district].

In Kilgad townland there is about 60 acres of good turf bog. It is 410 feet above the sea and 90 feet above the Kells water. Timber is found in it indiscriminately scattered about, chiefly fir. The stumps and roots remain in a growing position. The trunks appear to have broken off almost close to the roots. The trees, from their size, appear to have been of old growth. The depth of the bog averages from 4 to 10 feet.

In Ross townland there is a bog of about 50 acres, some part cut out, the other part affording good fuel. The depth is about 10 feet. The height above the sea is 400 feet and 60 feet above Kells water. There is fir and beech <beetch> timber much decomposed found in it.

In Maxwells Walls there is a small bog of good black turf. It is 600 feet above the sea and 260 feet above the Kells water. Fir timber is found indiscriminately scattered over it and oak is found in the margin. About 50 feet of an old fence formed

Parish of Connor

of hazel sticks above 2 inches in diameter was dug up in it a few years ago.

Woods

No remains of natural woods in the parish. In the townlands of Ross, Tawnybrack, Kells and Kildrum there is a considerable quantity of scattered planting consisting principally of fir and ash. With the exception of some few trees about farmhouses, the above-mentioned plantations comprise the entire wood of the parish.

Climate

No meteorological register has been kept. I obtained information of a farmer in Maxwells Walls townland: that there was now no difference in ripening of the crops in the mountains and plains, but in his time he could remember when there was a difference of 2 or 3 weeks. He could give no reason for this but that he thought the seasons were milder. His name is Samuel Eggleson. The crops are oats, flax and potatoes. Oats ripen in September and October. Flax is pulled in August, and potatoes are dug for winter use in November. Wheat is grown in the western part of the parish only. It ripens in August.

MODERN TOPOGRAPHY

Towns: Connor

There are 2 villages, Connor and Kells. Connor is situated about half a mile east south east of Kells. The road from Ballymena to Doagh passes through it. It is in length a sixth of a mile. The surrounding country is well cultivated. Where the church now stands, there were ruins of an old abbey which were demolished by a person looking for money. On the north east of the village there is an old fortification called the Trench. It is vaulted, but the entrance to the vault is covered, the present vicar having a flower garden over them. About 1 mile south west of Connor there is a clogh or standing stone. It is said that this stone marks the site to which the town once extended.

Public Buildings

There is a church and a Presbyterian meeting house. The former is a plain stone building 60 feet long and 30 feet broad. It was rebuilt in 1814. The cost was [blank] pounds, which was defrayed by [blank] [insert note: could not ascertain]. It will accommodate 200 persons. The general attendance is about 60.

The meeting house is a neat stone building 100 feet long and 40 feet broad. It was built in 1815 at an expense of 1,600 pounds, which was defrayed by a levy on the sittings and by subscription. It will accommodate 1,100 persons. The general attendance is 900.

Streets and Houses

The village consists of 1 irregular street varying from 26 to 30 feet broad. The houses are very small. They are in number 52 and contain 289 inhabitants. They are all built of stone, thatched and are mostly whitewashed outside. They have in general a very dirty appearance.

Employment and Economy

A great number of the people are employed in the mills of the neighbourhood, some are farm labourers, the remainder are mechanics. Fairs are held on the 1st February, 1st May, 2nd August and 28th October. The traffic is cattle, pigs and sheep. The village is not improving.

Village of Kells

Kells is situated 18 miles north west of Belfast, near the main road from it to Ballymena. [It] contains 16 houses of 2-storeys and 43 of 1-storey. The surrounding country is well cultivated. The scenery is pretty but not picturesque. There is a ruin of an old abbey on the west side of the village. The western gable and 2 large vaults are the only parts now standing. It is now used for a burying place. The houses are small but neatly built of stone and whitewashed, and are mostly slated. Their appearance is cleanly. Fairs are held here on the 8th January, 1st March, 10th June and 12th September. The traffic is cattle, pigs and sheep. The village is not improving.

Public Buildings

There is a [crossed out: Seceders'] meeting house in Carnaght townland [insert marginal query by J. Boyle: Covenanters ?]. It is a plain stone building 60 feet long and 30 broad. It was built in 1806 by public subscription at an expense of 400 pounds. It will accommodate 600 persons, the general attendance is 400. The minister's salary is 40 pounds per annum.

Gentlemen's Seats

The Glebe, the residence of the vicar, is situated in Connor townland. It was repaired and much improved in by its present inhabitant, the Reverend John Hobson. It is a neat stone building. The farm consists of 28 acres Irish, which has likewise been improved by him by draining and planting, chiefly fir.

Ross Lodge, the residence of Captain Millar.

Communications

The parish is well intersected with roads: the mail coach road from Ballymena on the west side, traversing south for 4 miles; the main road between Ballymena and Antrim, almost parallel to and on the east of the latter for 5 miles; the main road between Ballymena and Doagh through Connor, traversing south east for 5 and a half miles; the main road from Kells and Connor to Parkgate, traversing south east by south for 4 miles; the main road between Broughshane (through Doagh) and Belfast, joining the road between Ballymena and Doagh about 2 and a half miles east of Connor, for 3 miles; at this junction there is a continuation of the latter road to Larne and Ballyclare for 2 miles; the main road from Connor to Antrim for 1 and three-quarter miles; and the main road from Kells and Randalstown for 1 and three-quarter miles. These roads were made by the county and are kept in good repair by the half-barony, with the exception of the first, the repairs of which is paid one-half by the county and the remainder by the half-barony [of] Lower Antrim.

General Appearance and Scenery

The south east part of the parish is mountainous, but affords good grazing for cattle and sheep. The other parts are well cultivated and appear fertile. The scenery of the north is pretty and interesting, that part having a few scattered clumps of trees to relieve the great sameness which the traveller has met with in the south.

SOCIAL ECONOMY

Obstructions to Improvement

Some townlands in the parish are bishop's land and, from the short leases which are given on them, are an obstruction to improvement in these townlands. There are 12 of them. There are no other obstructions.

Dispensary

The introduction of a dispensary has been of great utility, the health of the people being much improved by it. It is situated in the village of Connor. It is supported by a subscription of 35 pounds per annum off the parish and the grand jury gives 35 pounds more. The house used for the dispensary is rented for about 8 pounds per annum, which is paid for by subscription.

Schools

There are several well-attended schools in the parish. The principal are in the townlands of Tawnybrack, Connor, Maxwells Walls, Tardree. The scholars learn reading, writing and some, but very few, arithmetic and accounts.

Table of Schools

[Table contains the following headings: name of townland in which situated, number of pupils subdivided by religion and sex, how supported, when established].

Connor, 68 Protestants, 28 males, 40 females, 68 total; Lord Ferrard gives 5 pounds per annum and pupils pay 1d per week; established for upwards of 80 years.

Maxwells Walls, 88 Protestants, 55 males, 33 females, 88 total; supported by a grant from Lord Ferrard, which in money, house and land amounts to 15 pounds per annum; the pupils pay 1d per week; established 1810.

Tawnybrack, 30 Protestants, 10 Catholics, 25 males, 15 females, 40 total; supported by a grant from the National Board of 10 pounds per annum, pupils 15 pounds per week; established 1810.

Tardree, 30 Protestants, 2 Catholics, 18 males, 14 females, 32 total; supported by each pupil paying 2d per week; established 1810.

Poor

There is no provision for the poor, with the exception of the collection which is made on Sundays at the several places of worship in the parish, each of which have a certain number to whom they give this charity.

Religion

The greater part of the population are Presbyterians. The proportions are Episcopalian 1, Presbyterian 36 and Roman Catholics 3 and a half. The number of the first of these is greatly improved of late years. It must be observed that Methodist Dissenters are included in it, and that Seceders are included in the Presbyterian. The income of the vicar is 70 pounds per annum of tithe from this parish and a glebe farm of 28 Irish acres. The

Parish of Connor

Presbyterian minister has 92 pounds 6s 1d 3 farthings per annum of regium donum and 50 pounds stipend, and a farm of 30 Irish acres worth 100 pounds per annum.

Habits of the People

The cottages are all built of stone and are mostly thatched and have all glass windows. They are in general 1-storey, but there are a few farmhouses of 2-storeys. They have from 2 to 4 rooms, are comfortable and in general are cleanly. The food of the people is potatoes and oaten bread principally. This is now and then varied with broth made with pork and vegetables and sometimes flesh meat and white bread. The usual number in a family is 4 or 5 and sometimes 6. There are no remarkable instances of longevity or early marriages. The fuel, of which there is a good supply, is turf. The people dress very well. The women all wear bonnets. Blue cloth coats and drab trousers are the favourite dress of the men. The women wear showy cotton prints. They have very little amusement. Dancing and singing parties are the principal resort in the evenings. They visit fairs and markets for recreation.

Emigration

Prevails to a small extent, chiefly to Upper Canada. Belfast or Liverpool are the favourite ports for embarkation.

Remarkable Events

During the rebellion of 1798 the centre arch of the bridge at Kells was destroyed, it is said, by the rebels on the northern side of the river, to prevent the military crossing for the purpose of suppressing them.

Local Government

Captain Ross is the only magistrate in the parish. He resides in Ross Lodge, is firm and respected by the people. There are 3 police in Kells (constabulary). Petty sessions are held in Ballymena. Illicit distilling is not carried on.

Parish of Cranfield, County Antrim

Emigration and Migration Statistics by J. Bleakly, March 1837

MEMOIR WRITING

Memoir Writing

Forwarded to Lieutenant Bennett, Royal Engineers, 22nd August 1840, [signed] James Boyle.

SOCIAL ECONOMY

Emigration

List of persons who have emigrated from the parish of Cranfield during the year 1835: Edward Irwin, 30, from Cranfield, Presbyterian, to New Orleans; Andrew Hume, 30, from Cranfield, Presbyterian, to New Orleans.

Migration

List of persons who migrate from Cranfield: John Duncan, 23, Roman Catholic, to Glasgow; Patrick Duncan, 30, Roman Catholic, to Glasgow; Charles McKowen, 20, Roman Catholic, to Glasgow. [Signed] J. Bleakly, 21 March 1837.

Notes on Antiquities by T.C. Hannyngton, 1835

ANCIENT TOPOGRAPHY

Cranfield Chapel and Cross

The ruins of Cranfield chapel are situated in the southern part of the parish, close to the banks of Lough Neagh. The architecture is very rude. None of the stones are hewn except the doorway and corner stones. They were placed in the wall in the same form as when lifted from the shore. They are not large, but of all shapes and not carefully fitted. The spaces between them are filled up with smaller stones about 1 lb weight each. The corners of the building are more carefully finished. The stones used for these are cut square. They are hard and shine when broken. The inhabitants say they are "composition." The doorway is formed of this stone and is still perfect. It is only 5 feet high and 3 in breadth. The windows are lined and arched with a kind of hard and large square brick, much closer in the grain than those used in the present day.

There is a holy well 94 yards to the east of the church. It is fine spring water and produces crystals. The country people assemble and take them out on May morning. They believe them to grow only on May Eve. These they take to America: their tradition is that no ship can be wrecked in which they are. A few very old thorns grow over the well.

Half a mile to the north of the church stands the remains of an old wooden cross. The portion still existing is 7 feet high and 3 across the shoulder. It is formed of a single log of black oak. The arms were mortised in. It was in a high state of preservation till 20 years ago, when some drunken Orangemen pulled it down. [Signed] T.C. Hannyngton.

School Statistics

SOCIAL ECONOMY

School Statistics

[Table contains the following headings: name of townland where held, name and religion of master or mistress, free or pay school, total annual income of master or mistress, description and cost of schoolhouse, number of pupils subdivided by religion, sex and the Protestant and Roman Catholic returns, societies with which connected].

Creve, master Hugh McDonnell, Roman Catholic; pay school, annual income 8 pounds; schoolhouse stone and lime, cost 35 to 40 pounds; number of pupils by the Protestant return: 16 Presbyterians, 5 Protestants of other denominations, 65 Roman Catholics, 44 males, 42 females; by the Roman Catholic return: 17 Presbyterians, 2 Protestants of other denominations, 61 Roman Catholics, 42 males, 38 females; connected with Kildare Place Society and London Hibernian Society.

Parish of Drummaul

Parish of Drummaul, County Antrim

Statistical Return by Lieutenant C.H. Mallock, August 1830

NATURAL STATE

Name, Situation and Boundaries

Name: Drummaul.

It is situated in the half-barony of Upper Toome, on the south border of the county of Antrim. It is bounded on the north by the parish of Ahoghill, on the south by Lough Neagh and south east by the parish of Antrim, on the south west by that of Duneane, on the west by Duneane and the grange of Ballyscullion <Ballyscullin>, on the east by the parish of Antrim, by the grange of Shilvodan and by the parish of Connor.

Extent and Divisions

It extends from the north to the south about 8 miles and from the east to the west about 6. It contains 20,742 acres. This includes 6 townlands which are situated in the south part of the parish of Duneane. It is divided into 47 townlands, including the 6 in Duneane. The whole of the parish is the property of Lord O'Neill. The farms throughout are held on short leases.

NATURAL FEATURES

Surface and Soil

It does not present any very marked features, but has throughout a very thriving appearance. Shane's Castle park, which is very extensive, being nearly 2,000 acres, the whole of which is well wooded and adds much to the beauty of the surrounding neighbourhood, is situated at the south east corner of the parish. The principal beauty of Shane's Castle park is derived rather from art than nature. There is very little of variety in the ground itself and, except when immediately on the lake shore, the lake is hardly seen from any part of the grounds. The River Main, which runs through the middle of the park, at one or two places affords pretty points of view. A considerable portion of the grounds are generally cultivated every year and appear from the produce yielded to be of a rich quality. The land throughout the parish appears to be good, but in some parts there are large tracts of bog. Of these, portions are reclaimed every year and repay well for the expense incurred.

Produce and Turbary

Oats, barley, wheat, potatoes and flax are all cultivated, but barley and wheat in but small quantities. On Shane's Castle ground turnips, mangel-wurzel and different forced grasses are cultivated with success. Turnips are also cultivated in the townland of Sharvogues.

There are extensive tracts of bog in all parts of the parish, all of which afford very good fuel.

NATURAL HISTORY

Geology

Limestone: not any; the nearest points from which it is obtained is from Carnmoney, about 16 miles distant, and from county Derry, about 10 miles distant. The supply is almost always obtained from Carnmoney, although the distance is greater and the roads not so level. This is in consequence of the heavy toll demanded for crossing the Bann at the Toome Bridge. Greenstone is almost the only description of stone found within the parish.

Minerals: not any.

MODERN TOPOGRAPHY

Towns and Villages: Randalstown

The town of Randalstown <Randlestown>, situated in the townland of the same name about the centre of the south end of the parish, on the west side of the River Main, and the village of Ballygrooly, on the east side of the River Main and which is in fact a part of the town of Randalstown, are the only places within the parish which can come under the designation of town or village.

Randalstown is 16 miles from Belfast and 8 from Ballymena. It is a post and market town. The mail from Dublin passes through at half past 4 in the evening and from Derry at 5 in the morning.

Wednesday is the market day. It is considered as being one of, if not the best grain market in Antrim. There is still much yarn and linen brought to this market, but every year the quantity becomes less and less. On the first Wednesday in each month is held the great market or fair. This was formerly very well attended, but then fell

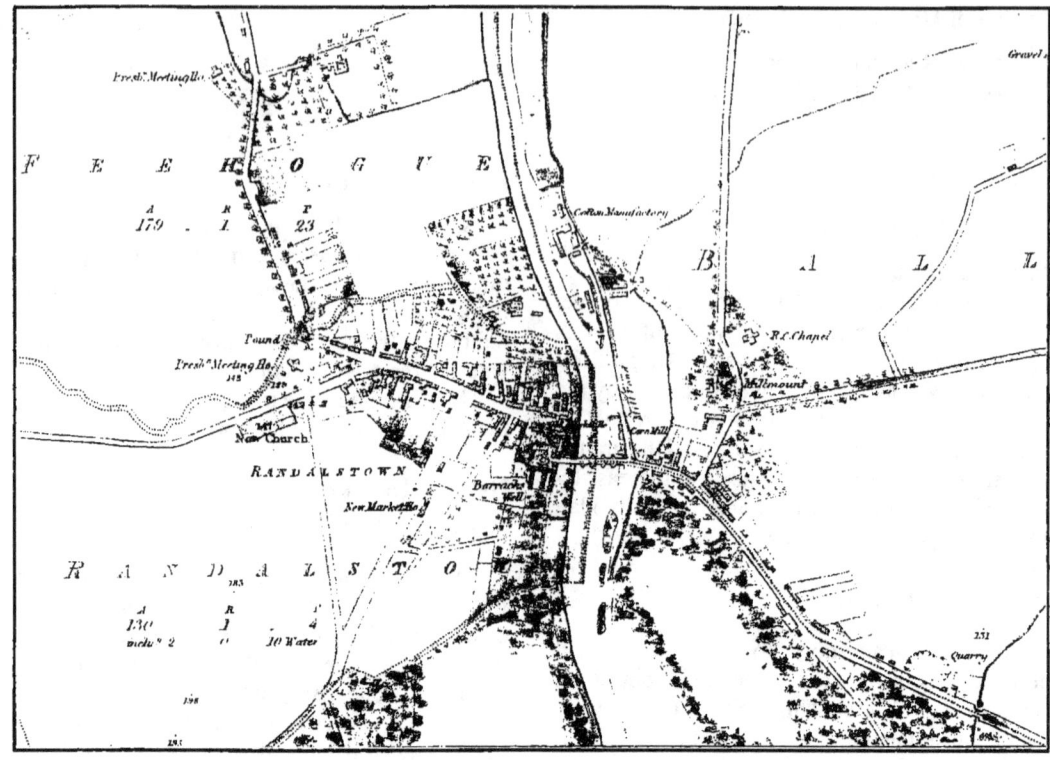

Map of Randalstown from the first 6" O.S. maps, 1830s

into disrepute and was entirely given up. In 1828 it was again revived and supported by all the principal linen merchants, and bid fair at that time to become one of the principal markets of the north. But I have since heard that it has again been almost given up. There are 2 fairs held in the year, one on the 16th July and one on the 1st November. Cattle of all descriptions are brought to these fairs.

Randalstown was formerly the headquarters for the Antrim militia. The barracks and parade ground, which are prettily situated on the banks of the river, are the property of Lord O'Neill. A new court and market house have lately been built. The parish church of Drummaul, now known as Randalstown church but anciently as Dunmore, is situated on the skirts of the town. The church is a small one and much out of repair, indeed so much so that it can hardly be repaired. There is a large meeting house in the town, and immediately adjoining a Catholic chapel and also a Seceders'. There is a large inn in the town, but it is not well kept. Post horses may be procured at it. A coach from Cookstown to Belfast passes through every other day. There is also a daily coach direct from Randalstown to Belfast.

The clergyman of the parish is the only gentleman who resides within the town.

Manufactories

There is a cotton manufactory a short distance above the town, on the River Main. About a mile higher up is a linen manufactory and bleach green. There is little business doing at either of the above mentioned. There is a large tanyard within the town, but nothing whatever doing in it. Formerly the family of every farmer was engaged in weaving linen. This is still carried on by a great number, but yields a very poor return.

Roads

The roads are most of them good, as far as the repair of them is considered, but little trouble appears to have been taken either to avoid or lower hills. This is particularly the case on the road to Cookstown, some parts of which is exceedingly steep. The road to Antrim is very good and nearly a dead level. The roads to Ballymena andND Ahoghill, the one on the east and the other on the west side of the River Main, are also good.

Natural Features

River Main

The River Main runs through a great portion of the parish. The falls on the river are but trifling, but the supply of water is always very great. At present it can hardly be said that any advantage is taken of the river for manufacturing purposes through any part of its course in the parish of Drummaul. Formerly there were a great number of salmon taken every year in Shane's Castle park, but the fish have been almost destroyed by poachers, so that the fishery is now given up. Lough Neagh, which bounds so large a portion of Drummaul, is not at present made to afford any advantages to the people. At Black rock in the townland of Gortagharn, on the Lough Neagh shore, there is a small quay and storehouse. Formerly lime and cobs were landed here, but of late this has been entirely given up.

Bogs and Woods

As before mentioned there are several large tracts of bog, all of which give good fuel, and when reclaimed, which has been the case on all the borders, it yields good crops, both of potatoes and oats. The only wood "except hedgerow timber" in the parish is that in Shane's Castle park, a little planting round the dwelling houses of Holybrook and Sharvogues, and a plantation in the townland of Craigmore. Although much wood in the grounds of Shane's Castle, there does not appear to be much that is valuable as timber. The present proprietor takes far more care of his game than of his plantations. The fear of disturbing the pheasants and hares, which are in great abundance, prevents the plantations from being properly thinned.

Social Economy

Population

The greatest number are Catholics, the next in number Presbyterians, then the Church of England. There are also a few Methodists and Seceders. In addition to the places of worship before mentioned, there is a Presbyterian meeting house in the townland of Craigmore, near the west side of the parish. The inhabitants generally are a very respectable class of people. The greater number are engaged in farming pursuits. A great number of horses are reared, but not bred in this parish. The general custom is to purchase 2-year-olds, work them on the farms for 2 years and then make them up for sale. In many instances the farmers go as far as Mullingar and Ballinasloe to purchase. They reckon upon the money to be made in this trade as being sufficient to pay the rents of their holdings.

Ancient Topography

Antiquities

There is little to be mentioned under this head, except the old forts <forths> and Shane's Castle, but here the name of O'Neill belongs rather to the antiquities of the country than do the ruins of the castle, they having the appearance of being those of a modern building. Adjoining the castle is a graveyard in which is the family vault of the O'Neills. A wide and high vaulted passage leads from the castle to the graveyard, the distance being about 100 yards.

In the townland of Drummaul there is also an old graveyard, in which the parish church was formerly situated.

Memoir by James Boyle, June 1838

Memoir Writing

Memoir Writing

This Memoir was originally commenced on the 12th April 1836 and completed on the 20th June 1838. The time employed at it is 497 hours or 55 days. *All* the information contained in it is complete and brought down to the present day. [Signed] James Boyle, 30th July 1838.

Natural Features

Hills

The parish of Drummaul is divided into 2 almost equal portions by the River Main, which traverses its centre from its northern to its southern extremity. Of these portions, the western embraces the southern extremity of the hilly ridge commonly known as the Killymurrays hills, which extends along the western side of the county from the parish of Finvoy, near its northern, to Lough Neagh at its southern side. The highest point in the ridge in this parish is Craigmore hill (a basaltic hummock near its north western side), 490 feet above the sea.

The ridge is of basaltic or trap <trapp> formation. Its descent from Craigmore hill to its southern extremity is at first broken and irregular, from the number of hummocks which diversify its summit, but gradually becomes more even, until it terminates in a low cliff in the shore of the lake. The descent eastwards from the summit of the ridge is abrupt at first, but becomes more gentle towards its base. The descent westward is interrupted by several little steps and ridges traversing its side. Towards the south of the parish these are in general more strongly marked and are frequently intersected by little valleys, which give a pleasing variety to the ground.

The eastern portion of the parish is almost flat, except immediately along its northern side, where its vast and dreary tracts of bog are somewhat varied by numerous insulated gravelly swells. The average elevation of this portion of the parish does not exceed 150 feet above the sea, nor 100 above Lough Neagh, towards which there is a trifling and unbroken fall. The principal points in the parish are Craigmore, 490 and Clonboy, 383 feet above the sea. These points are in its western portion.

Lakes

Lough Neagh, which washes the south western side of the county and southern extremity of the parish: within the confines of the former 48,342 acres 3 roods 19 perches, and of the latter 11,471 acres 3 roods 13 perches are included. Its depth in this parish is variable, being shallow immediately along its shore but gradually deepening towards its centre. Its rise in winter is of course affected by the wetness of the season, but may average 5 and a half feet. It never exceeds 6 feet and is seldom 5 feet. Its inundations are not in this parish attended with any injurious effects, as they are confined to the sandy and shingly strip which forms its beach and bed. The general direction of its coast is from east to west and its extent 5 and three-quarter miles. It consists of little craggy cliffs alternately with low sandy strands. The former do not exceed 20 feet in height. They present in 2 instances tolerably perfect specimens of columnar basalt.

Coast

The coast of this parish adds greatly to the beauty of the scenery of Lough Neagh, its low shores being covered with the dense plantations and woods in the demesne of Shane's Castle which fringe it to the water's edge and extend along it for more than 2 and a quarter miles. The terrace, conservatory and ruins of the ancient residence of the O'Neills are seen to great advantage from the water and from the opposite side of Antrim bay (the former being washed by the lake), while immediately behind them the lofty ruins raise their summits above the surrounding woods. [Insert marginal note: See sketch].

The views from the shore of this parish are very extensive, varied and beautiful, embracing almost the entire coast of the lake, its wooded shores along its eastern side and the numerous low points and promontories along its southern and western, presenting a pleasing contrast to the splendid mountain ridges in the adjacent counties of Derry, Tyrone, Down and Antrim.

River Main

The Main, which takes its rise in the parish of Killagan at an elevation of about 290 feet above the level of the sea and 242 feet above the level of Lough Neagh, into which it discharges itself. After pursuing a somewhat irregular and southerly course for 14 miles, during which it is considerably augmented by the Clough, Braid and several minor tributary streams, it descends to a level of 108 feet above the sea and 60 feet above Lough Neagh, and enters this parish at its north east corner. It forms the eastern boundary of this parish, separating it from that of Connor for about 2 and a third miles, when it is joined and considerably augmented by the Kells water (which flows from the mountainous districts to the eastward), and then enters this parish, through the centre of which it pursues an irregular but southerly course for 6 and two-third miles, and finally discharges itself into Lough Neagh 2 and a half miles south of the town of Randalstown, through which it passes.

The total length of this stream is 20 and two-third miles. In this parish its breadth varies from 87 to 186 feet and would average about 115 feet. It is, however, very irregular, sometimes contracting to its narrowest limits and then expanding into a wide reach. This irregularity of its breadth of course affects its depth, which varies from a few inches to 10 feet in ordinary weather. Its depth is still further affected by the irregularity of its bed and consequent variety and irregularity in its inclination or fall, long reaches of almost dead water alternating with shallow rapids which are, in ordinary weather, easily fordable by pedestrians, horses and carts, but from the frequency of its floods and their extreme rapidity in rising and subsiding, the fords are rather uncertain. Its mouth is obstructed by a bar of sand, which would impede the entrance of Lord O'Neill's steamer (a vessel of 100 tons) but for a dredging machine which his lordship keeps almost continually at work during summer; but, the bar being crossed, it is navigable for about a third of a mile for vessels of 50 tons burthen. It is, however, used only in this respect by Lord O'Neill, who keeps his steamer and other boats in it and uses it as a harbour for them.

It rises very rapidly and of itself subsides almost as much so, except in winter when a check is given to this discharge of its waters by the height of those of Lough Neagh, and it then inundates the almost level country through which it flows, towards the north of the parish, to a vast extent. In spring and summer it frequently commits much mischief by rising suddenly and sweeping off the loose soil or crops on the holmes <hoames> along it, and should it remain any time on the meadows or pasture grounds, the grass is invariably soured. The deposits are not attended with any perceptible effects. Towards the north of the parish the country through which it flows is almost flat.

Its banks are low and its bed soft and clayey. Further down its banks are somewhat higher, occasionally alternating with low holmes, while its bed is gravelly and stony; and for the last 2 miles of its course its banks are high and its bed (except at its mouth where it is sandy) is stony and uneven.

The average fall of this stream from its source to its mouth is 1 foot in 119 and from its source to the point where it enters this parish 1 foot in 901, and from that point to its mouth 1 foot in 792. The rapids are more numerous in the last 3 miles of its course, in which the average inclination is 1 foot in 360 feet. In Shane's Castle demesne there is one instance a fall of 5 feet in about 130. As these rapids generally alternate with long reaches of deep and almost dead water, the river is capable of furnishing a constant and regular supply of water power for machinery to almost any extent. It is therefore to be regretted that such a valuable stream should in this parish continue almost wholly unapplied to any one purpose, while it might be applied not only to machinery but also to the purpose of draining the vast tracts of useless flow bog which lie parallel and near to its eastern bank. Its situation for the purpose of irrigation is not, from the nature of the country, of any importance.

The Main flows through a tame and uninteresting country until it approaches the town of Randalstown, from which to its mouth its lofty and occasionally almost precipitous banks are clothed with a dense planting, which, unless its course be followed, quite conceal it from the view. The last 2 and a half miles of its course are through the demesne of Shane's Castle, to which, were it not so totally excluded from the view, it would form a great ornament. There are some delightful walks along its banks in the demesne, but from the drives an occasional glimpse of it is all that can be had.

Rivulets and Springs

There are numerous little rivulets and brooks in the parish, none of which, however, are entitled to the appellation of a stream. Most of them take their rise in the tract of swampy flow bog in this and the neighbouring parishes and, being gradually augmented by their uniting with others and by the contributions they receive when assisting in draining the land through which they pass, they wind a circuitous course through the numberless little valleys in the west side of the parish until they finally make their way into Lough Neagh. These rivulets are useful in their situation and might be rendered much more so in the drainage and consequent reclamation of the ground which, from its irregularity and their number and proximity to the lake and River Main, might be easily effected. In this parish, their waters being congregated and confined in dams or ponds by a breast work thrown across them, they are in 3 instances rendered applicable to the propelling of the humble machinery of the country and, except in the very dry seasons, afford a pretty constant supply of water. Irrigation is not much required and consequently is rarely attempted in this parish.

The supply of spring water is quite sufficient throughout the parish, and pumps or draw-wells are seldom sunk. There are not any hot or mineral springs.

Bogs

There are 3 extensive and several small tracts of bog in this parish. The most extensive is that known as Sluggan or Magheralane, situated in Magheralane and the adjoining townlands near the centre of the parish, and within a short distance of the River Main, to which it extends parallel for about 2 and two-third miles. Its extreme breadth is about 1 mile and its average breadth half a mile. Its total extent is about 852 acres. Its highest point is at its northern extremity, which is 163 feet above the sea and 56 feet above the nearest point of the Main water, which is 1 furlong distant. At its southern extremity it is 58 feet above the river, which at its nearest point is a mile and a quarter distant. It falls gently to both sides from the centre. Its extreme depth as yet known does not exceed 17 feet, but as it has been cut about the edges only, little is known of it. Its form would suggest an idea of its being much deeper towards the centre. Its bottom consists of tough bluish clay abounding with springs. White sand is said to have in several parts of it been found on the clay.

Its centre is said to have been the site of a lake, which has not existed within memory but is said to be laid down in some old surveys. It is growing very rapidly and in winter its consistency is so soft that no one has in that season been known to cross it in a direct line. Immense quantities of fir blocks and stumps (but few trunks) are imbedded in this bog, but from its rapid growth they are now more near to the bottom than the surface. Of these, 3 layers, one resting on the other, have been found. There is also some hazel and a little oak resting in the subsoil. The few trunks that are found have been broken off very close to the stump and lie with their heads to the north east. They all appear to have been broken off at the same height.

Along the edge of the bog the ground rises a little, forming as it were a barrier to its spreading, and then slopes gently to the River Main. This barrier is, however, in several places intersected by little valleys or hollows which seem to extend to the centre of the bog and from thence to the river. In one of these valleys, and near the north west extremity of the bog, the inhabitants had been in the habit of cutting their turf and had cleared away about 50 acres of the bog and cultivated the subsoil. Subsequently they commenced cutting the nearest portion of the main tract and, as the turf near the surface was almost useless, they sunk deeper until they cut through a sort of cordon or border of compressed bog, which seems to encircle the entire tract, and confined it to its former bounds. The only barrier at that point being thus removed, it soon burst forth as described hereafter.

Moving Bog

The following account of this phenomenon has been obtained from an eyewitness: "On Saturday the 19th September 1835, about 3 p.m., a hollow rumbling noise resembling distant thunder was heard in the bog by some persons working in the banks before mentioned. Soon after the bog began to heave and crack, and to move toward the banks at the head of the valley. This, however, caused but little alarm, as a similar occurrence took place about 7 years before, near the same spot. The bog remained rather stationary until Sunday night, when it commenced moving, but more rapidly, and it then overflowed about 15 acres of the reclaimed subsoil. It continued to overflow until it was arrested by the mail coach road from Randalstown to Ballymena, which, crossing the valley, stopped its progress until Tuesday night, when about 11 o'clock at night it burst over the road and continued to move very rapidly, until it had nearly reached the river, where its velocity suddenly increased to a such a degree that it not only filled the bed of the river but covered an acre of valuable land on its opposite side. The stream of bog, which averaged about 200 yards broad, had by this time covered about 100 acres of arable and cultivated land. After this it continued for 8 days to move into the river, large masses of bog with roots and stumps of trees and immense quantities of eels flowing down incessantly during that time."

Since then there has not been any further outbreak of the bog, but a small stream continues to flow down the centre of the bog deposited in the valley and which covers the land to a depth of from 5 to 10 feet. An idea of the rapidity with which it flowed may be formed from the fact that a man who was drawing corn from a field in its way was obliged to put his horse to a canter to escape it.

The probable cause of the bursting of the bog was its having been so fully saturated with water from the numerous large springs underneath it. Its consistence was too weak, without some barrier to keep it together. The circle of compressed bog which enclosed it having been removed, there was nothing further to confine this mass which was hourly becoming more fully saturated, and at the same time thinner and weaker in its consistence, and these circumstances, with the increasing pressure from the centre, may in all probability have caused its outbreak at the first point at which the barrier should have been removed. Had it burst forth at almost any other point on its western side, the mischief committed by it would have been much more serious, as the slope of the ground was unbroken and the space covered would have been considerably greater, and many of the houses along the road and in the fields might have been swept away by it. Only 1 house was blocked up by it and the bog about has since been removed.

The gulf or break opened near the north centre of the bog. From this it moved forward at first in

Parish of Drummaul

a north westerly but soon after in a westerly direction, until it reached the head of the valley. Except the chasm or valley thus left, and which is about 8 feet lower than the adjacent surface, the bog remains entire and unbroken. The general height of the ridge is, however, lowered about 10 feet, and trees, houses and other objects which could not formerly have been discerned by reason of its height are now to be seen across it. Some idea may be formed of the quantity of bog carried down the River Main when, even at the present time (May 1838), some of it is still to be found along the eastern shore of Lough Neagh, a distance of more than 9 miles from the place where it first entered the river. Hundreds of people came from all parts of the neighbouring districts to see the bog where it had burst, and so great was the concourse that tents for the sale of whiskey and refreshments and bread carts were established near it while it remained moving.

From its proximity to and elevation above the Main, this bog might be easily drained and rendered much more valuable. As it is at present it [is] worse than worthless, as from its state of moisture or swampiness it affects the climate of and retards the ripening of crops in its vicinity, by attracting and condensing the mists and vapours which follow the course of the stream from the lake, being wafted to the former by the prevailing southerly and south westerly winds.

Groggan Bog

There is another very large tract of bog in Groggan and the adjoining townlands, which extends along the western boundary of this and into the more northerly parish of Ahoghill for about 4 miles. It is narrow and is seated on the summit of the ridge extending along the west of the parish. Its average elevation above the sea is 430 and above the River Main 325 feet. Its centre, embracing its greater portion, is a swampy flow. It is therefore but little known, being cut for fuel about the edges only, and there its depth varies from 5 to 20 feet. The subsoil of this bog is a cold blue clay in which a few oak stumps (but no trunks) are found. About 4 feet above the subsoil a layer of fir stumps pervades the bog. The few trunks of fir which are found generally lie with their heads to the east and most of them, as well as of the stumps, bear marks of combustion.

In this bog there is a small partially-drained lake, the elevation of which above the sea is 400 feet. The entire bog seems to have been the site of a large lake, which has probably been partially drained by the numerous little streams issuing from it and which, if properly managed, might be now applied to it almost perfect drainage.

Sharvogues Bog

In the townland of Sharvogues, at the north east side of the parish, there is a large tract of bog approaching in form to convexity and extending over about 315 acres. Its elevation above the sea is 150 feet and above the River Main, from which it is distant from 50 to 400 yards, 33 feet. As it has been cut to a very trifling extent but little is known of it. It is said to be very deep and, as fir timber is found in large quantities about its edges in 2 layers, it has probably originated in the destruction of several successive forests. This bog approaches in form to convexity.

There are numerous smaller tracts of bog in the parish, almost all of which are in its western portion, occupying the hollows or valleys which so much vary its surface. They seem to have originally been the beds of lakes, upon the surface of which, from their partial drainage and stagnation, vegetable matter may have accumulated and thus caused their origin. Many of these tracts have been partially cut and found to contain a layer of fir stumps, with a few trunks of the same timber. Their subsoil, which is usually a greyish clay, is in general thickly studded with oak stumps, from which the trunks seem to have been broken very closely. Almost all the stumps bear marks of combustion and, as no trunks are found, it may be that the forest has been burnt to the ground, the roots only remaining.

Stakes found in Bogs

Rows of hazel stakes from 4 to 5 feet long and 2 to 3 inches thick have been frequently found in the bogs of this parish. They are invariably pointed at their extremity by 3 cuts of some sharp instrument, and are found at unequal distances of from 3 to 6 feet. The idea which prevails with respect to these rows is that the deer with which the country once abounded were driven into the marshes where the stakes were set and, from their being hidden, the deer staked themselves on them and thus were caught.

Woods

The tradition of the country is "that within a century a bird could have hopped from bough to bough along the shore of the lake from Toome

Bridge to the deer park at Antrim" (a distance of 16 miles). Of this vast forest the only remains now to be found in this parish consist of a few aged oaks and hawthorns and ash trees, and some hazel and sloe-thorn underwood in the demesne and deer park of Shane's Castle, and a few solitary old hawthorns and hazel and holly brushwood to be found about the raths of the country, which are indebted for their preservation to the superstition of the people. Holly seems to have been particularly indigenous to the parish, to judge from the size of its roots and the quantity of it to be found in its rocky and irreclaimable spots. One tree of it still remains uninjured in the townland of Drumsough. It measures at the butt 6 feet, and at 5 feet from the ground 5 feet 7 inches in girth. Its height is 24 feet.

The quantity of natural wood in Shane's Castle is very trifling, particularly when contrasted with the immense forest which once covered its entire extent (now 1,930 acres) and with the extent of its plantations. Occasional trees are now only to be found where once it is said there stood a dense and almost impenetrable forest, and their number is gradually decreasing by decay. The largest natural oak in the park measures in girth at the butt 17 feet. There are several others nearly but not quite so large: one ash tree measures at the butt 13 feet 5 inches. It is, however, much decayed. Many stumps of oak and some of ash, the trunks of which have fallen from decay, are still to be found in the deer park. The hawthorns in that part of the demesne are numerous and very old. The largest are to be found about the old raths or forts in it.

Climate and Crops

There is considerable variety of climate in this parish, owing to the situation of its different districts. It is, however, generally considered healthy, though moist and subject to rain. In the districts along the shore of the lake, owing to their southerly aspects and the gravelly nature of the soil, the seasons are much earlier than in the other districts of the parish, particularly those along both sides of the River Main, which are moist and subject to rain from the prevalence of westerly and south westerly and southerly winds, which waft the vapours collected about the marshy districts along the western and southern towards the northern and eastern sides of the lake, where, being attracted either by the River Main or the Bann, which flows parallel to and within 5 miles of it, they hover over the marshy and boggy tracts along either and are speedily condensed into rain. The large tracts of bog along the eastern side of the Main are therefore very injurious to the climate of the parish and materially retard the ripening of the crops and hardening of the grain in that portion of it. Along the western side of the river the acclivity of the ridge falling towards it is well cultivated and fertile, but here also the crops are longer in coming to maturity, owing to the same cause, added to the richness and heaviness of the soil.

The usual seasons of seed time and harvest throughout the parish are generally as follows: wheat is sown immediately after the raising of the potatoes, usually in the latter part of November and commencement of December. Its reaping commences in August, sometimes so early as the 12th of that month, and is generally finished by the first and second week in September. The usual time for sowing oats is from the 20th March to the 20th April. Its cutting down commences about the last week in August and concludes about the first week in October. The general planting of potatoes takes place during the last week of the month of April and the entire of May, and their raising during the month of November.

NATURAL STATE

Randalstown: Name

Randalstown, formerly called Mullynierin or "the iron mills", is said to have derived its former name from the ironworks which were at one time carried on there, as also from the circumstance of the iron ore having been procured from the hilly ridge at the base of which the town is situated. It is said to have retained this name until about the year 1680, when it received its present one from Rose O'Neill of Edenduffcarrick (now Shane's Castle), on her marriage with Randal <Randle> MacDonnell, Marquis of Antrim.

Locality

The market and post of Randalstown is pleasingly situated on the River Main, which is intersected by the main road from Belfast to Toome Bridge, the great pass between the southern portions of the counties of Antrim and Derry. The mail coach road from Belfast to Londonderry and the main road from Belfast to Portglenone unite here, the former at the eastern and the latter at the western end of the town.

Randalstown, according to the post office measurement, is 104 and a half miles north of Dublin.

Parish of Drummaul

It is 21 and a half miles north west of Belfast and 9 miles south of Ballymena. It is in the diocese of Connor, barony of Upper Toome, parish of Drummaul, manor of Edenduffcarrick and north east circuit of assize.

Extent

Randalstown chiefly consists of 1 street, extending for half a mile along the road from Belfast to Toome Bridge. From this a lesser street, consisting almost only of cottages, extends northerly for 264 yards along the road to Portglenone. The town is principally situated on the right bank of the river, towards which there is at first a rapid, but as it approaches it, a gradual fall. The extreme length of Randalstown is half a mile from east to west and 130 yards from north to south.

Scenery

The situation of Randalstown is very pleasing, possessing the advantages of being watered by a copious stream and almost embosomed in the dense woods and plantings of Shane's Castle, which extend along the southern side of the town and, with the rising ground on its eastern and western sides, almost completely exclude it from the view. The slender and graceful spire of its church is alone discernible from a distance and, being situated at the western end of the town, at once indicates its site and forms an ornament to the landscape.

HISTORY

History of Randalstown

Randalstown is said to be a place of considerable antiquity, but except the ruins of Shane's Castle, which are about 3 miles from it, there is not anything in itself or its immediate neighbourhood which could indicate this. It is said to have, from an early date, been connected with the family of the O'Neills and until within the last century to have been a place of trade and importance, though the extent of the town has never been greater than at present. Its origin is wholly involved in obscurity and its progress as to size and importance can only be conjectured to have resulted from the establishment of very extensive ironworks in it, sufficient proofs of the former existence of which are still to be found in the quantities of iron dross and cinders occasionally turned up about it. It is not, however, known when these works were given up. Within memory 3 distilleries of 550 gallons each and 3 very large malt kilns were in full work in Randalstown, but were in 1780 given up, owing to the duty either having been raised or set upon whiskey. An extensive bleach green and paper mills were established here within memory, but having been given up many years ago are now fallen into decay.

Previous to the union with Great Britain, Randalstown returned a member to the Irish parliament. It is said that this privilege was obtained for it by the celebrated Rose O'Neill, afterwards Marchioness of Antrim, but it is not known in what manner. The extent of the borough was but trifling and merely included the town. It was what was commonly but inelegantly termed "a potwalloping borough", that is any person [who] boiled a pot of yarn and resided within the limits of the borough had a right to vote. The elections seem to have been conducted in rather a curious manner. The O'Neills always nominated and returned whom they pleased and settled the entire business in the drawing room at Shane's Castle. The late Baron McClelland was the last member returned for Randalstown.

On the 7th June 1798 an engagement took place here between 50 of the Toome yeomanry and about 1,500 rebels, in which the former, having been beaten into the market house, were taken prisoners. 2 were killed and several wounded on each side. Next day more than one-half of the town was burned by the king's troops, commanded by Colonel Anstruther.

In the year 1818 the great monthly linen market, which for a long time had been almost the sole support of Randalstown, began to decline. In 1828 an attempt was made to revive it but without success, and it was in a short time wholly given up. The cause of its decline was its proximity to Ballymena. The fine yard-wide linen, the manufacture of which had hitherto been confined to the neighbourhood of Randalstown, being now also manufactured about Ballymena, and the principal buyers of that description also living in the latter town, the sale of it for the convenience of both was transferred to the great weekly market there. Randalstown, having been only a monthly market, was soon neglected by the weavers, who gladly availed themselves of the earliest opportunity of disposing of their cloth which the other presented. This was a serious injury to Randalstown, as since the abandonment of the linen market, the town has continued to decline, its other markets, except those for the sale of grain, being inconsiderable.

Modern Topography

Public Buildings

There are not any remains of ancient buildings in Randalstown. A church had stood near the site of the present one and was pulled down on its erection. It had not, however, been of any antiquity, as it is said to have been erected subsequently to that in the townland of Drummaul, the burial ground of which is still in use. The graves in the burial ground of Randalstown church are of comparatively modern date. The public buildings of Randalstown consist of the parish church, 2 Presbyterian meeting houses, a Roman Catholic chapel, 2 market houses, the barracks and a national schoolhouse.

Parish Church

The parish church is a plain but elegant building, situated on a gentle eminence at the western end of the town. Its form is that of an oblong square, measuring in the extreme 54 by 27 feet. It is built of whinstone, in rubble masonry, and has at each side 3 handsome Gothic windows with rich label mouldings of white sandstone. The chancel or east window is spacious and similarly ornamented, as are also 3 small Gothic windows in its western end. On its western gable is elevated a handsome square tower of masonry similar to that in the church, but ornamented at its angles with cut-stone pillars and pinnacles. From the tower springs a beautiful octagonal spire of white sandstone, of slender though symmetrical proportions. It has several deeply-throated mouldings at its base and is pierced by 2 storeys of little Gothic windows.

The interior of the church is equally plain and elegant. The roof is supported by metal [crossed out: principles] and is sheeted. At the western end is the chancel [crossed out: table] consisting of a handsome Gothic arch 11 feet 6 inches wide and 5 feet deep. At the opposite end over the private entrance is an excellent organ set in a Gothic niche, and presenting a handsome front. On each side of the organ is a private seat, the property of Lord O'Neill, each looking into the church through a Gothic arch. The church is well heated with hot air and is very comfortable. It contains accommodation for 256 persons.

It was erected in 1832 at a cost of 1,800 pounds, of which 1,500 pounds were advanced by the Board of First Fruits and 300 pounds contributed by Lord O'Neill, who also presented it with the organ which cost about 220 pounds, the stoves and the annual salary of the organist. The communion plate consists of a small flagon, a chalice and a very small paten, all of silver. They bear the inscription "Rose, Marchioness of Antrim, 1684." There is also a neat plated salver presented by the Reverend S.S. Heatley (the present incumbent) in 1818.

In the burial ground attached to the church Lord O'Neill has lately erected a capacious and very handsome vault, which has cost him 500 pounds. It contains niches for 18 coffins.

Presbyterian Meeting House

The Presbyterian meeting is situated in a hollow on the opposite side of the road from and within a few yards of the church. Its form is rather singular, being that of an elipse, the major diameter of which is 88 and the minor 48 feet. At its northern side stands a sexagonal porch, supporting a little wooden turret surmounted by a dome. The appearance of the building is plain and substantial, being well built of whinstone in common rubble masonry. The interior of the house is very comfortably and neatly fitted up, and contains a spacious gallery (to which there are 2 entrances from the porch) extending all around it. It contains accommodation for 1,106 persons in 134 pews. The ground on which the meeting house stands was originally granted by Rose O'Neill and an addition was made to it in 1790 by the late Lord O'Neill. It is enclosed by a stone and lime wall.

The erection of this meeting house (in 1790) cost the congregation 600 pounds. In 1828 it was newly roofed by them at an expense of 200 pounds, and between the years 1830 to 1832 1,054 pounds were expended in erecting the porch and gallery.

According to the tradition of the old inhabitants, the first Presbyterian meeting house was erected here about the year 1630 and consisted merely of a small thatched house which stood in the north side of the town. In 1670 the present site was granted to the congregation by Rose O'Neill (Marchioness of Antrim), who was a great friend to Presbyterianism, and a house was erected under the ministry of the Reverend William Taylor. It stood until the year 1790, when it was pulled down, and the first stone of the present house laid on the 12th July in that year, being the 100th anniversary of the landing of King William in Ireland. A small field or patch of land called the cowpark was then added to the meeting house yard by the Earl O'Neill.

Parish of Drummaul

Seceders' Meeting House

The Seceders' meeting house is situated to the north west side of the town, on the road leading to Portglenone. It is a plain old building of an oblong square form, measuring 42 by 30 feet inside. It is in bad repair and by no means a comfortable place of worship. It contains 35 pews, capable of accommodating 288 persons. It was erected by the congregation in 1753 and cost between 250 and 300 pounds.

Roman Catholic Chapel

The Roman Catholic chapel is prettily situated at the eastern side of the town, to the right of the road to Ballymena. It consists of a main aisle standing north and south and measuring inside 60 by 24 feet, to the west centre [of] which stands a lesser aisle measuring inside 26 feet 9 inches by 24 feet. The western end of the latter presents a neat front, being ornamented at its angles by cut-stone pinnacles and surmounted by a cross. The external appearance of this building is very neat, though plain. It is roughcast and kept in excellent order. The gallery contains 58 pews, but there are not any in the aisles. It contains in its present state accommodation for upwards of 1,000 persons. The main aisle of this chapel was erected in 1784 and the lesser one in 1824, when the house was almost rebuilt at an expense of 800 pounds, raised by subscription.

Old Market House

The old market house stands in the south side of the main street and near the centre of the town. It is a plain, uninteresting-looking building, 2-storeys high and measuring externally 60 by 25 feet. The ground storey is used as a weigh-house and for the storage of grain. There are also 2 apartments in it, which were formerly used as cells for the confinement of rioters etc. It opens to the street by 3 large, circular arched gateways with iron gates. The upper storey is now used as Lord O'Neill's office by his agent, for collecting or receiving his rents and transacting the business of his estate. It had formerly also been used for holding manor courts and petty sessions, and during the rebellion of 1798 the lower storey was used as a stable by the cavalry. This market house was erected in 1770 by the late Lord O'Neill.

New Market House

The new market house stands on the east side of a road called the New Street, a little to the south of the centre of the town. It is a plain substantially built edifice, 2-storeys high and measuring externally 62 feet 6 inches by 26 feet 6 inches. It is surmounted by a wooden cupola on which is elevated a gilt vane. The underfloor is used as a market for the sale of and for the storage of grain. It opens at each side by 3 lofty, circular arched gateways with wooden gates. 2 apartments on this floor are fitted up for the purposes of the dispensary. The upper floor is used as a court in which petty sessions, manor courts, courts leet etc. are held. This market house was erected in 1831 at an expense of 500 pounds, of which Lord O'Neill contributed 100 pounds. The remainder was assessed on the manor, his lordship paying his proportion of the assessment.

Barracks

The barracks are beautifully situated along the right bank of the river, extending from the western end of the bridge. The barracks consist of 3 parallel ranges of buildings. The front range facing the river consists of 4 contiguous houses 2-storeys high, 130 feet long and 20 feet deep. The second range consists of 1-storey houses and the third is occupied with offices for the others. The front range contains accommodation for 60 and the second for 20 men, but the first only are fitted up as barracks. They are occupied by the adjutant and staff of the Antrim Regiment of Militia, consisting of a sergeant-major and 8 sergeants with their families. In front of the barracks a very handsome parade ground 36 yards broad extends for 184 yards along the edge of the river. It is quite level and is kept well gravelled and in the nicest order.

The barracks were built by Lord O'Neill (colonel of the Antrim Regiment) in 1816 at a cost of 2,000 pounds, solely for the staff of that regiment on its being disembodied. The staff was then 97 strong, including 4 officers, but has since been several times reduced and now musters but 1 officer and 9 non-commissioned officers. These barracks afford comfortable quarters to the militia staff and the front range is [in] good repair, but they bear no resemblance to a regular barrack, either in their construction or fitting up, and do not in any respect differ from ordinary dwelling houses.

Schoolhouse

The national schoolhouse is a very neat little building, situated to the south of the town and near the church. It is 1-storey high and measures externally 36 by 24 feet. It is remarkably well fitted up inside and is kept in very good order. It contains accommodation for nearly 100 scholars. This schoolhouse was erected in 1833 at an expense of 188 pounds 18s 7d, of which sum 80 pounds towards its erection and 13 pounds for furniture were given by the Board of National Education, and the remaining sums of 90 pounds 13s 7d towards its erection and 5 pounds 5s for furniture were contributed by the Reverend Daniel Curoe, the parish priest.

Bridge

The bridge over the River Main is a clumsy old structure and must be of some antiquity, as it seems to have been twice widened, though it is in tolerable repair. It measures 193 feet in length and 29 in width within the parapets. It is supported by 9 circular-segment arches of unequal span.

Official Residences

The official residences in Randalstown are: Millmount, the residence of George Handcock Esquire, J.P., chief agent to the Right Honourable Earl O'Neill. The house, which is 3-storeys high, is modern and spacious, prettily situated on an eminence near the river and on the north east side of the town. The lawn is not extensive but is thickly planted, and the situation of the house retired though cheerful. A good garden and suitable offices are attached to the house. Lord O'Neill in 1825 purchased this place as a residence for his agent. Captain C.B. Carrothers, the adjutant of the Antrim Regiment of Militia, resides at the barracks.

The only private residence is that of the Reverend Samuel Heatley, vicar of the parish, who resides in a neat 2-storey house at the eastern end of the town.

Extent of Randalstown

Randalstown chiefly consists of 1 street, extending for half a mile along the road from Toome Bridge to Belfast. Towards its western extremity the street is slightly curved and near the river it makes an angular turn for a few yards southward to the bridge. The remainder of this street on the opposite side of the river is principally made up of a single row of cottages extending along the road for about 450 yards. This street varies in width from 29 to 47 feet and averages 38 feet. It is formed of broken stone and has on each side a narrow and rugged paved footway. From the north western end of this street a lesser one, chiefly consisting of cottages, branches north westerly for 246 yards, and from its centre another strikes off in a southerly direction for about 130 yards. This street has, however, been but lately commenced and as yet consists of but 6 houses.

Houses

Randalstown contains 1 3-storey and 70 2-storey houses and 135 cottages and cabins, all of which are built of stone and about one-half of them thatched. In their erection no regard whatever has been paid to uniformity or regularity, and not more than half a dozen have the slightest appearance of taste or neatness. There are not 10 good houses in the town and wherever there is even a middling one, it is invariably situated between 2 of an inferior description and the appearance of all thus destroyed. The better description of houses, those chiefly occupied by dealers, are about the centre of the town, but as they approach its outlets they dwindle into cottages and cabins. Almost all the houses and cottages are roughcast, but few of them are [in] good order and many of them in bad repair. The houses are of tolerable size and so far suited to persons in business. Some of the cottages of the tradesmen are substantial and comfortable, but many of them, particularly those occupied by labourers, are dirty and comfortless.

Speaking comparatively, the town is rather cleanly than otherwise. To this the inclination of the ground contributes in some degree, and it is said that since the cholera visited Randalstown in 1833, when 70 persons died of it, the inhabitants have been much attentive to cleanliness. A great drawback to the improvement of the appearance of the town is its distance from lime, the nearest lime-kilns being from 16 to 17 miles distant. No new houses are building or have been lately built, nor is the town likely to increase in size, there being at present 9 unoccupied houses in it.

SOCIAL AND PRODUCTIVE ECONOMY

Population and Occupations

The population of Randalstown amounts to 848 persons, of whom 419 are males and 429 females. Of these 122 are members of the Established Church, 348 are Presbyterians and 378 Roman Catholics. There are but 3 private families residing in the town. The people are of the middle or lower ranks and may be classed under the heads of dealers or persons in retail trade, tradesmen and mechanics, and servants and labourers (for a more detailed account see Table of Trades and Occupations, appendix).

The dealers are a respectable, industrious and frugal class, who, though they cannot be termed opulent, are mostly independent and comfortable in their circumstances. In addition to their trade they all hold some land. The tradesmen and mechanics are but indifferently well-off. They are not generally in constant employment and the rates of wages are rather lower than in the neighbouring towns. They are mostly well conducted and industrious, but many of them are improvident and intemperate in their habits, and they are consequently not unfrequently reduced to the verge of poverty. The labourers are a peaceable though not very provident class. They are rather industrious than otherwise, but as they are not kept in constant employment they are frequently in great want. A few labourers and most of the tradesmen hold a little land, generally from 2 to 3 acres.

Temperance Society

A temperance society was established here in 1834 and consists at present of but 40 members. It has not prospered here, nor has it produced any effect on the character of the inhabitants as to temperance, which is to be much regretted, intemperance being a vice to which both sexes are here much addicted.

Machinery

Randalstown is no longer a manufacturing town, though it had once been so, and though few towns possess the same advantages, in an unlimited and constant supply of water power for machinery, a population in want of employment and in its being within a reasonable distance from the port and market of Belfast, its manufactories now consist of: a small chandling establishment affording employment to but 2 men; a corn mill propelled by 2 breast water wheels, one of which is 14 feet in diameter and 3 feet 6 inches broad; the other is 12 in diameter and 5 feet 6 inches broad.

A cotton mill, now idle, is situated on the north east side of the town. It is a large building consisting of 4 floors. The machinery is propelled by an undershot water wheel 14 feet in diameter and 9 feet 9 inches broad. Near the cotton mills is a range of houses fitted up as workshops and containing 50 looms for weaving cotton. There are now only 65 persons employed in them, while in 1829 there were 75. To the rear of the workshops is a beetling mill, which has for many years been idle. The machinery is propelled by 2 breast water wheels, one of which is 15 feet 9 inches in diameter and 3 feet 8 inches broad; the other is 16 feet in diameter and 4 feet 6 inches broad.

Fairs

2 annual fairs are held in Randalstown, one on the 16th July and the other on the 1st November. These fairs are inconsiderable and are gradually becoming more so, a few cows and pigs, some yarn and pedlar's goods being almost the only articles exposed for sale. The customs levied in the fairs are 2d for each cow, 3d for each horse and 1d for each sheep or pig. They are the property of Lord O'Neill, the lord of the manor and soil, but do [not] amount annually to more than 1 pound 10s.

Markets

A large market is held here on the first Wednesday in each month. Formerly this market was well attended and the quantity of linen sold at it was very considerable. In the year 1828 the sale of linen ceased here, and almost the entire trade of the market has been absorbed by the great weekly one of Ballymena. A few pigs, some yarn and flax, pedlar's goods, earthenware and butcher's meat are now almost the only commodities exposed for sale, and even these in but small quantities.

The grain market is held on every Wednesday throughout the season for the sale of wheat and oats. The quantity of wheat brought to market here is annually decreasing, owing in a great degree to the non-attendance of purchasers, who now buy at the mills at Muckamore near Antrim, 7 miles distant, and at those at Crumlin, 12 miles distant. Besides, the farmers now prefer taking their wheat to Belfast, in order not only to obtain the highest price for it, but also that they may bring back lime from the kilns at Carnmoney on their way back. (A table showing the quantity of wheat and oats sold in Randalstown during the last 10 years will be found by referring to appendix). Grain, as well as the different commodities brought to this market, is conveyed to it in the carts of the farmer.

Provisions

Randalstown is miserably supplied with butcher's meat. The quality of that article sold here is of an inferior description, that required by the upper classes being procured from Antrim, 4 and three-quarter miles distant. Fish was until within the last few years very abundant, but is now scarce, owing to the breaking up of the cutts or weirs on the River Main, within a mile of the town. Lough Neagh trout and pullen taken along the shore of the parish of Antrim are sometimes brought here for sale. The supply of poultry, milk, eggs and butter is plentiful in their seasons. The only vegetables to be had are potatoes, leeks and onions. The former at all seasons and the latter in summer and autumn are abundant. Apples, pears, plums, black cherries and gooseberries are plentifully supplied and are cheap. There is not any market gardening nor grazing nor stall feeding for beef about the town. Grazing for milch cows usually lets for 3 pounds the Irish acre.

Building Materials

Belfast is the great mart from whence dealers are supplied with their various commodities of groceries, woollen drapery, cottons, timber, slates, iron and coals, the carriage of which to Randalstown costs from 6d to 8d per cwt. Slates, however, are rarely sold here, and the only description of timber for sale being planks and deals, those about to build or requiring these articles usually purchase them in Belfast. Pine timber and countess slates are the descriptions of these articles commonly used. Lime is procured either from the kilns at Carnmoney near Belfast, 17 miles, or from those in the county Derry, from 16 to 17 miles distant, and costs when laid down here from 1s 6d to 2s 7d per barrel. Bricks are procured from the banks of the Bann in the parish of Ahoghill, from 7 to 8 miles distant, and cost when laid down from 12s to 15s per 1,000. Whin and greenstone and the harder species of basalt admirably suited for building are abundant in the neighbourhood. Immediately adjoining the eastern side of the town is a capital quarry of the former description of stone.

Insurances and Employment

Only 3 houses and 1 life are insured in Randalstown. A fire here is a very rare event.

During the latter part of winter and the beginning of spring agricultural labourers are almost unemployed. At those seasons there is much distress and sickness, arising from their want of nutritive food among them. During the other seasons they are seldom unemployed. The tradespeople seldom suffer from want of employment.

Conveyances

Randalstown possesses every facility with communication with the neighbouring districts, as will be seen by referring to appendix. The mail from Dublin and Belfast arrives at 10 a.m. in summer and 11 a.m. in winter, on its way to Londonderry by Ballymena and Coleraine. It is dispatched for Belfast and Dublin at 4 a.m. There are 4 regular carriers to Belfast, who make the journey there and back in 2 days. The charge for carriage to Belfast is from 6d to 8d per cwt.

Dispensary

The dispensary was established here in 1813 and is supported in the usual manner, equally by the contributions of the inhabitants and landed proprietors and by the presentment of the grand jury. In a place like this, where there is much poverty, its effects have been perceptible, not only in administering to the wants of the poor, but also by its speedy assistance in checking the spreading of infection and in promoting habits of cleanliness in the persons and abodes of the lower class. For a detailed account of the funds of this institution and a table of diseases, see appendix.

Endowed Schools

There are 2 schools which are partly supported by benevolence, namely the parish and the national schools. The teacher of the former receives an annual gratuity of 4 pounds from Lord O'Neill and 3 pounds 10s from the London Hibernian Society, and the latter under the Board of National Education receives an annual sum of 12 pounds, besides school requisites from that society (see table of schools, appendix).

Donation

The only contribution for the support of the poor further than the weekly collection on Sundays is an annual one of 42 pounds from Lord O'Neill, to be distributed annually by the churchwardens among 40 poor persons in this parish.

Character of the People

There is now little or no taste for amusement, the industrious exertions of almost all being required to provide for themselves and their families. An idle day or two at Easter and the same at Christmas are now their only holy days. Sunday is by the better class spent after worship in strolling along the delightful walks in Shane's Castle demesne, to which the public have admission.

The character of all classes has been much changed by the decrease in the circulation of capital. They are now much more industrious and less social [than] formerly. Among the better description of people there is less intemperance, but still there is here among both sexes more than in the neighbouring towns. Otherwise, speaking generally, they are rather a moral people and are peaceable, civil and obliging, and rather humane and charitable.

Post Cars

5 post cars and horses, but indifferently appointed, are kept for hire. The usual rate of travelling is 5 miles Irish per hour. The charge per mile for 1 person is 8d and for 3, 10d.

Condition of the Town

Randalstown is improving in appearance as to cleanliness, but in every [other] respect it is declining. There is no trade or manufacture, no resident gentlemen of property, nor in fact anyone to take the slightest interest in it further than concerns their own. Its trade has been absorbed in the vortex of Ballymena, which has monopolised that of all the neighbouring towns and villages. There is no capital in the town, nor is there the slightest inducement, further than its natural advantages, for the investment of that of strangers.

Few towns possess more of the important requisites for establishing manufactures or machinery. There is a hardy, industrious and but half-employed population in the town and neighbourhood, a river capable of affording a constant supply of water power to almost any extent, excellent means of communication with the neighbouring towns and districts, and it is within a reasonable distance from the important market and harbour of Belfast. It is true there is not coal in the neighbourhood, but if not there is an almost unlimited supply of bog for fuel within 2 miles of the town, the removal or cutting of which would be an important benefit to the proprietor and the people. There is not the slightest excitement for enterprise among the inhabitants. Their trade or dealing is of a petty and trifling description, and any attempt to extend it might prove ruinous to them.

Ancient Borough

Antrim ceased to be a borough on the union of Ireland with Great Britain. For a long time subsequent to its enfranchisement it was a potwalloping borough, but the qualification to vote having been raised, the number of voters was reduced from upwards of 50 to 15, and again, on a second increase of the qualification, to 10. The last member returned for this borough was the late Baron McClelland.

MODERN AND ANCIENT TOPOGRAPHY

Public Buildings in the Parish

The only public building in the parish, beside those described under the head of Towns, is the Seceders' meeting house in the townland of Craigmore, 2 miles north west of Randalstown. It is a plain building, built of stone without being roughcast. It measures internally 37 by 22 feet and is pretty comfortably fitted up with 22 pews capable of accommodating 220 persons. It is a substantial edifice and is in good repair. It was erected by subscription in the year 1814.

Gentlemen's Seats: Shane's Castle

Shane's Castle, formerly called Edenduffcarrick, the ancient residence of the celebrated and noble family of O'Neill, and now that of the Right Honourable Charles, Earl O'Neill K.P., Lord Lieutenant of the County Antrim and colonel of the Antrim Regiment of Militia, who succeeded to the title and estates on the murder of his father in the town of Antrim by the rebels, on the 7th June 1798.

It must appear strange that little or nothing more than a few stories about ghosts and banshees should in its neighbourhood be known respecting a place so long and intimately identified with the history of the country. As to the date of its erection, nothing whatever can be locally ascertained, nor is it known who was its founder. Little therefore can here be given further than as to its present state. It is said that all the ancient manuscripts of the family were destroyed at the burning of Shane's Castle on the 20th May 1816. This, however, is to be doubted. This present noble proprietor appears totally ignorant on the subject of the history of his family and castle, though apparently willing to communicate everything in his power.

The ruins of Shane's Castle are situated on a little rise within a few yards of the shore of Lough Neagh and near the eastern side of the parish, and command a view of Lough Neagh from its northern to its southern extremity and, extending beyond it, to the distant mountains of Mourne on the south, those of Derry and Tyrone on the west, and a portion of the Antrim hills on the east. In the north of Ireland there is no rural scenery superior to that which the views from Shane's Castle, possessing as they do all the requisites of the richest landscapes in wood and water, with a beautifully outlined background, present. To the north the lofty woods of the demesne, which extend for 3 and a half miles from east to west, exclude a view which would be much less interesting, in the tame outline of the neighbouring mountains.

The ruins do not in their structure or masonry bear the stamp of antiquity. The portion still standing consist of 2 wings, standing north and south of each other and 76 feet apart. The part consumed and fallen down forms the centre or curtain which connected them and in the western side of which was the front. The wings are circular at their western ends. They extend eastwards for 57 feet and measure in width 22 feet. They are about 50 feet high and have had 3 floors. They are surmounted by stacks of brick chimneys, which give them the little effect they retain. Except a plainly cut-stone doorway in the northern wing there is no architectural ornament or device about them, and their roughcast and whitened walls but ill accord with the ideas associated with their history. A better idea of these ruins may perhaps be found by referring to appendix.

Shane's Castle was destroyed by an accidental fire which broke out in one of the bed or dressing rooms on the 20th May 1816, about 6 or 7 o'clock in the evening. The castle had been very gay at the time and a large party was assembled there that day. So rapid was the progress of the devouring element that scarcely anything was saved, and an immense quantity of plate, much of which had been but recently purchased, old family portraits, manuscripts, documents and books fell a prey to the flames. The fire is supposed to have originated in a chimney in the dressing room, in which some rooks had built.

Almost adjoining the southern wing of the castle is a handsome conservatory erected by the present earl. It is stocked with some rare exotics besides some remarkably fine orange and lemon trees. The conservatory presents a handsome front of 13 Saxon windows separated by moulded columns of sandstone. It has a southern aspect and extends for 105 feet along the northern side of the terrace of a battery, presenting to the lake, by which it is washed, a front of 328 feet. In depth the battery measures 132 feet and in height above the water 18 feet. It is surrounded by a parapet 4 feet 6 inches high, with embrasures for 21 iron 12-pounders, which are supported merely by upright legs. The battery and conservatory have a very good effect from the water, the former being well built of dark whinstone and inclining from the water to the cordon under the parapet at an angle of about 80 degrees to the former.

At the south west angle of the battery is a small triangular bastion, and at its south eastern angle a handsome circular tower 46 feet high from the water. A spiral stair descends from the terrace to a sally-port at the base of the tower.

The terrace is supported by a double row of 26 arched vaults, separated by a corridor extending from the western to the eastern side of the battery, where there are entrances from the water for the purpose of taking in coals or any other loading which might have been required. These vaults measure individually 46 by 12 feet and 8 feet high. They are almost quite dark, are wholly unoccupied and seem to have been erected merely for the support of the terrace. Communicating with the vaults is a very fine vaulted kitchen and several other underground apartments connected with the former kitchen, but now almost choked up with rubbish. From these a tunnel lit from above extended inwards for 90 yards. It was used for communicating with and conveying whatever was required to the underground apartments of the castle. It is 7 feet high and 7 feet wide. This, however, is also neary blocked up and of course unused and useless.

The ruins have not undergone much change for the last 3 or 4 years. This, from their exposed situation, is much to be wondered at. The southern wing discovers several fissures, but the northern is pretty sound and is likely to remain for years in its present state.

MODERN TOPOGRAPHY

Residence of Lord O'Neill

Since the destruction of the castle Lord O'Neill has continued to reside in some of the offices which he has fitted up. The offices stand about 600 yards north west of the ruins and are quite embosomed in trees and shut out from the public. They consist of 3 contiguous quadrangular courts or squares. In the eastern of these, the stable yard, are his lordship's apartments, extending almost along 2 of its sides, a third side being taken up with coach-houses and stables. The range on the north side of the square consists of a suite of apartments and a greenhouse on the ground, and sleeping apartments on the upper floor. This side of the square presents a brick-finished front and is enclosed from the yard by a low palisading. His lordship has some other private apartments in the

Parish of Drummaul

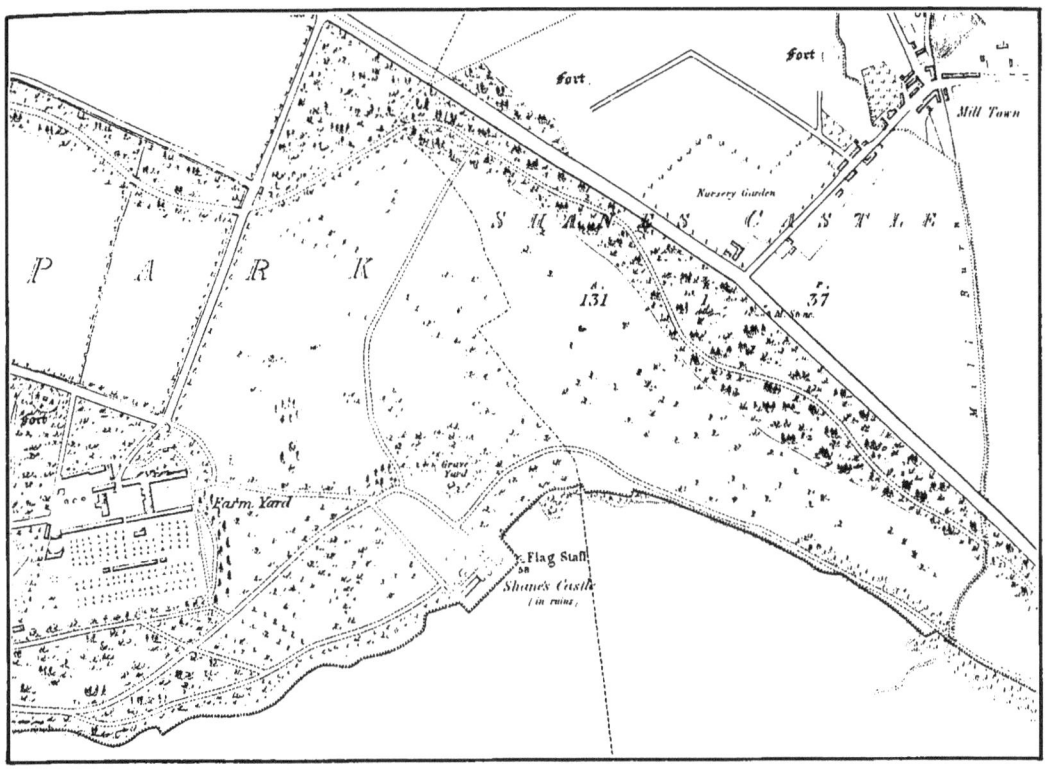

Map of Shane's Castle and neighbourhood from the first 6" O.S. maps, 1830s

western side of the square, which open to the gardens outside it.

The second square, occupied by domestics' apartments and offices, opens from the former by an archway surmounted by a cupola and gilded vane. Beyond this is the farmyard, with ranges of cowhouses, cart sheds etc. along each side, and stands for hay and cornstacks in the centre.

His lordship's library is modern and not very valuable, there are but a few paintings and these not deserving of particular notice or description, nor is there anything worthy of further notice in his residence.

Gardens at Shane's Castle

The gardens, which extend along the south side of the offices, are well worth visiting, being extensive, beautifully laid out, well stocked and in the nicest order. Their total extent, including the nursery, is about 6 acres. At one extremity of the flower or verdure garden is a very handsome greenhouse or conservatory, containing a valuable collection of rare plants. Its style of construction and design are very tasteful. In the centre of the front is a larger compartment, in which the family arms are richly displayed in stained glass.

The fruit and vegetable garden is extensive and well stocked. The grapery and pine [vine ?] pits are very large and the quantity of hothouse fruit, particularly grapes, produced here is very great. The nursery is not extensive, nor the quantity of young trees nor their variety of any consequence. These gardens are kept in the nicest order. The present gardener is a scientific person and exhibits no small proof of his professional skill in the specimens of his fruit and flowers displayed at the Belfast horticultural shows.

Shane's Castle Demesne

Shane's Castle demesne, including the deerpark, extends over 1,913 acres 23 perches, of which about three-fourths are under timber or planting. Its extreme length from east to west in a right line is 3 and a half miles. Its figure is that of a triangle, the base of which (at its western side) is 2 and a third miles long, while its sides are formed by the lake and the mail coach road from Randalstown to Belfast. It contains about 33 miles of avenues and roads or drives, most of which are kept in good order but not altogether well laid out, as from them an occasional glimpse of the lake or the river is all that can be obtained.

The demesne is watered by the River Main, a copious stream from 31 to 57 yards broad which winds its way for about 2 and a half miles through the western end of the park, from Randalstown at its northern to the lake at its southern side. Its banks at first tower to a considerable height, but gradually decline towards its mouth. They are clothed with a dense wood from their base to their summit, which almost wholly excludes the river from the view. Across the stream are 2 stone bridges, one of [blank] and the other of [blank] arches. They form the only means of communication across the stream and connect the main drive, which, commencing at Randalstown, winds its way along the stream, which it crosses twice and, running along the lake from its extremity, terminates near the eastern end of the demesne.

The grounds present but little variety of surface, being almost flat and inclining but gently towards the lake. The planting, however, being judiciously disposed, tends to relieve its monotony. It was put down about 30 years ago by the present proprietor, who then added considerably to the extent of the demesne by taking in the highway that then ran from Randalstown to Antrim and also a considerable space beyond it. He also then threw down several cottages and houses that stood in the demesne.

Woods of Demesne

There is not now much old timber either in the demesne or deerpark. A few aged oaks, ash trees, very large hawthorns and some hazel brushwood are all that remain of the vast woods of Shane's Castle. Among the most prevalent and finest timber are the elms, sycamores, beeches and horse-chestnuts. The sycamore and elms are particularly large and must have been growing for many years. The more modern planting consists of almost every variety of tree, but chiefly of fir, larch, beech and alder, which are thriving though badly taken care of, being in wretched want of thinning. A belt of planting extends from Randalstown for 3 and a quarter miles along the road to Antrim, which totally shuts out any view of the demesne.

Deerpark

The deerpark is included in the demesne but is not open to the public. It is situated at the western side of the river and contains about 700 acres. It is altogether, with the exception of what is under planting, laid down in pasture and is stocked with from 200 to 300 deer.

There are 2 lodges in the deerpark, one on the edge of the lake, a very pretty rustic stone cottage in which his lordship has some private apartments. The other is the residence of the park-keeper and is built of stone, in miniature imitation of the lodge of the ranger of Windsor forest. Attached to it is an aviary on a small scale, in which are some gold and silver pheasants.

There are 2 pretty rustic cottages of wood situated on the edge of the lake. His lordship very considerately had these erected for the accommodation of parties visiting the demesne.

Wildlife of Demesne

There is a heronry and a decoy in the demesne. The latter actually swarms with ducks, teal and widgeon, while the woods and plantings abound with pheasants. Woodcocks are numerous here in winter and thousands of wild duck live undisturbed along the shores of the lake and river. There is a numerous rookery here. A few years ago the rooks in returning to their abodes were overtaken by a dense fog, in which they lost their way and hundreds of them, flying over the lake until they were exhausted, were drowned in it and its shores were strewed with their dead bodies.

Entrances to Demesne

The entrances to the demesne, 2 in number, one being near its western and the other near its eastern end (on the Randalstown and Antrim road), are not at all in character with the place or the ideas associated with it. The one near Antrim merely consists of a miserable and ruinous wooded gate without pillars or lodge, there being merely a plain cottage on the opposite side of the road in which the gatekeeper resides. The other gateway is somewhat better. A large iron gate with wickets is swung from a pair of plain brick pillars. In a cabin nearly opposite, the person who opens the gate resides. His lordship is now erecting a 6 foot stone wall with Welsh coping along the demesne, on the road from Antrim to Randalstown. About half a mile has already been completed.

The public have access to the park every day except Sundays from May until October. It is much frequented by parties of pleasure from all the neighbouring towns and districts, but particularly from Belfast. Until the season before last the demesne was open to the public on Sundays, but on a remonstrance being made to Lord O'Neill by

Parish of Drummaul

some of the respectable inhabitants of the neighbourhood of Antrim, as to the thoroughfare it created in that town on that day, he very properly withdrew the lease for admission to it.

Machinery

The machinery of the parish, besides that described under the head of Towns, consists of 1 beetling mill, 3 corn mills and 1 flax mill.

The beetling mill is situated on the River Main and in the townland of Magheralane. Its machinery is propelled by 3 breast water wheels, 2 of which are 14 and 1 of them 15 feet in diameter.

The corn mill in the townland of Aghaboy is propelled by a breast water 16 feet in diameter and 5 feet 4 inches broad.

The corn mill in the townland of Killyfad is propelled by a breast water wheel 14 feet in diameter and 1 foot 6 inches broad.

The corn mill in the townland of Ballynacraigy, in the detached portion of the parish, is propelled by a breast wheel 14 feet in diameter and 2 feet broad.

The flax mill in the townland of Aghaboy is propelled by a breast water wheel 16 feet in diameter and 4 feet broad.

Communications

This parish is amply supplied with the means of communication in the numerous main and by-roads which traverse its surface. They are kept in repair at the expense of the barony of Upper Toome, in which the parish is situated, with the exception of the mail coach road from Derry to Belfast, which is kept up at the expense of the county at large.

This road forms the communication between Randalstown and the towns of Ballymena and Antrim, Ballymena being situated 9 miles to the north and Antrim 4 and a half miles to the south east of Randalstown. It traverses the eastern side of the parish for 4 and a half miles in a somewhat curvilinear direction from north to south, until it reaches Randalstown, where it strikes off almost at a right angle to the eastern extremity of the parish, a distance of 2 miles. Its total length in this parish is 6 and a half miles. Its average breadth from Randalstown to Antrim, including a footway 6 feet broad, is 60 feet, while from Randalstown to Ballymena its average breadth is but 30 feet. Its direction between the different towns could scarcely be improved. It is almost quite level, except towards the northern side of the parish where there is a trifling rise.

It is in general kept in pretty good repair. Between Antrim and Randalstown its breadth is almost twice too great and renders it more difficult to be kept in order. Added to this the dense planting along its southern side for its entire way prevents its drying so rapidly, and in winter it is consequently very heavy. As a mail coach road this line will be superseded by a new one direct from Antrim to Ballymena, which will not pass within 4 miles of Randalstown. The new line will be opened some time before next winter.

The road from Randalstown to Toome Bridge, on the western frontier of the county, traverses the western portion of the parish from east to west for 2 and a half miles. Its average breadth is 28 feet. Its direction is slightly curvilinear. It is kept in tolerable repair. This road is very badly laid out, passing over the summit of a steep hill 383 feet high, while by carrying it a third of a mile to the southward its elevation would not only be lessened by 104 feet, but the line might be continued in a good direction and with little variety of inclination for the entire distance. As it is at present it is wretchedly hilly. In the first mile and a half from Randalstown there is an average ascent of 1 in 24 feet, while in some places it is 1 in 14. In ascending the western side of the hill its inclination is very irregular and occasionally rapid.

A new line of road is much required instead of the present one, as this is the great leading road between the southern districts and the northern of Tyrone and Belfast, and the traffic of conveyances, carriers carts etc. on it is very considerable.

4 miles 1 furlong of the main road from Portglenone to Belfast through Randalstown pass through the western side of the parish. Its average breadth is 23 feet. The direction of this road is good and it is kept in pretty good repair.

4 miles 5 furlongs of the road from Toome Bridge to Ballymena traverse the western portion of the parish from south west to north east. Its average breadth is 24 feet. Its direction is good, but it might be much better laid out and its inclinations rendered less rapid in passing over the hilly ridge along the western side of the parish, by increasing its curvature. There is much necessity for improvement in this line, as there is considerable thoroughfare on it. It is not kept in very good repair.

By-roads

The by-roads are sufficiently numerous throughout the parish. In its north east district they are unnecessarily so. In the latter they have been chiefly made at the expense of Lord O'Neill or that of the manor, but speaking generally they have been made at the expense of the county and are kept in repair at that of the barony of Upper Toome. There are 29 and a half miles of by-roads in the parish. Their breadth averages 17 feet. Some of them in the eastern side of the parish are well laid out and tolerably level, but in its western side they are generally hilly and not in good repair. They are, however, everywhere sufficient for the purposes of the country.

The principal by-roads are that from Randalstown to Kells and Connor. There are 2 miles 3 furlongs of it in this parish. Its average breadth is 18 feet. Its direction is rather good, but it is not level nor kept in good repair.

The road from Randalstown to Ahoghill diverges from that to Portglenone and traverses the western side of the parish for 3 and a half miles. Its average breadth is 19 feet. Its direction is good and it is tolerably level and kept in pretty good repair.

A second road from Randalstown to Ballymena, diverging from that to Portglenone, runs along the western side of the River Main for 5 miles and unites with that from Toome Bridge to Ballymena. Its average breadth is 20 feet. It is kept in pretty good repair. The material used in the repair of the roads of this parish is broken stone of the harder kinds of basalt, which are abundant in all its districts.

Bridges and Fords

There are 2 bridges over the Main in this parish, one in the town of Randalstown, under the head of which a description will be found. The other is on the road from Toome Bridge to Ballymena and unites this parish with that of Ahoghill, in which a description of it will be found. These bridges are quite sufficient for the intercourse of the country. In summer the river may be easily and in many places crossed by carts, horses and pedestrians, but these fords, from the rapidity and velocity of its floods, are very uncertain.

General Appearance and Scenery

Except immediately along its southern side, which is for the most part densely planted and wooded, the general appearance of this parish is bleak and uninteresting. Large dreary tracts of bog are almost everywhere to be met with, and the bare aspect which they give to the neighbouring country is still further heightened by the miserable sod huts and cabins along their margins. The parish is sadly destitute of planting (with the exceptions alluded to). There are not even hedgerows to make up for its absence. Agriculture in most of its districts is in a backward state and in none of them in a forward state. The cottages and houses, however cleanly, want the neatness in outward appearance which lime only can give, but from which the cottages are too far distant to procure; and the general aspect of the country, besides being in itself uninteresting, tends also to convey the idea that the habits and ideas of its population are in an equally backward state of improvement and civilisation.

Immediately in the vicinity of Randalstown, and from it along the southern to the eastern confines of the parish, the aspect of the country is quite different, the thickly wooded demesne of Shane's Castle occupying all the intermediate space. The town itself is very prettily situated on the River Main and, though it is not in itself discernible from any distance, the very graceful spire of its church, rising above the neighbouring plantings, gives an exceedingly pretty effect to the landscape. It is, however, to be regretted that the woods of Shane's Castle are so dense and that there should not be a single opening or vista through which a view of the lake could be obtained from the almost level country which they border.

The views from the summit of the ridge and high grounds along the western side of the parish are not exceeded in beauty, variety or extent by any in the interior of the county. Looking southward the prospect embraces Lough Neagh from its northern to its southern extremity. Beyond are the Mourne Mountains raising their jagged outline. On the east and west are the Antrim and Tyrone hills, while nearer home the vast demesne of Shane's Castle, Antrim deerpark, the towns and spires of Antrim and Randalstown, and the rich shores of Killead present a landscape of no ordinary richness. Looking westward the entire western side of the county Derry, with its towns and villages and its chain of mountains, can be seen from its southern to its northern extremity. Lough Beg and the River Bann can also be traced for several miles. On the east the view extends to Knocklayd near the most northern point of the county and embraces most of its intermediate and central districts.

SOCIAL ECONOMY

Early Improvements

The inhabitants of this parish, with the exception of those in its detached portions in the parish of

Duneane, are almost exclusively of Scottish descent. Settlements of Scottish emigrants had taken place here about the year 1611, and also during the persecution of 1641, but the principal one took place between the years 1680 and 1695, when numbers came here in consequence of the encouragement they received from Rose O'Neill of Shane's Castle (afterwards Marchioness of Antrim) who was a zealous Presbyterian. [Insert footnote: To the present day an annual donation of 10 pounds is paid by the Shane's Castle family for a seat in the Presbyterian meeting house in Randalstown. This is said to have originated with Rose O'Neill]. She was maid of honour to Queen Mary and is said to have possessed vast influence at court.

The Scottish settlers seem to have in a great measure dispossessed the original inhabitants, as their descendants are almost only to be found in the detached portions of the parish, which are almost solely occupied by them. The townland of Portlee, one of these, is almost exclusively inhabited by Dowds, and in the other townlands the most prevalent names are those of McCann, McAteer, Fenton, Granny (sometimes pronounced Grant) and McAuley, all of whom are Roman Catholics and apparently descendants of the aboriginal inhabitants. The family of Hunter allege that their ancestors came to this country with Henry II.

Early Presbyterians

From some old records preserved by the Presbyterian congregation of Randalstown, it would appear that the Drummaul congregation had been established at an early period. According to them the Drummaul Presbyterian congregation is represented as being "vacant in 1655", and that "on the 21st May 1656 the Reverend John Cathcart was ordained to this congregation." In March 1661 the said Mr Cathcart stands in the list of ejected Presbyterian ministers, the entire number, 61, then officiating in Ulster having been ejected by Jeremy Taylor, Bishop of Down and Connor. In 1663 John Cathcart was one of those who consented to leave the kingdom, but was taken prisoner and sent to Athlone, where he remained in confinement for a considerable time. The next minister was the Reverend Richard Wilson, who was ordained to this congregation in 1689, since which time the congregation have had an uninterrupted succession of ministers.

The establishment of fixed ministers and of the Presbyterian religion, consequent on the colonisation of the parish by the Scots, may probably have been among the earliest and most important causes of improvement in the parish.

Marchioness of Antrim

The Marchioness of Antrim (Rose O'Neill) seems to have taken great interest in the prosperity of her tenantry and to have exerted herself in their improvement. To her exertions it is said Randalstown was indebted for the manufactories which were established in it, as also for its being created a borough, and she is said also to have encouraged habits of industry and regularity throughout her vast estates.

Progress of Improvement: Linen

Soon after, the linen trade sprung up in this country and was quickly established in this parish. It was a most important advantage to it until within the last year or two, as until then the great majority of its male population was solely engaged in weaving, while the females spun the yarn which the men manufactured into linen. Latterly, however, the weavers have been reduced to comparative poverty by the fall in the prices of linen which, had it not been for the introduction of mill-spun yarn, must have thrown them almost wholly out of employment, particularly as they had hitherto depended upon weaving as their sole support and held merely as much land as grazed a cow or grew potatoes for their use.

The introduction of mill-spun yarn in the year 1834, and its being given by manufacturers to weavers, not only has afforded them employment, with a fair remuneration for their labour, but also has saved them from the loss of time to which they had been subject in attending markets to purchase yarn and sell their manufacture, and also from the fluctuations in the prices of the latter. Still, however, the trade is very dull and the employment afforded by it far from being constant.

The introduction of the manufacture of "union" and calico about 4 years ago has given employment to many of the females and children, who would now otherwise have been unemployed. [Insert footnote: Union is a fabric resembling linen, and is so called from being made of linen and cotton yarn, the warp of the latter and weft of the former]. Boys and girls of 14 years of age can weave calico and earn 6d per day by it. The union requires rather more strength and yields about 8d per day to the weaver. The employment afforded by the manufacture of those articles is but partial and fluctuating.

A very beneficial result has been produced by the introduction of mill-spun yarn, in the increased demand for flax, which is now the most profitable crop cultivated here. Its cultivation has increased to a great extent, so much so that there is now an average weekly sale of 600 lbs at Ballymena market, while 8 years ago there were not 600 lbs weight of it sold there weekly. Its situation with respect to Randalstown as a grain market, to Belfast and Ballymena as markets for the sale of pork and butter, and to the great weekly general market at the latter town are matters of importance to the farmer.

Influence of Agent

Lord O'Neill's present agent (George Handcock Esquire) has by the course he has pursued effected a greater change in the conduct and character of the people during the last 4 years, than had previously been produced by any individual or by any event, social or otherwise. By combining mildness with firmness and decision, and by evincing a regard for the comfort and interests of the tenantry, he has gained the goodwill of all parties and managed them in a manner to which they had before been strangers. The consequences are that arbitration between neighbours are now substituted for litigation, there is less rioting and quarrelling, and the people are much more orderly and regular in their general conduct. Reference to the table of cases brought before the Randalstown petty sessions (see appendix) will more clearly illustrate this.

For a short time after the passing of the act empowering magistrates to fine drunkards on the spot, intemperance was diminished considerably, but as it was but for a short time strictly enforced, drunkenness is now as prevalent as it had previously been.

Obstructions to Improvement: Lord O'Neill

The system pursued by Lord O'Neill in the management of his vast estates (of which this parish forms a portion) is not only a serious obstruction to any improvement taking place in the moral or social condition of his tenantry, but it is also calculated to reduce them to and retain them in a state of recklessness as to industry, education, comfort or respectablity of character. To this the more extensive farmers of course form an exception. They, however, constitute but a very small portion of the population.

The system pursued by Lord O'Neill is equally injurious to himself and his tenantry. In the selection of a tenant he is not guided either by the solvency or character of the individual, but by the sum or rent which he proposes to pay: the consequence of which is that a respectable and solvent person is rarely selected, as he is in general outbid by one who is aware of Lord O'Neill's object, and who at the same time takes the land with all its encumbrances at a rent which he quite well knows is beyond its value and which he also knows he has little intention of paying. Having taken the farm and paid Lord O'Neill all the arrears of tithes and rent on it, he is left without a fraction of capital, and therefore to purchase farm stock and seed he is obliged to give a promissory note and a high credit price for them. When the notes become due the price of his crops, which should have paid his rent, is expended in paying the former, and here in the very first year he is in arrears of rent and also in debt for provisions for his family.

The second year leaves him still in arrears, and in the third year he is ejected, having held the land for 3 years and merely paid off some of the previous arrears on it. Besides this, the land is impoverished by each tenant taking the most he can out of it and the farmhouse and offices are left in a state of ruin. By this system both landlord and tenant are injured, and the latter, from having no stake as to property or character, is rendered wholly regardless of respectability either as to his own acts or those of his family, and from the uncertain tenure upon which he knows he occupies the land, careless of and inattentive to any opportunity of improvement.

Lord O'Neill has therefore a large nominal rental, but he is unpaid and his tenantry, particularly the humbler class, are in distress. The number of ejectments annually served on his estate are almost incredible, and in the depth of winter many a family is annually turned adrift without a house to shelter them. Though he has a most excellent agent, and one in every way qualified for the situation, still his duty is almost wholly confined to the receiving of rents, the disposal and allotment of farms being entirely managed by himself.

He takes no other interest in his tenantry, either in alleviating their annual distress (in spring), nor in contributing to their mental or social improvement in any respect. [Insert footnote: NB In confirmation of this assertion, I can positively state that Lord O'Neill's total annual contributions towards education, relief of the poor on his estate, dispensaries and all other charitable institutions in his property in this county do not amount to 90 pounds. Towards education he contributes 4 pounds annually, and this to a school which has been almost wholly abandoned from the wretched state of the house in which it is held. His lordship's gross rental is 30,000 pounds. Though almost constantly residing within 4 miles of the town of Randalstown, he has not been in it thrice during the last 15 years]. They have no confidence in or dependence upon his care for their comfort, and he is equally distrustful of them by (instead of creating a mutual spirit of confidence) keeping a regular core of bailiffs and underagents in various capacities, upon whom alone he relies for the payment of his rents.

Subletting of Farms

The subletting of farms, and the letting of small portions of bog to poor families, has been another drawback to improvement in this parish. Along the edges of the larger tracts of bog, and also the highways traversing that in the eastern portion of the parish, Lord O'Neill some years ago let many portions of bog of generally a rood each to labourers' families, at an annual rent of 10s 6d or 2 pounds 2s per acre. There was of course great demand for such holdings, and the bog soon became studded with sod huts of the most wretched description. The little tract attached to them was soon enclosed and cultivated, but it of course was quite inadequate towards supplying the family with provisions and, in consequence of the great increase in the number of labourers consequent on the migration to this from neighbouring districts, there was of course a proportionate decrease in the quantity of employment afforded.

The result has naturally been that, out of a family of 5 or 6 or, what is more usual, 7 individuals, not one receives daily employment throughout the year. In the spring and winter they are almost wholly out of employment and, as the reclamation or culture of the bogs is very far from keeping pace with their increase of population, they are obliged to resort for their subsistence to unfortunate alternatives. The children, generally accompanied by the mother, beg through the neighbouring parishes and generally succeed in one day in obtaining support for themselves and the remainder of the family for the following. They have abundance of fuel, their rent is but light and but little care therefore devolves upon the head of the family, who soon becomes indolent and unwilling to work. Begging creates immorality of various descriptions and is in general but a step preparatory to that of possessing themselves of the property of others in a less ceremonious manner, as the farmers in the neighbourhood of the bogs have too good reason to know.

Spirit Licences

The facility for procuring spirit licences, and the indiscriminate manner in which they are now granted, has, by increasing their number in almost every district of the parish, been for it, in common with others, an unfortunate measure.

Payment of Tithe

The opposition offered by Lord O'Neill to the payment of the tithes on his estates, for which he is accountable to the several incumbents, however justified he may be, has in such a district as this been an unfortunate step. The parish of Drummaul is a vicarage, the rectorial tithes of which have for years been litigated by Lord O'Neill and by such of the tenants for whom he is not accountable. There are heavy arrears due by both to the lay impropriator and of course heavy costs are also accruing upon them. Besides this, Lord O'Neill has (and it is said, unadvisedly) litigated the payment of such of the vicarial tithes as he was liable for, and the tenants at will, following his example, have done the same. Lawsuits have of course ensued and terminated in favour <favor> of the incumbent, but are again renewed. The latter is not only kept in a state of embarrassment, but an unfortunate feeling has been created between him and his parishioners and his utility thereby considerably affected. The tenantry, without considering the motive or principal upon which Lord O'Neill acts, merely imitate his example, which for all parties has been a most unfortunate one.

The want of a resident gentry, who by their influence or by their example could tend towards the improvement of the social condition of the people, or who by the employment they could afford, or the circulation of capital which they might in many ways create, is here hardly felt. The people are almost wholly left to themselves, and though there are few parishes more easily, from its natural state and resources, susceptible of improvement, there are few which in all its districts, but particularly in its more retired ones, which have advanced so little in any respect.

Local Government

There is but 1 magistrate resident in the parish, namely George Handcock Esquire, whose residence at Randalstown is conveniently situated. He deservedly possesses the confidence and respect of all classes and parties, and combines decision and firmness with impartiality and mildness. He is chief agent to Lord O'Neill. Earl O'Neill, lieutenant of the county and colonel of the Antrim Regiment of Militia, resides at Shane's Castle near the eastern side of the parish. 5 constabulary are stationed in Randalstown.

Petty Sessions

Petty sessions for the district in which this parish is included are held at Randalstown on every alternate Tuesday. 2 magistrates, of whom Mr Handcock is one, the other coming from some of the neighbouring parishes, preside here. The cases tried at these sessions are not of any importance, consisting chiefly of private quarrels, minor assaults, disputes about wages and trespass, and other causes of similar unimportance. Petty theft such as stealing turf are not unusual, but there is no symptom of agrarian or party disturbance in any of the causes brought before this bench. The number of cases annually tried is on the decrease, which is solely to be attributed to the exertions of Mr Handcock, who exercises the influence which as Lord O'Neill's agent he possesses among the farmers, in arranging their disputes by means of arbitrations. The number and nature of the cases tried at these sessions for a series of years will be found in [Fair Sheets].

Manor Courts

Manor courts and courts leet for the manor of Edenduffcarrick, in which this parish is situated, are held at Randalstown, the former once a month and the latter once in 6 months, for the recovery by civil bill process of sums not exceeding 20 pounds. At the latter the fiscal business of the manor is also transacted. Major James Higginson J.P. and D.L., seneschal, Earl O'Neill, lord of the manor.

The parish, as has before been stated, is comparatively free from party or political outrage, and the nature of the crimes brought before the authorities is of but trivial importance. There is a spirit of resistance to the payment of tithes and there is an inclination to oppose the letting of the farm of which a tenant has been dispossessed, but this spirit has not as yet been attended by any acts of outrage.

There is not, nor has not been, any illicit distillation known in the parish for several years.

Insurances

There are only 3 life assurances and but 5 fire insurances in this parish. The insurance of farm stock is unusual and, as accidents from fire are rarely known, the insurance of property is not likely to become more general. [Insert footnote: Lord O'Neill's life is insured at the Globe Insurance Office (Dublin) for 120,000 pounds, which he borrowed about 5 years ago from one of that company for the purpose of paying his creditors. The person who lent him the money nominated his agent].

Dispensary

A dispensary was established at Randalstown in the year 1813 for the relief of the poor of Lord O'Neill's estate in this and the adjacent districts and has since then been supported by an annual local subscription, to which the county grand jury add a similar sum. This institution has been of infinite service in this parish, but more particularly in its western districts, where there is so much poverty, where there is such an equality as to the grade and circumstances of the people and where many of them could not otherwise obtain the assistance which it affords.

There has not been an apparent decrease in any particular complaint or disease: on the contrary, fever, sometimes of a very malignant nature, rheumatism and consumption are on the increase, the first proceeding from increasing want of sufficient nutritive food (in fact from poverty), the second from the increased moisture of the climate and the third complaint arising from both these causes, to which the early age at which children are put to work adds not a little inducement. But still, the prevalence of infectious and contagious diseases is materially checked by the ready assistance it affords, and the inculcation of attention to cleanliness is not least useful of its objects.

The district included in the range of this dispensary is much too extensive for 1 medical man. It embraces the parishes of Cranfield and Duneane, the latter of which would afford ample employment to 1 person. There is neither system or regularity in its management and, although the present surgeon is both humane and attentive, still there is much room for improvement and alteration in the entire system, if system it can be termed, at present pursued in affording relief, and also in the general management of this institution. A statement of the funds of this dispensary and a table of the diseases and cases treated at it will be

Schools

520 children are at present receiving instruction at the day schools in this parish. The proportion the number of pupils bears to that of the entire population is as 1 to 19, being considerably less than in the more easterly parishes. There are several causes to be assigned for this disproportion between the number of children receiving instruction and that of the population. The chief of these is the want of sufficient funds to endow schools, so that the means of instruction may be placed within the reach of the poorer families who constitute so large a portion of the population; the want of sufficient clothing to enable the children to attend school during the winter; the early age at which in summer children are employed; and the want of encouragement or excitement to acquire knowledge.

The only one in the parish who has taken any pains with respect to the education of the lower class is the Reverend Daniel Curoe, the present parish priest, whose exertions in the course of education have been most energetic and tolerably successful. Through his instrumentality the 3 national schools in this parish were established. 2 of them have been recently erected, and towards them he has contributed munificently. These schools are well managed and are much resorted to by the Roman Catholics and a few of the Presbyterians, but the members of the latter persuasion consider the system an irreligious one, and if they are able, prefer sending their children almost any distance to other schools. If unable to pay for their education, they prefer keeping them at home.

The only other endowed school is the parish school, to which Lord O'Neill annually contributes the sum of 4 pounds 4s, but in consequence of the ruinous state of the house, the school is badly attended, and a Sunday school which had been established in it in 1836 was, in November 1837, totally given up. The teacher of this school also receives 3 pounds 10s per annum from the London Hibernian Society. It is much to be regretted that greater facilities for education are not afforded here, and that the better class do not make some exertions to afford its advantages to a people [who] would, if they were enabled, avail themselves of them. Sunday schools are pretty well attended and have been attended with perceptibly beneficial effects; but there unfortunately seems to be a greater difficulty in obtaining teachers than pupils. See tables of schools, appendix.

Poor

Owing to the causes before stated, the poor of this parish bear a more than ordinary proportion to its population. Their numbers are also continually fluctuating and changing according to the seasons. In winter and spring they are most numerous, for at these seasons, owing to the want of employment, they migrate or stroll through the neighbouring parishes in quest of assistance. In their own parish, except along its southern side, there is but little relief to be obtained in this manner, the people being too much on an equality as to circumstances, but still are humane and charitable to the extent of their power in affording relief either in potatoes or meal. The farmers say that a tax of 6d per acre would be considerably under what they annually contribute in charity, but at the same time they would prefer giving one-half more than that sum at their own door to paying it in the shape of a tax or rate.

The "beggar's curse" so much feared throughout Ireland has no terrors here, but the beggar's blessing is acceptable, and the farmer's wife undoubtedly delights receiving it, whether it be from the vanity she feels in being able to bestow what she has also the power to withhold, or whether derives the pleasure from another and a more praiseworthy motive. The least charitable class are the shopkeepers, who, though they derive their support from the lower class, are the least liberal in affording them assistance. Monday is the day upon which beggars are assisted in Randalstown and on this day they receive something from every householder who can afford to give.

There is not any regular provision for the poor of this parish. Lord O'Neill annually contributes 42 pounds among 40 poor persons. The collections at the parish church which are distributed among the poor of the parish average weekly 2s 9d. The collections at the Presbyterian meeting house in Randalstown average 8s 6d weekly, which except about a quarter are distributed among the poor of the congregation. The collections at the Seceders' meeting house in the townland of Craigmore average 3s weekly and is, with a trifling deduction, distributed among the poor of the congregation. The weekly collection at the Roman Catholic chapel at Randalstown averages

7s, which is distributed among the Roman Catholic poor of the congregation.

Religion

According to the revised census of 1834 there are in this parish 465 members of the Established Church, 5,108 Presbyterians of different sects, 4,062 Roman Catholics and 93 others, whose religions could not accurately be ascertained. There is sufficient and suitable accommodation at the different places of worship for the members [of] these persuasions. In the Established Church this parish is a vicarage in the presentation of the Marquis of Donegall. The rectorial tithes are in the hands of a lay impropriator. The vicarial tithes, amounting to 450 pounds per annum, are paid to the vicar, the Reverend Samuel S. Heatley. There is not, however, a glebe or glebe house.

In the Presbyterian church there are 3 distinct congregations of different sects, namely Presbyterians of the Synod of Ulster, Seceders and Primitive Seceders or Burghers. In the congregation in connection <connexion> with the Synod of Ulster, the stipend paid to the minister amounts to 85 pounds per annum and the regium donum to 100 pounds per annum. The members of this congregation worship in the meeting house in Randalstown. In this congregation a schism took place in the year 1836 (in the month of March), owing to a disagreement as to the choice of a minister. The more humble portion of the congregation opposed the minister chosen by the upper class, though he had been legally and regularly elected. The former seized the meeting house, which they actually garrisoned by keeping several armed men in it until the month of May 1838, when a sort of compromise, as yet (June) unfinished, commenced. In the meantime service has been performed in the new market house by the minister elected.

The Seceders' congregation, which worship at the Seceding meeting house in the town of Randalstown: they pay their minister 40 pounds per annum. He also receives a regium donum of 50 pounds per annum.

The Primitive Seceders or Burghers worship at the meeting house in the townland of Craigmore. They accept of no assistance from government, but pay their minister a stipend of 40 pounds per annum. The members of these congregations are not merely confined to the parish of Drummaul. In the Presbyterian church a congregation is formed of such persons as take seats in the meeting house and pay stipend for them, without any reference to their residence.

In the Roman Catholic church this parish is united to those of Antrim and Donegore, and the grange of Shilvodan. There is a Roman Catholic chapel in this parish, as also in that of Antrim, and a third in the grange of Shilvodan. The Reverend Daniel Curoe is the parish priest. He resides in Randalstown. His income (he says) amounts to but 150 pounds per annum. The public assert that it amounts to 600 pounds per annum. A list of the original clergy of these congregations will be found in appendix.

Habits of the People: Occupations

By the census of 1831 the population of the parish of Drummaul amounts to 9,737 individuals, or 1,733 families, giving an average number of (as nearly as possible) 5 and two-fifths to each family. This, however, is only the average, for in the neighbourhood of the bogs, and in the poorer districts of the parish, the families are in general much larger than those of the more comfortable and independent class of farmers and dealers. The families of the latter do not exceed an average of 5 individuals, while those of the cottiers and poorer labourers fully average 6 each.

According to the same census 1,659 families were chiefly employed in agriculture and 538 in trade or dealing. 182 farmers or persons occupied land [and] gave employment to labourers, and 510 persons holding land cultivated it without employing labourers. 778 labourers were employed in agriculture, 13 in manufactories and 776 persons in retail trade or handicraft. There were 63 included under the head of professional or educated persons. There were 279 male and 19 female servants.

Decline of Linen Trade

Since 1831 there has, however, been a very great alteration in the occupations of the people. At that period a much greater proportion of the population were engaged in some branch of the linen trade, which about that time had begun to decline. The great bulk of the adult male population of this parish had for a century depended solely upon the manufacture of linen for their support, and held as much land only as was sufficient to provide their family with meal and potatoes, and a little flax. They took the land at a high rent when trade was prosperous, they paid no attention to agriculture and consequently were unprepared to meet the very great reverse which has latterly befallen them. Heretofore the males of the family were engaged in weaving, the grown-up females in spinning and preparing the flax and the younger members of the family in winding the yarn upon bobbins for the weavers.

Weaving was also carried on in almost every farmer's house, either by the sons of the farmer during the dead seasons or by his apprentices or journeymen, who occasionally assisted at the farm during the busy seasons of seed time and harvest. They wove the yarn spun by the females of the family from flax grown on the farm. Thus almost every member of every family was kept in a continual and profitable employment, and it is not therefore to wonder that agriculture should have been so little attended to and that the people should have been so little fitted for the change which has within the last 7 or 8 years taken place in their mode of support.

Now not more than two-thirds of the number of adult males formerly employed in and depending on weaving for their support are employed in it, and added to this the females and younger members of the family are thrown out of employment by the introduction of mill-spun yarn, which has so far superseded that manufactured by the hand that spinning is now resorted to more as an alternative to being idle than from anything which can be earned by it. As the linen trade had commenced declining before the introduction of mill-spun yarn, it is probable that but for it a much greater number of weavers would have been thrown out of employment and the distress of the parish increased. Its adoption is now daily becoming much more general and the wages which it affords, either when purchased by the weaver or when given out to be woven by the manufacture, together with the saving of time in not being obliged to attend fairs or markets, are fair and commensurate with the decline in the price of provisions.

Weavers

The weavers are, however, in a very different condition from their previous one. Their houses are necessarily dry and are therefore pretty comfortable, being built of stone and lime, generally thatched, lit by 2 or perhaps 3 "lead" or small sash windows and consisting of 2 apartments, in one of which the loom or looms are set up. Their floors are earthen and their appearance from the want of lime (which at nearest is 16 miles distant) neither neat nor cleanly. Their furniture is but scanty and there is but little regard to cleanliness in their interior or exterior. A pigsty rests against one end of the house and a turf stack against the other. In front is the almost invariable accompaniment of a cesspool or manure heap. From 1 to 4 acres are generally attached to these tenements, though many of the weavers hold no land. In the general cultivation of it the women are now employed, as also in preparing the turf in the bogs. Few of the weavers have cows, their livestock generally consisting of a pig and about a dozen head of poultry, all of which are for sale.

Potatoes and salt herrings now constitute their principal food. One-fourth of the quantity of meal formerly consumed is not now made here, the farmers and others preferring, indeed being obliged, to sell the raw grain to pay their rent. Their holdings being so small, added to their ignorance as to economy, they cannot manage to keep a cow.

The green crop system is almost unknown, and there is no one who manifests any interest in their comfort by introducing it among them. Their little gardens contain a few early potatoes, cabbages, leeks and onions. Their consumption of animal food is now very trifling, a little salt beef or bacon being the only description now used.

They are rather intemperate than otherwise and are prevented from being more so only by the want of means. They are not an immoral class and are generally peaceable, humane and industrious, though very improvident.

Labourers

In proportion to the decrease in the number of those employed in weaving, that of the agricultural labourers has increased and is now so great that the distress arising from want of employment is annually increasing. Many of those formerly employing labourers have ceased to do so since the females of their families have been thrown out of employment by the introduction of mill-spun yarn. Besides, the farms or holdings throughout the parish are too small and too numerous, and most of them afford employment only to the family of the farmer. The distress endured in the seasons of winter and summer is now very great. In the summer of 1837 it was particularly so, many families having been for 24 hours without tasting food. The most to be pitied of this class are those who had been weavers and, having held no land, depended solely on their trade. Many of these, who had been honest and industrious, were now reduced to starvation and still could not bring themselves to ask charity, while those who merely worked when inclined and kept their children employed in begging, suffered but little.

The agricultural labourers are generally, particularly those living along the edges of the bogs and in the detached portions of the parish, an improvident race, very indolent and apathetic, and perhaps from habitude quite willing to remain in their present comfortless and half-civilised state, than to increase their comforts by industry and exertion. Their general character differs very much from that of the weavers, the former being almost altogether Scotch in their extraction, in their habits and ideas, and of the Presbyterian religion, while the latter, who are mostly Roman Catholics, possess many traits of the Irish character and are apparently of Irish descent. Many of them have latterly settled here, as it would seem from their mode of life, merely from their proximity to fuel and to be able to gain a subsistence without working for it.

Their abodes are generally little more than miserably small sod huts, damp, dirty, comfortless and scantily furnished, dark with smoke, which makes its exit by a hole in the roof near the gable. The principal light is from the doorway, as that received through a little lead window is too faint to admit of any occupation being pursued inside. But a small proportion of labourers have comfortable cottages, even those which are built of stone and lime being damp and filthy and badly furnished. Very few of them hold any land or possess a cow, and not more than half of them have got pigs. They depend upon potatoes for their subsistence and they, with salt herrings and a little milk, may be said to constitute their food.

On an average not more than one out of each family is constantly in employment. Those about the bogs are merely employed during the seasons of seed time and harvest, and at the cutting and preparing of the turf. A few of these, perhaps not more than 14, have got donkeys or ponies and small carts, with which they are employed in drawing turf for sale to the neighbouring towns, chiefly to Antrim. During the seasons at which provisions are scarce and dear, the families (the females) of the cottiers in the bogs stroll into neighbouring easterly parishes and beg. The idle life thus commenced and the habits thus acquired are not easily dropped. On the contrary, they increase and spread, and the feelings of all soon become habitually blind to any sense of shame.

There is a good deal of immorality among this class. They are prone to whiskey drinking and have but little anxiety for the education of their children. They also marry very early and much more so than the other classes in the parish. Marriages of women under 17 and of men under 21 are not unusual among them.

Farmers and Manufacturers

The farmers and manufacturers, who constitute the remainder of the population of this parish, are a blunt, honest and respectable class, possessing a large share of intelligence and generally well educated and enlightened. They are very industrious and frugal, at the same time evincing a taste for comfort in their style and manner of living. Most of them are in comparatively comfortable circumstances, and some of them, particularly the manufacturers, are wealthy, having realized their property by the manufacture of linen. The extent of their farms varies from 10 to 50 acres; might average 18 acres. Their houses are in general neat and comfortable looking, and they are every day evincing signs of improvement in the construction of new ones. They are generally 2-storeys high, substantially built of stone and lime, and slated. Many of them are neatly furnished and have got a parlour, which is often to be found fitted up with some pretension to neatness. It is not, however, always in use, as the family and servant generally eat together. A kitchen where the family all sit, with 2 or sometimes 3 other apartments on the ground floor, and a loft on which the servants sleep, generally constitute the extent of the 1-storey houses or cottages of the farmers.

A few bushes or trees, generally ash or sycamore, surround the houses. Their gardens are but small, cabbages and onions being almost the only vegetables cultivated. Potatoes, meal made into porridge, baker's bread (now in general use), bacon, hung beef, milk, butter and eggs constitute the food of this class. Tea is used at least once a day by the better description of farmers. They are rather fond of whiskey, though not often to be found in a state of inebriety. They are, generally speaking, a moral and well-conducted race.

All classes are civil, obliging and hospitable, peaceable and amenable to the laws. There is now but little party spirit; it formerly was carried to great pitch here. The sabbath is outwardly very strictly observed, but in reality there is more drinking and mischief upon that than any other day.

Dress and Fuel

All classes dress neatly and comfortably in their respective stations. This seems to be the only exception to the general change which has taken place in them. They now dress as well as ever and

Parish of Drummaul

their appearance at their places of worship, fairs or markets is very respectable. In the more westerly districts of the parish they do not dress quite so neatly. The low price of printed cottons and the importation of cast wearing apparel, which is now sold at a very cheap rate at the markets and fairs throughout the country, have tended to place the article of dress within the reach of all. Among the farmers clocks are common, but watches are not nearly so much so as in the more southerly and easterly parishes. Turf, which is everywhere abundant throughout the parish, is the only fuel used.

Longevity

There are several instances of persons of from 80 to 90 years of age in full possession of their faculties. In the year [blank] a man named Whitney, who had been a pensioner for 50 years, died in the townland of Feehogue, at the advanced age of 107 years. Persons of from 70 to 80 years of age are to be found in almost every townland.

Amusements

Though they may possess the same taste as ever for amusement, they now evince but little of it. The pressure of the times has called for every increased energy which they can afford to support themselves. They have not now the means of enjoying themselves and their amusements are now confined to attending one or two of the summer fairs, an idle day or two at Christmas and Easter, and attending an occasional dance. Formerly they were very fond of dancing. Wakes also were attended for amusement. Cock-fights were frequent, particularly at Easter, and card-playing was more common. There is still a little card-playing, but it is carried on privately. Fires are burned on St John's Eve, but this custom has nearly disappeared. Its origin is not known among the people, who suppose it to be symbolical of some political event. Freemasons celebrate the 24th June by walking in procession and, until the late act against party processions, the Orangemen celebrated the 12th July in a similar manner. Ribbon societies are generally believed to exist in the parish.

Traditions

An implicit belief exists in ghosts, fairies and banshees, in enchantments and in the power which the fairies so wantonly exercise in depriving cows of their milk, nor are these notions confined to any particular sect or denomination. The Irish cry, which was formerly sung at the funerals of Roman Catholics, has for some years been given up, and hymns are now sung in its stead. Their legends and traditions are not nearly so numerous or interesting as might have been expected, when their vicinity to Shane's Castle is considered. There is not a single tradition in the parish which in the slightest degree bears either on its history or on that of the family connected with it. The only traditions are absurd stories relative to ghosts and the banshee Neeny Roe, who has haunted the O'Neill family for ages. The more interesting, or rather the least absurd, of these will be found in the appendix.

There is not any ancient music in the parish. The people have to a certain extent a taste for music, but it seldom exceeds standing for half an hour at a fair listening to a ballad singer, or being able to play a few common tunes on a flute or violin.

At the Presbyterian meeting house the entire congregation join in singing. The tunes to which their psalms are set are only 12 in number, and are those used by the Covenanters of old. There is something devotional in them, and they are well suited for embracing the variety of voices in a congregation, but at the same time there is a want of harmony or melody in the music at the meeting houses in this parish.

Physical Appearance

There is no peculiarity in the habits or appearance of the people of this parish, except that those along its western side, and as they approach that district of the parish, are less civilised and enlightened in their appearance and ideas than the inhabitants of the more easterly and southerly parishes, and that in the same respects they are rather superior to those of the adjacent western and northern ones. Their dialect, idioms and phraseology are strictly Scottish, but rather less so immediately along the south west side of the parish. As is usual in manufacturing districts the men seldom exceed the middle stature and are narrow-shouldered and not robust in their appearance, though really strong and wiry. The females are not generally good-looking.

Emigration

In the year 1835 24 individuals emigrated from this parish to America. Of these, 13 were Protestants (of different sects) and 11 Roman Catholics. In the year 1836 22 individuals, of whom 16 were Protestant and 6 Roman Catholics, emigrated to America; and in the year 1837 47 individuals, of whom 37 were Protestant and 10 Roman Catholics emigrated to America, and 1 person emigrated to Glasgow and 1 to Liverpool.

All of those who embarked in 1835 emigrated to the United States, chiefly to New York and New Orleans. Of those who emigrated in 1836, 3 sailed for Quebec and almost all the others for New York or New Orleans. Of those who emigrated in 1837, 13 sailed for Quebec and all the others except 5 for the United States.

With but a very few exceptions the emigrants from this parish have taken out little or no capital with them. They are chiefly either holders of small farms or agricultural labourers. Few mechanics or tradesmen have emigrated from the parish and very few emigrants have returned. In this, as in most districts, the industrious and well conducted are almost the only emigrants, while the able-bodied idlers and disorderly characters are but rarely known to leave the country. Spring is the usual season of embarkation. Belfast until the last 2 or 3 years was the port at which they embarked, but Liverpool is the one from which emigrants from the north of Ireland now sail.

Migration

There are 51 individuals in this parish who are in the habit of annually migrating to the Scottish or English harvests. Of these, 23 are Protestants and 28 Roman Catholics; 44 go to the Scottish and 7 to the English harvests. They almost invariably return when they are over. This custom is not now so general as formerly, there not being the same encouragement for Irish labourers. For some of those who pursue this practice it is a profitable one, but for the majority it is not, as they generally remain in a state of idleness until the sum which they have brought home is expended. They are usually stout, active young men, most of whom are unmarried.

Remarkable Events

Except the movement which took place in Sluggan bog (see Natural Features), this parish has not been the scene of any remarkable event of which there is any local record, nor has it given birth to any remarkable person, if the members of the O'Neill family be excepted.

ANCIENT TOPOGRAPHY

Ecclesiastical: Burial Ground

The only ecclesiastical remains in this parish are 2 graveyards or burial grounds, namely that in the townland of Drummaul and that near the ruins of Shane's Castle.

In the former of these, which is situated towards the western side of the parish, stood the ancient parish church of Drummaul, of which nothing but the foundations and a small portion of the eastern gable now remain. The church stood in the centre of the burial ground and bore nearly due east and west. The foundations measure 40 by 25 feet and are 3 feet thick. The style of the masonry is rude, the stones being undressed, rather small, and such as are generally termed field stones. The cement used seems to have been grouting.

The burial ground now includes a space of about 49 by 46 yards. In the year 1828 (having been found much too small) a perch in breadth almost all round it was added to it at the expense of the parish. It is pretty well enclosed, but is otherwise very irregularly kept, and from its being a favourite place of interment, the graves are piled one upon another and its surface thereby considerably elevated above that of the adjacent ground.

No ancient nor remarkable family bury here. It is, however, the favourite place of interment for the inhabitants of the surrounding districts and is said to have been so for centuries. There is not any record of any of the O'Neills having been interred [in] it, nor is it supposed that such has been the case. There are not any curious monuments nor headstones, nor any of antiquity or interest, to be found in this burial ground. The oldest date is that of 1721, on a stone erected to the memory of a man named King.

Nothing is known concerning the history of this church, either as to when or by whom it was built or at what period it ceased to be used. It must have been of considerable antiquity and it must also have for a very long time been in ruins, for in the year 1725 it was known as Old Drummaul.

It is probable that this church ceased to be used in the time of Rose O'Neill (Marchioness of Antrim), when that in the town of Randalstown was erected about the year 1690. The old church of Randalstown was pulled down in 1831 to make way for the present one, which stands near its site.

Burial Ground at Shane's Castle

The ancient burial ground in Shane's Castle demesne is situated 90 yards north east of the ruins of the castle and is quite secluded in a dense grove of rather modern planting, among which are some very old ash trees. The burial ground includes a space of 190 by 132 feet, partially enclosed by a low stone wall. It has not been used for nearly 40

Parish of Drummaul

years, and to prevent its further use Lord O'Neill enclosed a portion of ground for about a mile to the north of it for the purpose of a graveyard.

In this burial ground is a very curious vault (of which a drawing etc. will be found in [appendix]) erected by French John O'Neill in 1722, "for a buryal place for himself and family of Clanneboy." Its dimensions are 24 by 27 feet. The height of the gables is 14 feet. Its side walls do not exceed 3 feet high. Its walls and roof altogether built of stone and lime, in ordinary rubble masonry. In its eastern gable is a common doorway and strong wooden door, over which is the inscription (which will be seen in appendix) specifying its date and building. In the western gable is a vertical slit for the purpose of admitting air. Except the inscription stone there is no architectural nor other ornament nor device about it.

The first person of whose interment here there is any record is French John's wife, "Charity O'Neill, alias Dixon, who dyed in Edenduffcarrick 30th November 1726 and was buried in my own vault there." (See appendix). John himself was the next person interred here. He died in 1739.

There is not any local record of the interment here of any of the O'Neills until that of the late lord, who was killed by the rebels in the action at Antrim on the 7th June 1798. Since that time the vault has not been opened, nor will any others of the family be interred here. Lord O'Neill has built a costly and capacious vault in the churchyard at Randalstown, in which he is to be laid, and it is said that he intends removing thither the bones of those interred at Shane's Castle.

The other tombstones in this burial ground possess no interest whatever, either as to antiquity or to the families over which they are erected, who were merely the villagers of Shane's Castle or the inhabitants of the immediate neighbourhood. The stones are about 20 in number. They are simple slabs set upright. The oldest legible bears the date of 1684. The graves are not numerous, and from the flat surface of the ground it would not seem to have been much used for interment. It is said that a chapel once stood here, but within memory there has not been the slightest trace of it.

Military: Shane's Castle

Shane's Castle, now in ruins, is now the only remnant of any building which approaches in appearance to, or would seem to have been capable of being applied to, any military purpose. Its present remains possess but few pretensions to this character, as they consist merely of 2 wings, 76 feet apart and connected by a curtain or centre building, without the slightest trace of any outworks or defences. The situation of the ruins in the vast demesne of Shane's Castle, within 35 yards from the southern shore of Lough Neagh and about 23 feet above it, is not conspicuous except from the water or from the eastern shore of the lake, though at the same time the views from them embrace the scenery along both sides of the lake to its southern extremity. The ground on which the ruins stand is almost flat, falling very gently towards the water. It is in general densely wooded, so much so as, on all sides but the one, wholly to exclude them from the view.

Shane's Castle consisted of a centre building or pavilion, standing nearly north and south and measuring 76 by 40 feet. At each end of this is a wing measuring 57 by 22 feet. The western extremities of these wings are circular, and in each is a doorway or entrance. The wings are about 50 feet high and consisted of 3 storeys. They are standing, but the centre has fallen to the ground. The principal entrance was in the western side. The windows are principally square and of modern dimensions. Some of them have circular heads. There is no architectural ornament nor cut stone about them or the doorways, except a plain modern frieze over one of those in the western side.

The walls are roughcast and whitened, built of stone and lime with brick facings and arches, all in modern and at the same time indifferent rubble masonry. Their thickness varies from 2 feet 6 inches to 3 feet, but they are chiefly of the former thickness. The wings are castellated at the summit, and over the southern one are stacks of high brick chimneys similar in proportions to those of the Elizabethan style of architecture. Underneath were some vaults consisting of numerous small apartments, now mostly covered with rubbish. None of the floors and only a small portion of a beautiful spiral stair of cut stone now remain.

On the eastern side of the southern wing, and about 30 feet from its base, is a face of black stone known as Edenduffcarrick or "the black face of stone", from which the manor is said to take its name. (A description of this will be found hereafter).

This was the entire extent of Shane's Castle. It was consumed by a fire which broke out in it on the 20th May 1816, when many strangers were on a visit at the castle. Almost all the family documents, records and papers were consumed.

It may appear strange that absolutely nothing should be locally known concerning the history of Shane's Castle, its date of erection, or the name of its founder, but such is the case; and little therefore except a mere topographical description of it can here be given. The vulgar tradition in the neighbourhood is that Shane's Castle had been originally a nunnery, but at what period is unknown; that Rose O'Neill, Marchioness of Antrim, who afterwards married her cousin Henry O'Neill, was the one who raised it to its present size; and that in the interval between the destruction of the nunnery and Rose O'Neill's becoming its proprietor, that it had been a small strength or fortress belonging to the family.

The village of Shane's Castle extended eastward along and nearly parallel to the shore for about quarter of a mile. It was thrown down and the ground on which it stood, and also the high road from Antrim to Randalstown which ran through it, added to the demesne in 1803-4. Races which lasted for several days took place here annually and at them some of the best horses in Ireland are said to have been entered. The late Lord O'Neill was a great patron of racing. According to an old song still common in the neighbourhood, he had an iron chest full of gold which he won on the turf. The racecourse was in front of the village and along the lake, but all trace of it, as well as the village, has been quite obliterated. At Lord O'Neill's residence here there is a painting of Shane's Castle and the village, representing the races. It is, however, but an indifferent production.

There is nothing in the ruins of Shane's Castle, if the ideas associated with them and their situation be accepted, to excite either interest or curiosity, and their thin whitewashed walls but ill accord with the deeds and history of the family with which they are identified.

Dunmore Castle

About 2 miles to the west of Shane's Castle, and in the demesne as it is at present, there stood within memory the ruins of an ancient building commonly known as Dunmore Castle, but of which not the slightest vestige now remains. It is more than 30 years since all trace of these ruins has been removed, and now except the name nothing further is remembered or known relating to them. They were removed on the enlargement of Shane's Castle demesne and at the time when it was totally altered and improved by the present Lord O'Neill.

Pagan: Giant's Grave or Tumulus

On the summit of a little swell (147 feet above the sea) in the townland of Barnish, near the eastern confines of the parish and about a third of a mile to the right of the road from Antrim to Randalstown, are the imperfect remains of a tumulus, or giant's grave as it is by some termed, while by people in the neighbourhood it is more generally known as the Rock, probably from the hill on which it is situated being of basaltic formation, though partially coated with a shallow gravelly soil. From the mutilation which it has undergone, but an imperfect idea can now be formed concerning it, and by a reference to plan and drawing (appendix) it will perhaps be more clearly understood.

It seems originally to have consisted of a circular tumulus or cairn of small stones, enclosed by a row of large ones, occupying the summit of the knoll and probably about 90 feet in diameter. Inside there seems to have been other rows of enormous stones, which, however, do not now retain any regular form, and near the centre is the grave, bearing west south west by north north east. The portion of the cairn now remaining (somewhat less than one-half of the original extent) is about 4 feet high. The grave, or rather what remains of it, measures in extreme length 18 feet and in breadth on the inside only 9 and a half inches. It is formed of large slabs laid longitudinally on their edges, a few inches apart but firmly and uniformly set. They vary in height in the inside from 3 to 4 feet. At the eastern end of the grave is a large upright slab 6 feet high, 5 feet broad and 15 inches thick. The stones at its western extremity have been removed. There are not any coping or roofing stones to the grave, though from the uniformity in height of those forming its sides, there may have been such. The bottom of the grave is not paved nor flagged, nor are there any further traces of what it has been.

An irregular row of large stones, perhaps from 2 to 3 tons weight, extends eastwards from the extremity of the grave to that of the cairn, along which several others are placed. In one instance here a stone measuring 6 feet by 2 feet 6 inches by 2 feet is placed upon another 4 feet high by 4 feet long and 3 feet broad. The summit of the cairn is on a level with that of the stones forming the grave and those around it. It seems to have been higher, but the larger stones have been removed from time to time to form the fences round the field in which it is situated.

About 20 years [ago] a standing stone, fully 6 feet high, 3 feet broad and 1 and a half feet thick, was removed from the western side (probably the western extremity) of the grave.

Parish of Drummaul

Standing Stone

On the summit of a conspicuous hill (420 feet above the sea), and in the townland of Muckleramer near the eastern side of the parish, is a standing stone 4 feet high and 2 by 2 feet 4 inches thick.

Forts

There are 39 forts in this parish, all of which are constructed of clay. Within memory as many have [been] destroyed by the farmer, from their having interfered with his operations, and those which still remain have with a few exceptions undergone more or less mutilation. The most perfect are those in Shane's Castle park. There are 15 within its confines. 3 of these are rather remarkable for their form and situation. Plans of them and the other forts in the parish will be found in appendix.

Dunmore Fort is situated on the summit of a very steep bank overhanging the River Main, above which the summit of the fort is elevated 86 feet. It is situated on the right bank of the river, in Shane's Castle demesne, and about a fifth of a mile below the town of Randalstown. A low and almost level holme extends along the opposite [side] of the river.

This fortification consists of a somewhat oval-shaped mound raised to an elevation of about 34 feet above the ordinary level of the bank. Adjoining the southern side of this, but less elevated by 30 feet, are the traces of an almost square fort, or rather a hollow, the front or eastern parapet of which is formed by the face of the bank; and adjoining the southern [end] of this is a circular fort, the parapet of which has been almost wholly raised. 25 yards west of the latter are 2 little mounds, elevated from 1 and a half to 2 and a half feet above the adjacent ground. One of these is of an oval form and measures 28 by 18 feet. The other is circular, its diameter is 14 feet.

The mound in form is somewhat oval. At the base its diameters are 104 and 64 feet. It is very steep, particularly at its northern side, where a small circular platform 22 feet in diameter is raised on its summit. On the western side of the mound a rampart or sunken road 13 feet wide extends about half-way round it. To this there is a sort of ramp or approach leading from the centre fort and another from the more distant of the 2 mounds before alluded to. The ground falls gently westward from the western side of the principal mound.

The central fort measures internally 40 by 50 feet. The interior has been sunk and the parapets, which are from 3 to 7 feet high, thereby formed. The southern of the 3 forts is from 2 to 5 feet higher than the centre one. It consists merely of a circular platform from 5 to 7 feet higher than the adjacent ground. It is 79 feet in diameter. There are faint traces of a parapet which enclosed its summit.

One and three-quarter miles south of the former, and on the summit of the same bank, is a second fortification, consisting of an oval and a circular fort with a small circular platform or outwork attached to each. The oval-shaped fort is the larger of the two. It is situated on the summit and at the verge of the bank, which is within 500 feet of the river, above which it is elevated 70 feet. The bank is pretty steep but smooth in its declivity. This fort measures in extreme length 218 feet and in breadth 160 feet. It is enclosed by 2 parapets, between which is a ditch from 6 to 10 feet wide. The inner parapet is from 2 and a half to 4 feet high in the inside and from 4 to 8 feet high in the outside. The outer parapet is from 2 to 4 feet high above the ditch and from 1 to 2 feet high in the exterior side. It averages about 7 and a half feet in thickness but has been partially removed. The fort is divided near its centre by a ditch from 1 to 3 feet deep and 5 feet wide, on the southern side of which are the traces of a parapet. In the northern division are the remains of [a] circular platform 38 feet in diameter and about 1 foot high. On its western side is a second platform, nearly circular and 44 feet in diameter.

The circular fort is situated 38 feet to the south west of the former and 110 feet from the edge of the bank. Its extreme diameter is 152 feet. It consists of a circular body enclosed by a parapet from 5 to 7 and a half feet high and 12 feet thick, beyond which is a shallow ditch 11 feet wide. On the south eastern side of this fort is a circular earthen outwork 58 feet in diameter and 3 feet high.

The circular and the oval have each 2 entrances, namely one at their northern and one at their southern sides.

The fortifications which have just been described would, were the ground clear of timber, be discernible from each other, but as it is, the intermediate ground is densely planted and wooded. On these forts are several ash and other trees, which from their extreme age are partially decayed. A plan of this fort will be found in appendix.

680 yards further down, and on the opposite side of the river, are the remains of a very large fort, which have been so mutilated as to retain but

little of their original form. It is situated on a low and almost level holme and on the very brink of the river, which would seem to have worn part of it away, either by its increasing in breadth or by its having changed its course. The former is, however, the more probable cause.

The fort consists of a mound or body 134 feet in length by 29 feet broad, 16 feet high above the river and 12 feet above the ditch around its eastern side. It is encompassed by a ditch from 15 to 18 feet wide and 3 feet lower than a parapet beyond it, which seems to have been of immense thickness, but all have undergone such mutilation that it is now impossible to give a more accurate or detailed description of them. A plan of this fort will be found in appendix. It could but for the planting be easily discerned from the one previously described. Some ash and other trees of great age are growing upon this fort.

There is not anything worthy of particular notice or description in the other forts in this parish. Their form and style of construction may perhaps be more easily understood by referring to the plans in the appendix than by any other mode of description.

Coves

There are not at present in this parish any coves which are open, or into which an entrance (without some difficulty) can be effected. There are, however, 9, the situations of which are precisely known, but from their having interfered with the cultivation of the land in which they are, they have all been dug away or closed up and the ground over them cultivated, so that their site is known only to the farmer. 2 of these, situated in the townland of Barnish and near the giant's grave, were remarkable for their extent. They were, however, demolished about 19 years ago.

There is one in the townland of Caddy, the entrance of which is now too small for admission, in which there are 2 chambers turning off at right angles. There is one in the townland of Ballytresna, which from a similar cause cannot be entered; one in the townland of Drumsough, the entrance to which is obstructed by a lodgement of a quantity of water in it; one in Craigmore, now blocked up; one in Feehogue, now cultivated over; one (which has been wholly removed) in the townland of Procklis; and one in Shane's Castle demesne, the ground over which is now level.

Many others, the sites of which are now uncertain, have within memory been removed, either from the view, by cultivating the ground over them, or by their total demolition. There is not a townland, except those chiefly occupied with bog, in which there has not been one, and in those where the soil is light or gravelly, they have been more frequently found.

Giant's Chair

In the townland of Craigmore, near the summit of the craggy hill of the same name, is [a] rock or large stone somewhat in form resembling a chair, and to which the name of the Giant's Chair has been conferred; but as this name is of but modern application it is not worthy of further notice.

Ancient Bell

The bell here alluded to is now in the possession of Adam McClean Esquire of Belfast. It was given to him many years ago by a man named Mulholland, who had been a schoolmaster and had educated Mr McClean. In his latter days Mulholland (who had resided near Shane's Castle) had been in reduced circumstances and, having been almost wholly supported by Mr McClean, left him at his death this bell and a very old bible. The bell in itself is rude in the extreme, both in form and workmanship, and from its worn state must be of immense antiquity. Intrinsically it is not worth anything, but a clear idea of its value and the veneration in which it must have been held can easily be found from the richness and costliness of its cover, of gold, silver and precious stones of the most curious and exquisitely elaborate workmanship, the intrinsic value of which, without taking into consideration the time and labour its manufacture required, is very considerable. From its size the bell could not have been used in a belfry, and from its tone also it is more probable that it had been used in the interior of some building.

[Insert footnote: Drawings of this bell and cover had been made and have been or are being engraved by the Royal Hibernian Academy. I need not attempt a description of it, as without a drawing it would be useless. Mr McClean has the original drawings from which these were made and which are faithfully correct. I have already written to Lieutenant Bennett concerning them [signed] J. Boyle].

The Mulhollands were a very ancient family and had possessed large estates both in this county and the county Derry, all of which were confiscated by King William, chiefly on account of the assistance they gave in persecuting the Protestants and in opposing the English settlers

Parish of Drummaul

Coat of arms from Shane's Castle

and garrisons in the north. In 1688 they went in great numbers to assist the army besieging Derry and this is supposed to have sealed their doom. The district along the Crumlin water, and in the parish of Killead (on the opposite side of Antrim bay from Shane's Castle), which still retains the name of Kilmacavert, was held by them until the confiscation, and as it had been a portion of the O'Neill estates or territories, an alliance existed between their families.

It is supposed that the last Roman Catholic of the O'Neill family (it is said the great-grandfather of the present lord), on his adopting the Protestant faith gave this bell, which had hitherto for centuries been in the possession of his family, to a lineal ancestor of Mulhollands, who was a Roman Catholic and his bosom friend.

The bible, which is one of the earliest printed copies, contains several entries of births and deaths in the O'Neill family, which tally precisely with those in the appendix as quoted from a document of French John's. The Mulhollands handed the bell from father to son until it came into the possession of the one who gave it to McClean.

The bell is well known by the old people in the neighbourhood, as it had within their memory been used for swearing by, a purpose to which, it is said, it had for ages been devoted, and so great was the veneration with which it had been regarded that many who would have been unscrupulous in their asseverations by other forms, would not have ventured being so by this. It was principally appealed to in cases of theft, when anyone was suspected, and was either obliged to "clear" himself or did so voluntarily.

Arms of the O'Neills

The arms (as shown in drawing) are said to have been erected over one of the principal entrances of the castle. They are now lying among mortar and rubbish in the present farmyard. The stone is a whitish sandstone, such as is not common in the county Antrim. The workmanship is good, but they have been sadly broken and in some instances defaced.

Edenduffcarrick

Edenduffcarrick (as it is vulgarly pronounced) or "the black face of stone" is the face represented in drawing. The face is evidently intended to represent that of a female, and has a mournful expression. It is about 9 inches long, 6 inches broad and 3 inches thick. The stone of which it is formed is quite black. It is stuck in or against the outside of the eastern wall of the south wing of the castle,

Edenduffcarrick from Shane's Castle

about 30 feet from the summit and 30 feet from the base. As there are some open or rather roofless vaults at the foot of the wall, it is higher from the ground than it had formerly been and cannot now be approached.

There is neither legend, tradition or history relating to this face. All that is known is its name, and that that of the manor is taken from it. Its name might have derived from that of the castle, which until the time of French John was Edenduffcarrick, and this name may have been derived from the black crags or little cliffs extending westward from the castle along the shore. The word would admit of being interpreted as "the black face of stone" or "the face of a black rock"; but it is more probable that the face is that of someone connected with the early history of the castle, and that from it the castle and consequently the manor took their names.

Baptismal Fonts

The stone, of which 2 drawings are shown in [appendix], was found in one of the Three Islands, which are off the south western coast of this parish and are included in the confines of one of its detached portions. It is precisely similar, as respects the dimensions of the hole or font, to many others which have been found in old burial grounds and about old churches in this county. There are several cuts or hacks as if made with some sharp instrument about the font. The stone, which is of hard greenstone, is rough and unhewn and measures 3 feet 4 inches by 2 feet 2 inches. The font is somewhat oval. It measures 13 by 10 inches and 7 and a half inches deep. It is very smoothly cut.

About 50 feet from the eastern gable of Old Drummaul church is a square stone, quite flat on the surface, with a circular hollow 9 inches in diameter and 5 inches deep, very smoothly cut. It is now set up as a headstone. It is said that a quantity of gold was many years ago found under this stone by a man named Robert Dickey, but this statement is not worthy of credit, and it is probable that it is nothing more than one of the old fonts commonly found in such places.

Rings of Copper

About 6 years ago a man named Adam Davison, living in the townland of Aghaboy, found in a field 30 copper rings each 1 and a half inches in diameter and linked together. They have since

Parish of Drummaul

unfortunately been lost. They were considerably corroded and bore no marks of having been ornamented.

Stone and Brass Weapons

Stone and brazen spears and hatchets and flint arrowheads are frequently picked up in the fields in this parish, particularly in the vicinity of the forts. Drawings of some of these will be found in appendix. The hatchets are of almost every size, but all apparently of a similar period or age of manufacture, being beautifully smooth and of a hard greenstone, while the flint arrows and spears are of almost every variety of workmanship, from the earliest and rudest to the later and almost perfect.

These articles are scarcely found until they are again lost to the country, either by itinerant ragmen who collect the brazen instruments to sell as old brass, or by the collectors for public and private cabinets, but chiefly for the Belfast museum.

Coins

Old silver coins are very frequently picked up in the fields in this parish. Those of the reign of Elizabeth are particularly numerous. Besides those, coins of the reigns of Edward the I, II, III and VII [sic], Henry II, III, IV, VII and VIII, Robert Bruce, James I, and copper coins of Charles II and James II are occasionally found. They are almost invariably brought to the watchmakers, who purchase them as old silver and afterwards sell them as such in Belfast.

Querns

Querns <quearns> are frequently found, not only in the fields but also in the bogs in this parish. They present great variety in size, and also in form and style of workmanship, varying in diameter from 7 and three-quarters to 20 inches, some of them being handsomely carved while others are very rude, and in one instance, as shown in drawing[s], being furnished with 3 feet and grooved in the centre to admit the other portion.

One quern in the possession of the Reverend Hugh Smith of Craigmore has its upper part handsomely cut. It is, however, broken in two.

The quern shown in drawing[s] is of a sort of hard gritty sandstone, quite dissimilar from that of any of the others, which are all of a species of basalt.

A quern of the ordinary description was lately found in a bog in the townland of Magheralane, at a depth of nearly 10 feet from the surface, but still not at the bottom of the bog.

Old Clock

At Shane's Castle is a little clock in an ebony case, which was presented to Rose O'Neill (Marchioness of Antrim) by Queen Mary (consort of King William III), to whom she had been maid of honour. This clock had a narrow escape at the burning of Shane's Castle and was preserved by the exertions of the housekeeper.

Appendix to Memoir by James Boyle

SOCIAL ECONOMY AND HISTORY

Original Clergy

No further record of the successive clergy of the Established Church has been preserved than that given below. The first remembered by the oldest inhabitant was the Reverend Barry, who was succeeded by the Reverend Phipps, the Reverend Hudson, the Reverend Scott, the Reverend Lang, the Reverend Charles Henry Crookshank, the Reverend William Henry Pratt, who was in 1815 succeeded by the present vicar, the Reverend Samuel Shenton Heatley.

Presbyterian and Seceding Ministers

The first Presbyterian minister of whom there is any record was the Reverend John Cathcart, who in 1661 was one of the ministers ejected by Jeremy Taylor, Bishop of Down and Connor. He was succeeded by the Reverend Richard Wilson, ordained in 1689 and who died in 1694; the Reverend William Taylor, ordained in 1697 and who died in 1727; the Reverend William Henderson, ordained in 1732 and who died in 1781; the Reverend James White, ordained in 1746; the Reverend Thomas Henry, ordained in 1786 and who died in 1830; the Reverend Archibald Jameson, ordained in 1826 and who died in 1835; and the Reverend Alexander Crawford, ordained in 1837.

The first Seceding minister in this parish was the Reverend John Smith, ordained to it in 1786. He emigrated to America and was succeeded in 1816 by the Reverend Thomas Reid, the present minister.

Roman Catholic Clergy

The earliest parish [priest] remembered was the Reverend McGregor, who was succeeded by the Reverend Neeson, the Reverend Peter Boyle, the Reverend Bernard McAuley (who succeeded Mr Boyle in 1819) and the Reverend Daniel Curoe, the present priest, who was appointed to this parish in 1825.

Document relating to O'Neills

Copy of a document in the handwriting of French John O'Neill (1), great-grandfather of the present Earl O'Neill. [Insert footnote: I copied this from the original document. See notes to this paper].

"The deaths of my relations and friends. My grand-uncle Sir Henry O'Neill died at Blackheath in 1638, near Stratford Le Bow in England, was brought into Ireland and buried in the church of Carrickfergus.

I know not when my grandfather Brian O'Neill died, but I believe it was in the year 1669. He was buried in the church of Skerry (2).

My grandfather Captain Phelim O'Neill died in the year 1677 and was buried in the church of Skerry.

Dame Martha O'Neill, relict of Sir Henry O'Neill and daughter of Sir Francis Stafford, died in Ballymagarry in April 1678, lay in state in Edenduffcarrick (3) and was buried in the church of Carrickfergus.

Captain John O'Neill, second son of Sir Arthur O'Neill, died in the year 1687 in London and was buried in St James' there.

My grandmother O'Neill alias O'Hara died in Edenduffcarrick in 1690 and was buried in the church of Skerry.

Ensign Arthur O'Neill, second son of Captain John O'Neill, was murdered by a mob in Mechlin in Flanders in 1694 and was buried in or near the town.

Rose O'Neill, Marchioness of Antrim, relict of Randal, Marquis of Antrim, and daughter of said Sir Henry O'Neill, died at Edenduffcarrick the 27th April 1695, lay there in great state and was buried in great state in the church of Carrickfergus on the 4th July following.

Henry O'Neill Esquire, eldest son of said Captain John O'Neill, was drowned in the bay of Dublin, coming from England in the year 1696, and his corpse was never found.

My mother Elinor O'Neill alias Magenis died the 7th February 1704 and was buried in the church of Skerry.

My sister Martha O'Neill alias Hagan died at Dunmore 14th February 1704 and was buried at Cranfield.

Colonel Cormack O'Neill, eldest son of said Arthur O'Neill Esquire, died at Broughshane 10th December 1706 and was buried in the church of Skerry.

Major Con Magenis, my double cousin-german, died in Broughshane 26th February 1713-14 and was buried in the church of Skerry.

Charles O'Neill Esquire, third son of said Captain John O'Neill, died 2nd May 1716 in London and was buried in St James' there.

My brother-in-law Captain Arthur Hagan died at Ardbo (4) 17th September 1717, and [was] brought to Cranfield (5) and buried there beside my sister.

My brother-in-law Robert Dixon Esquire died in Dublin 5th March 1726 and was buried in Kilcullen church, county Kildare.

My wife Charity O'Neill alias Dixon died in Edenduffcarrick 30th November 1726 and was buried in my own vault there."

John O'Neill Esquire died at Shane's Castle 1739 and was buried in his vault there. [Insert footnote: This was French John himself, who built the vault at Shane's Castle or Edenduffcarrick in 1722].

"Deaths of my friends. Randle McDonnell, Lord Marquis of Antrim, died at Ballymagarry (6) 2nd or 3rd February 1682 and lay in state there, and was buried on the 14th March following in the vault at Ballymagarry.

Sir Neal O'Neill was wounded at the battle of the Boyne in 1690 near Slane, was carried to Dublin and from thence to Waterford, where he died of his wounds by the negligence of his surgeons.

Alexander McDonnell, Earl of Antrim, brother to the late marquis, died at Thistleworth near London in the year 1699 and was buried at Holywell in Wales.

My old comrade Major Charles Stewart (7) of Ballintoy died in London about the middle of November 1710 and was buried in St James' church there.

Captain Edmond Stafford (8) died in Portglenone in August 1713 and was buried in the church of Aghoghill, by whose death I lost a kind and dear friend.

Clotworthy Skeffington, Lord Viscount Massereene (the first of that Christian name), died in the castle of Antrim 13th March 1713-14 and was buried in the church of Antrim, by whom I lost a good friend.

Mrs Abigail Parnel (9) died in Antrim Castle 4th February 1715-16 and was buried in the church of Antrim.

Captain William Shawe, my old comrade, died at Bush (10) 3rd November 1719 and was buried in Templepatrick.

Randle McDonnell, Earl of Antrim (son of Earl

Alexander), died in Dublin in October 1721 and was buried in Christ's Church there.

Joshua Dawson Esquire died 12th March 1724-25 at Castledawson and was buried in his own chapel there, by which I lost a very kind and dear friend.

Colonel Clotworthy Upton died at Castle Upton 6th June 1725 and was buried at Templepatrick, by which I lost a good friend.

My old friend Mr James McCullock died at Grogan (11) 9th July 1725 and was buried in Old Drummaul.

My old friend and schoolfellow Henry McCullock Esquire died at Fehogue (12) 16th January 1728-29 and was buried in Old Drummaul.

Charles Campbell died at (New) Grange 29th October 1725 and was buried at [blank], by which I lost a kind and dear friend.

William Connolly died in Dublin 30th October 1729 and was buried in great state in Celbridge, alias Kildrogheda, in the county Kildare, by which I lost a special good friend.

Rachel Hungerford, Viscountess Dowager Massereene, relict of the above Lord Viscount Massereene, died in Antrim Castle in January 1731-2 and was buried in the church of Antrim, by which my family lost one of the best friends.

My kind friend Brigadier-General Richard Kane alias O'Cahan died the 30th December 1736 in the island of Minorca, of which he was chief governor for the King of England."

Notes to Document on O'Neills

(1) "French" John O'Neill was the 13th child of John O'Neill of the Largywood and, besides his having so many seniors, his delicate health and appearance rendered the idea of his succeeding to the estates a very improbable one. He obtained his soubriquet from having been educated in France. [Insert footnote: The Largy or Largywood is in the parish of Ahoghill. This family of O'Neills were known from their trade as "The Basketmakers"].

(2) Skerry: many of the O'Neills are interred in Skerry, which was at one time a favourite burial place of the family. The old church of Skerry is situated in the parish of the same name and near a residence of the O'Neills, a short distance from the village of Broughshane. Skerry church is said to have been built by St Patrick.

(3) Edenduffcarrick, now Shane's Castle, and so called after this same John O'Neill: the manor still retains the original name, said to be derived from Eden-dhu-carrick or "the black face of stone"

from a face or head of some kind of black coloured stone on the east side of the ruins of Shane's Castle (a drawing of this face will be found in [appendix]).

(4) Ardbo or Ardboe, in the parish of the same name, in the county Tyrone and on the shore of Lough Neagh: on a point or low promontory on the shore are the foundations of a very extensive monastery and church, and also a remarkably large and curiously carved stone cross (from 12 to 15 feet high) said to have been erected there by St Patrick.

(5) Cranfield: the little parish of Cranfield adjoins the south eastern corner of that of Drummaul. It occupies the extremity of a low point running into Lough Neagh and is remarkable for the antiquity of its church (now in ruins), which is said to have been founded by St Patrick. Within a few yards of the church is a holy well, which until within a few years was frequented by hundreds from this and the neighbouring counties, who came to be cured of their diseases by it. They assembled for several days at it in the month of June, but it latterly had become such a scene of riot and drunkenness that the Roman Catholic clergy were obliged to forbid their flock attending it. Captain Hagan's tomb is still in preservation.

(6) Ballymagarry, in the parish of Dunluce and on the north west coast of this county: the McDonnells had a castle here, of which there are now but faint vestiges. It is about 1 mile south of Dunluce Castle.

(7) Major Charles Stewart of Ballintoy: Ballintoy Castle was formerly the residence of the Stewarts. It was also a strong Protestant garrison during the wars of 1641, but was soon after allowed to fall into decay. The Stewarts were also the proprietors of Ballymoy Castle in the adjoining parish of Billy, which stood about 3 miles north west of Ballintoy. They were, however, obliged to fly from it in 1641 by Sir Phelim O'Neill, who then burned the castle to the ground. The Stewarts have now but little property about Ballintoy. The castle is no longer in their possession, and the lineal descendant of the family has taken the name of Moore and resides in the neighbouring parish of Derrykeighan. There is still a Major Stewart, a branch of the family alluded to, residing in the parish of Ballintoy.

(8) Captain Edmond Stafford commanded the garrison at Portglenone, which was attacked by the advanced guard of King James' army when proceeding to the siege of Derry. An ancestor of his also commanded the garrison placed here by

Queen Elizabeth to keep Sir Phelim O'Neill in check.

(9) Mrs Abigail Parnel: the plate in Antrim church was presented to it by this lady and bears an inscription to that effect.

(10) Bush, a townland within 1 and a half miles of Antrim: there is not now any trace of a respectable residence in it, except one which has recently been erected, nor is there a single tree of any kind in it.

(11) Grogan, a townland within 2 miles of Randalstown: there is not any trace of a respectable residence in it.

(12) Feehogue, a townland adjoining the town of Randalstown: there is a gentleman's residence in it, but it does not bear any marks of antiquity.

Legends of the O'Neills: Banshee

Legends and traditions connected with the O'Neill family. The most remarkable legend connected with the O'Neill family is that relating to the banshee which has for centuries haunted them: Neinn Roe "my red-haired daughter" is the proper name of the banshee, but Neina Roe or Neinny Roe, which is locally interpreted as Catherine O'Neill, is the name applied to her (improperly) by the country people. [Insert footnote: Neinn in Irish signifies "daughter." Neinna is the plural of neinn. Roe signifies "red", and when coupled with any name always relates to the colour <color> of the hair [signed] J. Boyle].

This creature is said to have been a daughter of one of the O'Neills, but more relating to her history is not known. Always previous to the death of any of the family, or previous to any afflication or calamity befalling them, she has been heard to forbode it, by her usually mournful wailing "och, och, och, och", and never has her prediction been unfulfilled.

For some time previous to the burning of Shane's Castle she had been heard by several, but particularly by Bernard Moore the underbutler, but since the fire she has never been heard. An apartment (a bedchamber) is said, and with truth, to have [been] appropriated for her use and, though she never has been seen, still her impression was regularly found in the morning on the bed in it. The common idea is that she was a beautiful virgin who was enchanted by the fairies and sent by them to forewarn her family of the approach of any calamity.

On the evening on which the fire which consumed Shane's Castle took place, a large party of visitors were staying there. The fire broke out in a dressing room, in the chimney of which the rook had built and which is generally supposed to have been the cause of the fire. One of the company, the late Captain Greer of Randalstown, a magistrate of the county, who with others had rushed out to the grounds, distinctly saw a figure in armour several times appear at and pass one of the windows on the second floor. This Mr Greer has frequently stated, at the same declaring that it could not have been the effect of imagination or fright. There were neither figures nor paintings in the room in which he saw the apparition and besides, everyone had at that time left the castle. [Insert footnote: I have frequently heard Captain Greer relate this strange story [signed] J. Boyle].

The story of the Bloody Hand is too well known to be repeated here.

PRODUCTIVE ECONOMY

Randalstown: Table of Trades and Occupations

Apothecaries and surgeons 3, bakers 3, butchers 2, blacksmiths 3, bonnetmakers 4, clergymen 3, carpenters 5, cartmakers 2, chandlers 1, carmen 3, clockmakers 2, constabulary 5, dressmakers 9, woollen drapers 2, glaziers 1, grocers 10, hotelkeepers 1, houses of lodging and entertainment 6, hosiers 1, innkeepers and publicans 14, leather cutters 2, masons 2, milliners 2, magistrates 1, militia 9, nailers 2, physicians 1, pensioners 15, ragmen 2, reedmakers 2, shoemakers 7, schoolmasters 4, schoolmistresses 2, saddlers 2, tailors 3, weavers 6, total 142.

Randalstown Grain Market

A statement of the quantity of wheat and oats sold in Randalstown grain market from the year 1826 to the year 1837 inclusive.

1826: wheat, 530 tons 19 cwt 1 quarter 10 pounds; oats, 769 tons 8 cwt.

1827: wheat, 684 tons 11 cwt 1 quarter 16 pounds; oats, 790 tons 13 cwt 1 quarter 22 pounds.

1828: wheat, 991 tons 16 cwt 1 quarter 14 pounds; oats, 811 tons 16 cwt 6 pounds.

1829: wheat, 857 tons 8 cwt 2 quarters 7 pounds; oats, 1,065 tons 12 cwt 1 quarter 6 pounds.

1830: wheat, 910 tons 4 cwt 8 pounds; oats, 976 tons 16 pounds.

1831: wheat, 717 tons 13 cwt 2 quarters; oats, 913 tons 9 cwt 6 pounds.

1832: wheat, 592 tons 18 cwt 3 quarters 2 pounds; oats, 1,101 tons 11 cwt 3 quarters 2 pounds.

1833: wheat, 454 tons 10 cwt 1 quarter 8

Parish of Drummaul

pounds; oats, 878 tons 10 cwt 3 quarters 8 pounds.

1834: wheat, 360 tons 5 cwt 3 quarters 18 pounds; oats, 910 tons 5 cwt 1 quarter 16 pounds.

1835: wheat, 210 tons 4 cwt 1 quarter 6 pounds; oats, 1,210 tons 4 cwt 3 quarters 8 pounds.

1836: wheat, 193 tons 5 cwt 3 quarters 11 pounds; oats, 811 tons 5 cwt 1 quarter 27 pounds.

1837: wheat, 171 tons 2 cwt 1 quarter 20 pounds; oats, 734 tons 13 cwt 2 quarters 9 pounds.

Conveyances

[Table contains the following headings: description, hours of departure and arrival, time passing through Randalstown, fare from Randalstown inside and outside, days of plying].

Mail coach from Derry to Belfast, leaves Derry at 6 p.m., arrives in Belfast at 7 a.m., in Randalstown at 4 a.m., fare inside 5s 6d, outside 3s 6d, daily.

Mail coach from Belfast to Derry, leaves Belfast at 7 a.m., arrives in Derry at 8 p.m., in Randalstown at 10 a.m., fare inside 20s, outside 16s 6d, daily.

Pair horse car from Cookstown to Belfast, leaves Cookstown at 4 a.m., arrives in Belfast at 11 a.m., in Randalstown at 7.30 a.m., outside fare 3s, daily except Sundays.

Pair horse car from Belfast to Cookstown, leaves Belfast at 2.30 p.m., arrives in Cookstown at 9 p.m., in Randalstown at 5.30 p.m., outside fare 3s, daily except Sundays.

Four-wheeled conveyance from Magherafelt to Belfast, leaves Magherafelt at 5 a.m., arrives in Belfast at 11 a.m., in Randalstown at 7.30 a.m., outside fare 2s, daily except Sundays.

Four-wheeled car from Belfast to Magherafelt, leaves Belfast at 2 p.m., arrives in Magherafelt at 6 p.m., in Randalstown at 5 p.m., outside fare 2s 6d, daily except Sundays.

2 one-horse cars from Randalstown to Belfast, leave Randalstown at 5 a.m., arrive in Belfast at 9.30 a.m., outside fare 1s 6d, on Tuesday and Friday.

2 one-horse cars from Belfast to Randalstown, leave Belfast at 4 p.m., arrive in Randalstown at 8.30 p.m., outside fare 1s 6d, Tuesday and Friday.

SOCIAL ECONOMY

Randalstown Dispensary

A statement of the funds of the Randalstown dispensary. [Table contains the following headings: income from the county, from legal subscriptions, surgeon's salary, medicines, house rent, contingencies, number of patients. Surgeon's salary for each year 50 pounds, house rent for each year, except 1826, 5 pounds 10s].

1825: from the county 58 pounds 3s 4d, legal subscriptions 58 pounds 3s 4d, medicines 15 pounds 8s 1d.

1826: from the county 38 pounds 2s, legal subscriptions 38 pounds 2s, medicines 23 pounds 8s 8d, house rent 6 pounds 15s 7d, contingencies 9 pounds 8s 9d, number of patients 1,610.

1827: from the county 34 pounds 16s, legal subscriptions 34 pounds 16s, medicines 10 pounds 15s, contingencies 6 pounds 15s 7d.

1828: from the county 42 pounds, legal subscriptions 42 pounds, medicines 10 pounds, contingencies 5 pounds 14s 1d, number of patients 1,922.

1829: from the county 39 pounds 11s 6d, legal subscriptions 39 pounds 11s 6d, medicines 15 pounds 17s 2d, contingencies 4 pounds 16s 7d.

1830: from the county 37 pounds 5s, legal subscriptions 37 pounds 5s, medicines 15 pounds 1s 4d, contingencies 3 pounds 5s 2d.

1831: from the county 34 pounds 7s 6d, legal subscriptions 34 pounds 7s 6d, medicines 11 pounds 7s 8d, contingencies 1 pound 3s 1d, number of patients 2,891.

1832: from the county 34 pounds 7s 3d, legal subscriptions 34 pounds 7s 3d, medicines 22 pounds 17s 7d, contingencies 15 pounds 9s 9d.

1833: from the county 31 pounds 11s 10d, legal subscriptions 31 pounds 11s 10d, medicines 17 pounds 9s 1d, contingencies 5 pounds 12s 2d, number of patients 2,531.

1834: from the county 35 pounds 15s, legal subscriptions 35 pounds 15s, medicines 19 pounds 8s, contingencies 4 pounds 10d, number of patients 2,336.

1835: from the county 39 pounds 10s 6d, legal subscriptions 39 pounds 10s 6d, medicines 5 pounds 13s, contingencies 3 pounds 14s 7d, number of patients 2,477.

1836: from the county 33 pounds 7s 5d, legal subscriptions 33 pounds 7s 5d, medicines 16 pounds 4s 7d, contingencies 2 pounds 4s 8d, number of patients 2,491.

1837: from the county 36 pounds 3s 1d, legal subscriptions 36 pounds 3s 1d, medicines 17 pounds 1s 5d, contingencies 6 pounds 18s 2d, number of patients 2,762.

Randalstown Dispensary: Table of Diseases

Asthma: 1822 47, 1831 92, 1834 72, 1837 69.

Boils: 1831 88, 1834 60, 1837 71.

Consumption: 1822 21, 1831 46, 1834 46, 1837 49.

Chronic cough: 1822 120, 1831 201, 1834 157, 1837 183.

Cholera morbus: 1822 20, 1831 92, 1834 72.

Colic: 1822 45, 1831 53, 1834 53, 1837 76.

Dysentry and diarrhoea: 1822 17, 1831 58, 1834 58, 1837 61.

Dyspepsia: 1822 143, 1831 44, 1834 49, 1837 98.

Dislocations and fractures: 1822 2, 1831 19, 1834 29, 1837 20.

Dropsy: 1822 23, 1831 52, 1834 52, 1837 47.

Erysipelas: 1822 27, 1831 56, 1834 59, 1837 62.

Hysteria: 1822 35, 1831 198, 1834 148, 1837 137.

Whooping <hooping> cough: 1831 90, 1834 97, 1837 71.

Inflammation of the bowels and chest: 1822 126, 1831 209, 1834 129, 1837 118.

Inflammation of the ear and kidneys: 1822 12, 1831 52, 1834 49, 1837 56.

Inflammation of diseased parts and mortification: 1822 70, 1831 89, 1834 79, 1837 83.

Herpes, lepra and various disorders of the skin: 1831 112, 1834 100, 1837 117.

Liver complaints: 1822 19, 1831 30, 1834 34, 1837 26.

Rheumatism: 1822 67, 1831 24, 1834 39, 1837 31.

Scurvy and itch: 1822 123, 1831 112, 1834 69, 1837 101.

Scald head: 1831 67, 1834 67, 1837 41.

Scrofula: 1822 20, 1831 84, 1834 89, 1837 72.

Typhus: 1822 311, 1831 601, 1834 451, 1837 509.

Ulcerated and inflammatory sore throat: 1822 24, 1831 195, 1834 124, 1837 133.

Wounds and ulcers: 1822 70, 1831 61, 1834 69, 1837 88.

Worms: 1822 137, 1831 166, 1834 116, 1837 141.

[Totals]: 1822 1,479; 1831 2,894; 1834 2,361; 1837 2,650.

I could not obtain a list of the cases for any other years than those given here [signed] J. Boyle.

Emigration

[Table gives year, age, capital, occupation, religion and sex of emigrants]. 1835: 3 under 10 years, 3 over 10 and under 20, 15 over 20 and under 40, 3 over 40; capital: 1 under 50 pounds and over 20 pounds, 3 under 20 pounds and over 10 pounds, 20 under 10 pounds; occupations: tradesmen 1, labourers 22, others 1, Protestants 13, Roman Catholics 11, males 15, females 9, total 24.

1836: 6 over 10 and under 20 years, 16 over 20 and under 40; capital: 3 under 20 pounds and over 10 pounds, 19 under 10 pounds; occupations: labourers 20, others 2, Protestants 16, Roman Catholics 16, males 11, females 11, total 22.

1837: 2 under 10 years, 11 over 10 and under 20, 28 over 20 and under 40, 6 over 40; capital: 5 under 50 pounds and over 20 pounds, 7 under 20 pounds and over 10 pounds, 35 under 10 pounds; occupations: tradesmen 2, labourers 40, others 5, Protestants 37, Roman Catholics 10, males [blank], females [blank], total 47.

National and Parish Schools

[Table contains the following headings: name, situation and description, when established, income and expenditure, physical, intellectual and moral instruction, number of pupils subdivided by age, sex and religion, name and religious persuasion of master or mistress, date on which visited].

Parish school, situated in the town of Randalstown; the house is in a dilapidated state and almost wholly unfit for the purpose, established 1820; income: from the London Hibernian Society 3 pounds 10s per annum and from Lord O'Neill 4 pounds 4s per annum, [total] 7 pounds 14s, from pupils 4 pounds; expenditure on salaries: the teacher receives the sums granted and also that paid by the scholars; intellectual instruction: books of the London Hibernian Society, *Gough's* and *Thomson's Arithmetic*, *Murray's Grammar* and *Thomson's Geography;* moral instruction: church catechism taught by the master, Authorised Version of the Scriptures read, occasionally visited by the vicar; number of pupils: males, 10 under 10 years of age, 8 from 10 to 15, 18 total males; females, 10 under 10 years of age, 7 from 10 to 15, 17 total females; total number of pupils 35, 21 Established Church, 14 Presbyterians; master Andrew Moore, Established Church; the visits of the vicar are irregular, few and far between.

National school, in the town of Randalstown; an exceedingly neat and well built house 36 feet by 24 feet, dry and airy and kept in nice order, erected at a cost of 188 pounds 18s 7d, of which 95 pounds 18s 7d was contributed by the Reverend Daniel Curoe, parish priest, and the remainder by the Board of National Education, established 1833; income: from the Board of National Education annually 12 pounds, from pupils 12 pounds; expenditure on salaries: the teacher receives both these sums; intellectual instruction: the books of the Board of National Education only; the instruction embraces spelling, reading, writing, arithmetic and grammar; moral instruction: visited by the priest, a portion of each day and Saturday set apart for religious instruction, all versions of Scripture read; number of pupils: males, 29 under 10 years of age, 20 from 10 to 15, 5 above 15, 54 total males; females, 10 under 10 years of age, 6 from 10 to 15, 16 total females; total number of pupils 70, 38 Presbyterians, 32 Roman Catholics; master James Gribben, Roman Catholic; the visits of the priest, though frequent, are not at stated periods.

National school, in a very neat, dry, airy and suitable house, built for the purpose at a cost of 101 pounds 18s 3d, of which 62 pounds 3s 3d was contributed by the Reverend Daniel Curoe, parish priest, and the remainder by the Board of National Eduation; situated in the townland of Drumsough (measuring 30 feet by 16 feet), established 1834; income: from the Board of National Education annually 8 pounds, from pupils 4 pounds; expenditure on salaries: the teacher receives both these sums; intellectual instruction: the books of the Board of National Education only; the instruction embraces spelling, reading, writing, arithmetic and grammar; moral instruction: visited by the priest, a portion of each day and Saturday set apart for religious instruction, all versions of Scripture read; number of pupils: males, 10 under 10 years of age, 20 from 10 to 15, 30 total males; females, 5 under 10 years of age, 15 from 10 to 15, 20 total females; total number of pupils 50, 4 Presbyterians, 46 Roman Catholics; master John Martin, Roman Catholic; the visits of the priest, though frequent, are not at stated periods.

National school, situated in the townland of Magheralane; a suitable house 28 by 13 feet, thatched, warm and dry; originally built for the purpose of a school by subscription; original date of establishment unknown, placed under the National Board 1833; income: from the Board of National Education annually 10 pounds, from pupils 5 pounds; expenditure on salaries: the teacher receives both these sums; intellectual instruction: the books of the Board of National Education only; the instruction embraces spelling, reading, writing, arithmetic, and grammar; moral instruction: visited by the priest, a portion of each day and Saturday set apart for religious instruction, all versions of Scripture read; number of pupils: males, 30 under 10 years of age, 30 from 10 to 15, 4 above 15, 64 total males; females, 20 under 10 years of age, 12 from 10 to 15, 32 total females; total number of pupils 96, 3 Established Church, 5 Presbyterians, 88 Roman Catholics; master James Martin, Roman Catholic; the visits of the priest, though frequent, are not at fixed periods.

[Totals] income: 37 pounds 14s from public societies or benevolent individuals, 25 pounds from pupils; expenditure on salaries 53 pounds 4s; number of pupils: males, 79 under 10 years of age, 78 from 10 to 15, 9 above 15, 166 total males; females, 45 under 10 years of age, 40 from 10 to 15, 85 total females; total number of pupils 251, 24 Established Church, 61 Presbyterians, 166 Roman Catholics.

These schools were visited in June 1838, [signed] J. Boyle.

Kildare Place Society Schools

Situated in the townland of Caddy; the schoolhouse measures 20 by 16 feet, is thatched and is in tolerable repair, and suitable for its purpose; built by subscription, established 1830; income from pupils 15 pounds; expenditure on salaries 15 pounds; intellectual instruction: books of the Kildare Place Society, with *Gough's Arithmetic, Murray's English grammar, Manson's Spelling book;* moral instruction: visited occasionally by the vicar, Authorised Version of Scriptures read daily and church and Presbyterian catechisms taught on Saturdays; number of pupils: males, 12 under 10 years of age, 11 from 10 to 15, 2 above 15, 25 total males; females, 3 under 10 years of age, 6 from 10 to 15, 9 total females; total number of pupils 34, 32 Presbyterians, 2 Roman Catholics; master Thomas Birkby, Established Church; visited occasionally but not frequently nor at stated periods by the vicar.

Situated in the townland of Cloghogue; the house, which was originally built for the purpose by subscription, measures 21 and a half by 16 and a half feet; it is thatched and in but middling repair and indifferently fitted up, established 1817; income from pupils 15 pounds; expenditure on salaries 15 pounds; intellectual instruction: books of the Kildare Place Society, *Gough's Arithmetic, Manson's Spelling book* besides *Thomson's Arithmetic* and Pinnock's *Catechism of geography;* moral instruction: visited occasionally by the vicar, Authorised Version of Scriptures read daily and church and Presbyterian catechism taught on Saturdays; number of pupils: males, 8 under 10 years of age, 4 from 10 to 15, 12 total males; females: 8 under 10 years of age, 3 from 10 to 15, 11 total females; total number of pupils 23, 17 Presbyterians, 6 other denominations; master Samuel McCracken, Moravian Protestant; visited occasionally, but not frequently nor at stated periods, by the vicar.

Situated in the townland of Terrygowan; the house, which measures 20 by 16 feet, was built for the purpose by subscription; it is thatched and in sufficent repair, established 1809; income from pupils 12 pounds; expenditure on salaries 12 pounds; intellectual instruction: books of the Kildare Place Society and *Gough's Arithmetic;* moral instruction: visited by the Presbyterian clergy, Authorised Version of the Scriptures daily and Presbyterian catechisms on Saturdays; number of pupils: males, 25 under 10 years of age, 5 from 10 to 15, 30 total males; females, 10 under 10 years of age, 5 from 10 to 15, 15 total females; total number of pupils 45, 1 Established Church, 44 Presbyterians; master John Robinson, Covenanter; frequently visited by the Presbyterian ministers but not at stated periods.

Situated in the townland of Ballydunmaul; the house was originally built for the purpose by subscription; it measures 20 and a half by 15 feet and is suffecntly commodious and in tolerable repair, established 1823; income from pupils 12 pounds; expenditure on salaries 12 pounds; intellectual instruction: books of the Kildare Place Society, also *Thomson's Arithmetic and bookkeeping, Bonnycastle's Algebra, Thomson's Geography, Murray's Grammar;* moral instruction: not visited by the clergy, Authorised Version of Scripture daily, Presbyterian catechism on Saturdays; number of pupils: males, 9 under 10 years of age, 3 from 10 to 15, 12 total males; females, 5 under 10 years of age, 3 from 10 to 15, 8 total females; total number of pupils 20, all Presbyterians; master Hamilton Dixon Malcom, Seceder <Seceeder>; not visited by the clergy.

In a suitable house in the townland of Leitrim [crossed out: built for the purpose by subscription], measuring 18 and a half by 15 and a half feet; the school is attached to a dwelling house and [no further information], established 1825; income from pupils 12 pounds; expenditure on salaries 12 pounds; intellectual instruction: books of the Kildare Place Society, also *Thomson's* and *Gough's Arithmetic, Jackson's Book-keeping, Bonnycastle's Mensuration, Goldsmith's Geography;* moral instruction: visited by the vicar and Presbyterian minister, Authorised Version of Scriptures daily, church and Presbyterian catechisms on Saturdays; number of pupils: males, 12 under 10 years of age, 6 from 10 to 15, 6 above 15, 24 total males; females, 7 under 10 years of age, 5 from 10 to 15, 12 total females; total number of pupils 36, 1 Established Church, 28 Presbyterians, 7 Roman Catholics; master Peter Aicken Black, Seceder; visited occasionally by the vicar and Presbyterian minister but not at stated periods.

[Totals] income: from public societies or benevolent individuals 37 pounds 14s, from pupils 91 pounds 10s; expenditure on salaries 129 pounds 4s; number of pupils: males, 145 under 10 years of age, 107 from 10 to 15, 17 above 15, 269 total males; females, 78 under 10 years of age, 62 from 10 to 15, 140 total females; total number of pupils 409, 26 Established Church, 202 Presbyterians, 175 Roman Catholics, 6 other denominations.

These schools were visited in the month of June 1838, [signed] J. Boyle.

Private Schools

Female school, situated in the town of Randalstown; a small private room not in good repair and indifferently furnished, dry but cold, established 1819; income from pupils 6 pounds; expenditure on salaries 6 pounds; intellectual instruction: books of the Kildare Place Society, *Manson's Primer and spelling book;* reading, plain needlework also is taught here; moral instruction: Authorised Version of Scriptures are read daily in this school; number of pupils: 8 under 10 years of age, 2 above 15, total 10; total number of pupils 10, all female, 3 Established Church, 6 Presbyterians, 1 Roman Catholic; mistress Mary Clark, Presbyterian; visited 2nd June 1838.

English and classical school, held in a room suitable for the purpose in the new market house in the town of Randalstown, established 1836; income from pupils 25 pounds; expenditure on salaries 25 pounds; intellectual instruction: grammar, geography, history, *Chamber's and Bryce's Mathematics,* all the Latin authors usually read, *Nelson's Greek grammar,* Greek Testament and other works of a similar kind; moral instruction: Authorised Version of the Scriptures; number of pupils: 4 under 10 years of age, 11 from 10 to 15, 1 above 15, total 16; total number of pupils 16, all male, 1 Established Church, 12 Presbyterians, 3 Roman Catholics; master Reverend Hugh Smyth, Seceding minister; visited 16th May 1838.

Parish of Drummaul

In the townland of Lenagh, a small room 13 and a half by 11 feet, tolerably comfortable; it is private property and is rented by the teacher at 1 pound 7s 6d per annum, established 1831; income from pupils 10 pounds; expenditure on salaries 10 pounds; intellectual instruction: *Manson's Primer and spelling book,* writing, *Gough's Arithmetic,* reading, English grammar; moral instruction: the Authorised Version of Scriptures read daily; number of pupils: males, 15 under 10 years of age, 2 from 10 to 15, 3 above 15, 20 total males; females, 5 under 10 years of age, 5 from 10 to 15, 10 total females; total number of pupils 30, 15 Presbyterians, 15 Roman Catholics; master John Dunlop, Presbyterian; visited 20th May 1838.

In the townland of Ballytresna, in an excellent house 22 by 16 feet, thatched, warm and comfortable; this school is of such ancient date that its original establishment is unknown; rebuilt in 1836; income from pupils 18 pounds; expenditure on salaries 18 pounds; intellectual instruction: *Murray's Reader and English grammar, Manson's Primer and spelling book, Gough's Arithmetic,* writing; moral instruction: visited occasionally by Presbyterian clergy, Authorised Version of Scriptures taught on Saturday; number of pupils: males, 15 under 10 years of age, 15 from 10 to 15, 30 total males; females, 10 under 10 years of age, 15 from 10 to 15, 25 total females; total number of pupils 55, 1 Established Church, 49 Presbyterians, 5 Roman Catholics; master William McCarroll, Presbyterian; visited 9th May 1838.

[Totals] income from pupils 59 pounds; expenditure on salaries 59 pounds; number of pupils: males, 34 under 10 years of age, 28 from 10 to 15, 4 above 15, 66 total males; females, 23 under 10 years of age, 20 from 10 to 15, 2 above 15, 45 total females; total number of pupils 111, 5 Established Church, 82 Presbyterians, 25 Roman Catholics.

Sunday Schools

[Table contains the following headings: situation and description, when established, superintendence, number of teachers, number of scholars, books read, hours of attendance, societies with which connected, remarks].

In the town of Randalstown, a school held in the national schoolhouse described before, established 1826; under the superintendence of the Reverend Daniel Curoe, parish priest; 5 male teachers, total 5; number of scholars: 202 Roman Catholics, 101 males, 101 females, total 202, 120 exclusively Sunday school scholars; books read: the books used in the day school; hours of attendance from 3 until 5 p.m.; though unconnected with any society, the school is held in the national schoolhouse; the system [?] allotted is the monitorial, similar to that of the day school; the school is given up during the winter months.

School held in the meeting house in the townland of Craigmore, established 1824; superintended by Thomas Butler, John Boyd and James McMullin (farmers), Presbyterians; 8 male and 6 female teachers, total 14; number of scholars: 8 Established Church, 84 Presbyterians, 8 Roman Catholics, 50 males, 50 females, total 100, 29 exclusively Sunday school scholars; books read: Authorised Version of Scripture, *Manson's Primer and spelling book,* the property of the children; hours of attendance from 8 to 10 a.m. and from 5 to 7.30 p.m. in summer and from 8 to 10 a.m. in winter; societies with which connected: none; this school originated and is well attended by the farmers and ministers.

School held in the national schoolhouse in the townland of Magheralane, established 1833; under the superintendence of the Reverend Daniel Curoe, parish priest; 3 male and 1 female teacher, total 4; number of scholars: 10 Presbyterians, 38 Roman Catholics, 23 males, 25 females, total 48, 12 exclusively Sunday school scholars; books read: the books used in the day school; hours of attendance from 8 to 10 a.m.; held in the national schoolhouse and books of the board read, otherwise unconnected with it; this school is held from the 1st of May to the 1st of November.

School held in the national schoolhouse in the townland of Drumsough, established 1834; superintendence: under the patronage of the Reverend Daniel Curoe, parish priest, John Martin, the day schoolmaster, superintendent; 4 male and 2 female teachers, total 6; number of scholars: 8 Presbyterians, 112 Roman Catholics, 64 males, 56 females, total 120, 90 exclusively Sunday school scholars; books read: books used at the day schools; hours of attendance from 3 until 5 p.m.; held in the national schoolhouse and books of the board read, otherwise unconnected with it; this school is held from the 1st of May to the 1st of November.

Held in the day schoolhouse in the townland of Ballytresna described [before]; when established: one of the oldest Sunday schools in the country, re-established in 1837; superintended by Messrs George Jackson and James Reside (farmers), Presbyterians; 6 male and 3 female teachers, total 9; number of scholars: 90 Presbyterians, 10 Roman

Catholics, 40 males, 60 females, total 100, 50 exclusively Sunday school scholars; books read: books published by the Sunday school society; hours of attendance from 8 to 10 a.m. and from 5 to 7 p.m. in summer, and from 8 to 10 a.m. in winter; connected and supplied with books and cards by the Sunday School Society; this school is well attended by both teachers and pupils.

Establishments for the Indigent

[Table of benevolence contains the following headings: name, object, when founded, management, funds from public bodies and from private individuals, expenditure on house rent and salaries, relief afforded, number relieved].

9 schools supported either wholly or in part by charitable individuals and benevolent societies; object: the removal of ignorance; when founded: at sundry periods; management: by sundry societies and by local committees and patrons; funds from public bodies: 30 pounds per annum from the Board of National Education and 3 pounds 10s per annum from the London Hibernian Society, [total] 33 pounds 10s; from private individuals: from Lord O'Neill annually 4 pounds 4s; salaries: the teachers receive the sums granted and also that paid by the pupils; relief afforded: school requisites; the number of children at present receiving daily instruction is 409.

Charitable donation; object: the relief of 40 poor persons and to prevent them being obliged to have recourse to street begging; when founded: not precisely known; management: distributed annually by the churchwardens; funds from private individuals: from Lord O'Neill 42 pounds; relief afforded: 1 pound each per annum to 40 poor persons; number relieved: 40.

[Totals]: from public bodies 33 pounds 10s, from private individuals 46 pounds 4s.

Dispensary, object: affording medicine and medical advice to those who are unable to purchase it; when founded: 1814; management: by a committee of governors, a secretary and treasurer who meet annually; funds from public sources: the average sum annually granted by the county grand jury for the last 12 years is 42 pounds 10s 11d; from private sources: the average sum annually locally subscribed for the last 12 years is 42 pounds 10s 11d; annual expense of management, house rent: previous to 1830 5 pounds 10s was annually paid for house rent, but since then a free house has been granted; the surgeon's salary is 50 pounds; number relieved: the average number annually relieved for the last 12 years is 2,294; relief afforded: the surgeon atttends at the dispensary on Tuesdays and Thursdays, for the purpose of affording medicine, and in areas where patients are unable to attend they are visited in their houses by him; average expense of patients: the average annual expense for the last 12 years is 85 pounds 1s 11d 3 farthings.

Drawings

Map of Randalstown, showing boundary of the ancient borough.

Ruins of Shane's Castle, front view looking from the west [showing 2 wings and round tower with 2 figures in the foreground].

Inscription on a stone over the doorway of the vault in the ancient burial ground at Shane's Castle: "This vault was built by Shane Brien Phelim Shane Brien Phelim O'Neill Esq. in the year 1722, for a burial place to himself and family of Clanneboy."

Plan of the Rock tumulus or giant's grave in townland of Barnish, with dimensions and orientation.

Giant's grave in townland of Barnish.

Plan of Dunmore Fort, Shane's Castle demesne [in relation to the River Main], scale 1 inch to 80 feet.

Plan of ancient fortification, Shane's Castle demesne, scale 1 inch to 80 feet.

Plan of fort, Shane's Castle park [in relation to the River Main], scale 1 inch to 80 feet.

Plan of 8 forts in Shane's Castle park [with numbers], scale 1 inch to 80 feet. [Insert footnote: The figure prefixed denotes the number of that description of fort in the townland].

Plan of 8 forts [with townland names recording instances of the fort type occurring in each: Lenagh, Magherabeg, Lisnagreggan, Sharvogues, Ballybollen, Groggan, Clonboy, Aghaloughan, Ballynacraigy, Lurgan West, Artresnahan, Randalstown, Ballytresna, Downkillybegs, Kilknock, Tanaghmore, Killyfad, Drumsough].

Arms sculpted on a stone found near Shane's Castle, townland of Shane's Castle.

Edenduffcarrick or the "black face of stone" on the outside of the eastern wall of Shane's Castle, townland of Shane's Castle.

Baptismal font on the Three Islands, view and section with dimensions.

3 flint spears, flint arrow, brazen hatchet and stone hatchet, full size.

Ornamented quern, upper and reversed views with section, scale 1 inch to 1 foot; upper part of quern: view and section, diameter 18 inches.

Parish of Drummaul

Draft Memoir by G.W. Hemans, with comments by Lieutenant R.K. Dawson, May 1835

MEMOIR WRITING

Memoir Writing

Received May 11 1835. Memo: No notice is taken of the detached portions of the parish to the westward. Their position, boundaries etc. will of course be described under the head Locality, but there may also be some peculiarities or details to notice under the heads of Natural Features and Modern Topography [signed] R.K. Dawson.

Memo: Mr Boyle has completed the above heads in this parish and has the Memoir in his own hands at present, [signed] J. McGann, 24th January 1837.

NATURAL FEATURES

Hills

There is a good deal of bog on the east side of the River Main <Maine>. The ground on the west side rises gradually to an average height of 400 feet.

River Main

At present it cannot be said that any advantage is taken of the river for manufacturing purposes through any part of its course in the parish of Drummaul. It is shallow with a sandy bottom, often crossed by fords and stepping stones. At times it overflows its banks, many parts of which are very little above the water and the slight deposit it leaves is so immaterial that it neither improves nor injures the surrounding cultivation. In the time of great floods the mill wheels on the banks cannot work. The scenery on the banks [is] dull and monotonous. [Insert query by R.K. Dawson: Maine or Main? It is said that "no advantage is taken of the river for manufacturing purposes" and subsequently mills are spoken of. How are these 2 statements to be reconciled?]

Bogs

There are extensive tracts of bog in all parts of the parish. [Insert note by Dawson: More particulars wanted].

Lough Neagh Fisheries

The fisheries on the north coast have greatly declined of late for want of success, which is owing to the increasing scarcity of fish. The only kinds caught there are pullens (which are said to exist only in 2 lakes in Europe: Lake Constance and Lough Neagh) and trout. The pullens are white and somewhat larger than herrings.

There are now only 3 fishing boats between Toome and Antrim, each of which is the property of 3 persons conjointly. [Crossed out: The fish are so scarce that] They consider an average of 3 a night in each net very good, and in winter they do not get so many. [Insert footnote: This report has appeared so incorrect in comparison with others that although actually given by a fisherman, it must be doubted, 200 or 300 being sometimes caught in a night]. In summer they set their nets a mile or even 2 from the shore, but in winter they dare not go further than half a mile, for fear of the weather. The fish caught by these 3 boats' companies is all consumed by themselves, though in the other coasts of the lake they produce a good market. The men assert that a cut at the mouth of the River Bann at Coleraine would greatly improve the fishing, by allowing the small fry to come up the river, [signed] G.W. Hemans.

Woods

The only wood except hedgerow timber in the parish is that in Shane's Castle park, a little planting around the dwelling houses of Holybrook and Sharvogues, and a plantation in the townland of Craigmore. [Insert note: This is badly described. The description of Shane's Castle park given under the head General Appearance should come in here].

Coast

The Lough Neagh coast in this parish has a pebbly beach, craggy banks, which in 2 different places in Lord O'Neill's demesne present very good specimens of the columnar basalt of the Causeway.

General Appearance

The scenery about Randalstown is very pretty. The Main water ripples down a pebbly shallow bed into Lord O'Neill's demesne, where it becomes lost to view among the thick woods and foliage, unless you follow its banks. The whole of Shane's Castle park is thickly wooded, in some places with beautiful oak, but the most abundant trees are larch and fir. The demesne is plentifully stocked with game and the deerpark well filled with roe deer.

Modern Topography

Towns: Randalstown

Randalstown is situated on the main road from Belfast to Moneymore. Its public buildings consist of a church, 2 meeting houses and a Roman Catholic chapel.

The court house was built in 1770 at the sole expense of Charles Earl O'Neill; the market house built in 1831.

Places of Worship

Randalstown contains 1 Protestant church. It was erected in the year 1832 by the Board of First Fruits and is meant to contain 266 persons, and cost 1,800 pounds. [Insert footnote: The Board of First Fruits lent the parish 1,500 pounds at 4 per cent, to be paid back by annual instalments, the interest paying the principal. To this sum borrowed from the board, Lord O'Neill added 300 pounds, so that the whole amount expended on the building is 1,800 pounds].

One meeting house, belonging to the Synod of Ulster, built in the year 1790, the original cost of which was 600 pounds. In the year 1828 a new roof cost 200 pounds, and between the years 1830 and 1832 a gallery and porch cost 1,054 pounds, total expended on the building up to 1835, 1,854 pounds. It was built to contain 1,000 persons. [Insert query by Dawson: Style of the building. Is there not some mistake here? Can it be possible that the gallery and porch cost so much more than the original building, together with the new roof?]

One Seceders' meeting house, built in the year 1753, the original cost of which was, according to the most accurate accounts which can be obtained, from 250 to 300 pounds. About 100 pounds have been since expended upon it. It was built to contain from 550 to 600 persons. [It] was originally the Burgher Associate Synod, now the Presbyterian Synod of Ireland, distinguished by the name Seceders.

One Roman Catholic chapel, large and of rather handsome construction. [Insert note by Dawson: Give particulars outside].

[Insert footnote: Further particulars concerning this chapel were requested of the Roman Catholic priest, who seemed unwilling to grant them, and although he had promised to ascertain date, cost etc., never communicated his answers].

Markets and Fairs

There is a small market held every Wednesday in Randalstown, principally for grain, and the first Wednesday of every month a larger, to which are brought cattle, pigs, sheep etc. but no horses. There was formerly a good linen market in this town, but it gradually declined and finally died away about the year 1825. The cause of this was the vicinity of Ballymena linen market, which absorbed all the Randalstown trading by possessing a more central position in the county, greater facilities of communication with Belfast [insert marginal note: query this], more resident merchants etc. On Mondays there is also a grain market, to which a large quantity is brought: counted 90 carts, containing on an average 4 sacks each.

2 fairs are held annually in Randalstown, one in winter, on the 1st November, the other in summer, on the 16th July. They are both nominally horse and cattle fairs, but very few horses are ever brought to either.

Streets and Houses

There is only 1 street in Randalstown, from which various dirty lanes and narrow alleys diverge. The pavement is bad and the town is not lighted at night. The houses are all built of stone and are all very poor in their appearance. Towards the end of the street they die away into thatched huts. The houses are stone, but low and generally thatched, none of them more than 2-storeys high. Very few are insured.

Social Economy

Local Government

2 magistrates reside in Randalstown, who form a bench at petty sessions once every fortnight on Tuesdays. There are never more than 2 magistrates on the bench. The police barrack contains a sergeant and 4 men. The 2 above-mentioned gentlemen are not stipendiary magistrates.

Dispensary

There is a dispensary in Randalstown, supported by a number of subscribers who pay a certain sum annually. The amount of the sum paid by the subscribers is laid on at the assizes. Number of patients subscribed for in the year 1834: 1,927. The following return of patients between the years 1830 and 1831 is the only one which could be procured.

From 1st July 1830 to 30th June 1831 inclusive: typhus 601, inflammation of the bowels and chest 209, inflammation of the ear and kidneys 52, diseased parts and mortification 89, chronic

Parish of Drummaul

cough 201, asthma 92, consumption 46, liver complaint 30, cholera morbus 92, cholic 53, biles 88, rheumatism 24, ulcerated and inflammatory sore throat 195, dysentery and diarrhoea 58, dyspepsia 44, worms 166, hysteria 198, scrofula 84, erysipelas 56, wounds and ulcers 61, scurvy and itch 112, dropsy of the abdomen 52, scald head 67, herpes lepra and diseases of the skin 112, dislocation and fracture 19, whooping cough 90.

Conveyances

The mail from Dublin now passes through Randalstown at 10.15 in the morning, the mail to Dublin at 4 in the morning. There are 3 other coaches pass through this town for Belfast in the week, 2 every day, the third every alternate day. The 2 regular coaches pass at 7 in the morning and return at 5.30 in the evening, the alternate one at 10.30 in the morning and 3 in the evening. The alternate coach comes from Derry, the 2 regular ones from Cookstown. The carter's charge from Randalstown to Belfast is 10[d ?] per cwt, for grain 6d per cwt, distance 16 miles Irish.

MODERN TOPOGRAPHY

Mills

A corn mill close to Randalstown bridge, diameter of wheel 14 feet, breadth of buckets 3 and a half feet, undershot, fall of water 3 and a half feet. Same mill possesses another wheel, diameter 12 feet, breast 6 feet 6 inches, fall of water 3 and a half feet, undershot.

One cotton factory a little higher up, diameter of wheel 14 feet, breast 9 feet 9 inches, fall of water 3 and a half feet, undershot.

A corn mill belonging to Mr Davidson, diameter of wheel 17 feet, breast 4 feet 6 inches, fall of water 18 inches, breast wheel.

[Insert query by Dawson: Another corn mill is marked on the index map, in the detached portion of the parish to the westward].

Communications: Bridge

The Randalstown bridge over the Main water was formerly very narrow, but was widened in 1816.

Schools

[Table contains the following headings: name of townland where situated, number pupils divided by religion and sex, how supported, when established].

Randalstown, total 105 pupils; under the National Board of Education; the master receives 12 pounds from the board and 14 pounds from scholars, established 1834.

Randalstown, 44 Protestants, 6 Catholics, 25 males, 25 females, total 50 pupils; under the Kildare Street Society, the master supported solely by the scholars, established 1831.

Randalstown, 14 Protestants, 12 Presbyterians, 4 Catholics, 15 males, 15 females, total 30 pupils; founded by the parish of Drummaul, established 1804.

Randalstown, 5 Protestants, 11 Presbyterians, 4 Catholics, 14 males, 6 females, 20 total pupils; a private school, opened September 1834.

Maghereagh, 10 Protestants, 10 Presbyterians, 24 Catholics, 35 males, 19 females, 54 total pupils; supported solely by the scholars, established 182[last figure blank].

Magheralane, 4 Protestants, 54 Presbyterians, 2 Catholics, 60 total pupils; 8 pounds from National Board of Education, rest from scholars.

Gentlemen's Seats

Shane's Castle park, on the shore of Lough Neagh, is the property of the Earl O'Neill.

Shane's Castle is now a ruin. It was burned about 23 years since. There is a terrace with battlements overhanging the lake. There are 22 12-pounders mounted on it. They are cast iron guns. About a quarter of a mile to the west of the castle, close to edge of the lake, a beautiful specimen of columnar basalt appears. The basalt are perfect as those of the Causeway and are 9 feet high [drawing].

Holybrook: unoccupied.

Sharvogues: Hugh Lang Esquire.

SOCIAL ECONOMY

Table of Occupations in Randalstown

Surgeons and apothecaries 2, grocers 15, bakers 2, whiskey shops 8, innkeepers 1, private inns 1, milliners 3, smiths 1, reed makers 1, houses of entertainment for the poorer classes 5, tailors 1, nailers 1, saddlers 1, booksellers 1, schools 4.

Extracts from Fair Sheets by John Bleakly, 9th April to 25th June 1838

MEMOIR WRITING

Memoir Writing

County of Antrim, parish of Drummaul: commenced 9th April 1838, completed 25th June 1838, 186 hours employed, [signed] J. Bleakly.

Forwarded to Lieutenant Bennett, Royal Engineers, 1st August 1838, [signed] James Boyle.

SOCIAL ECONOMY AND MODERN TOPOGRAPHY

Income of the Clergy

The stipend of the Reverend Thomas Reid, Seceding minister of the first congregation of Randalstown, amounts to 40 pounds per annum. The stipend of the Reverend Alexander Crawford, Presbyterian minister of Randalstown, amounts to 40 pounds per annum. Information obtained from the Reverend Thomas Reid, Seceding minister. 30th April 1838.

Original Presbyterian Clergy

On the 21st May 1656 the Reverend John Cathcart was ordained in this parish, which was then under the Antrim presbytery. The second minister, in 1689, was the Reverend Richard Wilson; he died in 1694. Third, Reverend William Taylor in 1697; he died 1727. Fourth, Reverend William Henderson in 1732. He bequeathed 4 pounds per annum to the Presbyterian congregation of Drummaul. His will is dated 31st March 1781. He died some 6 months after his will was perfected, a copy of which is in the hands of John Brown of Randalstown. Fifth, in 1746 Reverend James White. In 1786 Reverend Thomas Henry; he died in 1830. In 1826 Reverend Archibald Jameson; he died in 1835. And in 1837 the present, the Reverend Alexander Crawford; but since that a dispute arose about the choice of a minister between the members of the congregation, in consequence of which the meeting house was closed up and a division took place. Mr Crawford is necessitated to preach in the upper room in the new market house. 9th April 1838.

Presbyterian Meeting House

From traditional statements of the old residents, the original place of meeting was a small thatched house on the north side of Randalstown, at the back part of the tenement at present occupied by Thomas Macartney, then occupied by Michael King. The present site is said to have been granted to the congregation about the year 1670 by Lady Marchioness McDonald, whose maiden name was Rose O'Neill, a great friend of Presbyterians. This lady was married to the Marquis of Antrim. The contract of marriage was that the estates of each should revert to the several families if they should die without issue, which they did. About this time the old meeting house was built, and under the ministry of the Reverend William Taylor. It stood till the year 1790, when it was pulled down and the foundation of the present house laid on the same site, on the 12th July, that day 100 years after the landing of William III. The seats of the old house were so broken during the long contest that they had not been repaired until Dr Henry set about building the present house. When the walls were about 3 feet high his lordship (the present Lord O'Neill's father) came to see the work and was as well pleased with it that he gave the ground before the door, called the cowpark, to be attached to the house.

The present meeting house has been shut up since August last, 1837, until Sunday 8th March 1838, in consequence of a split in the congregation about the choice of a minister, as before stated. From the Reverend Alexander Crawford, Presbyterian minister, and Mr David Moore, watchmaker.

The average collection, at the new market house of the Presbyterian congregation at Randalstown, i.e. Reverend Alexander Crawford minister, amounts to 8s 6d. From John Brown and John Cooper.

Original Catholic Clergy

The first of the Roman Catholic clergy remembered by the oldest inhabitant was the Reverend McGregor, second Reverend Neeson, third Reverend Peter Boyle, fourth Reverend Bernard McAuley, who succeeded Boyle in 1819, fifth the Reverend Daniel Curoe, who came in 1825 and still continues. Information obtained from Mr Davey Moore and James Hunter, Randalstown.

Roman Catholic Chapel

The Roman Catholic chapel stands north east of the village, in the rear of the agent's house and on the eastern side of the Main water. The front possesses some architectural beauty, namely 4 cut-stone pinnacles and a cross. This edifice is of this shape: [ground plan, "T" shape]; (a) is the front or new part, which was built in 1824 and measures 26 feet 9 inches by 24 feet inside; (b) is the original part and was built in 1784. It measures 60 by 24 feet inside, all in a good state of repair. The gallery contains 58 single pews. 36 of these pews are each 8 by 2 feet 2 inches and 22 are each 10 by 2 feet 2 inches. It has 13 windows square, each 5 feet 7 inches wide, and 3 square doors. The front door is 5 feet 3 inches wide, the other 2 are each 3 feet wide, the whole in good repair.

Parish of Drummaul

The average collection at the Roman Catholic chapel at Randalstown amounts to 7s per Sunday.

The average collection for the poor on each Sunday at the Randalstown church amounts to 2s 6d per [Sunday]. From the vestry book and Mr Davey Moore.

Seceders' Meeting Houses

The Seceding meeting house at Randalstown is situated a short distance from the town on the road leading to Ahoghill. It measures 42 by 30 feet inside and contains 34 single pews, each 8 by 3 feet, and 1 double pew, 8 feet by 5 feet 8 inches. Each single pew would contain 8 persons and the double pew 16 persons. The pews are in bad repair. It has 14 windows, each 5 by 2 feet 8 inches. 11th April 1838.

The second Secession Presbyterian congregation of Randalstown worship in the meeting house situated at the end of the town, on the left of the road leading from Randalstown to Ahoghill. It is of an oval shape and exhibits much architectural beauty. The intended belfry in front is of a sexangular form, with a pinnacle on top ornamented with a gilded ball. This edifice measures 80 by 42 feet inside and contains 134 single seats or pews, each pew on an average 9 by 3 feet, all in good repair. Built in 1790, vide stone over front door, Thomas Henry, minister; the late repairs, viz. new gallery, new roof etc., in 1832. It has 24 Gothic windows: 14 are 11 feet 3 inches by 4 feet 9 inches, the other 10 are smaller. 6 doors: 3 of the largest are each 5 feet 9 inches broad. Each pew would contain 9 persons: at 1 foot for each person would amount to 1,106 persons. Aisle is 6 and a half feet wide, 3 smaller aisles below, each 3 feet 10 inches wide. This congregation has no regular minister. From Thomas Courtney and John Brown. 12th April 1838.

The Seceding meeting house in Craigmore is on the road leading from Randalstown to Portglenone. It contains 18 single pews, each 8 and a half by 2 and a half feet, and 4 double pews, each 8 and a half by 5 and a half feet. This meeting house would contain 240 persons at 1 foot per person. It has 10 windows, each 6 by 2 feet 9 inches, and 1 square door.

The average collection at the Craigmore meeting house amounts to 3s 6d per Sunday. 13th April 1838.

Old Market House

The old market house stands in the centre of the town. It measures 60 by 25 feet outside. The upper part is used as an office for Earl O'Neill's agent to collect the rent, the under part [as] a weigh-house, with a small room which was formerly used as a black hole. The agent's office was formerly used as the manor court room for the manor of Edenduffcarrick. During the rebellion of 1798 the weigh-house was used as a stable for the cavalry horses.

New Market House

The new market house is situated at the south west end of the town. This edifice measures externally 62 and a half by 26 and a half feet. The upper storey consists of 3 rooms, viz. 1 for the magistrates' petty session room and 2 jury rooms. The lower part is a weigh-house, a dispensary and another smaller room.

Three Islands Cottage

The Three Islands Cottage was built or commenced 17th March 1811, but now is in a dilapidated state, the roof only on part of the cottage. It is 3 years since it was used. The walls are of brick, 7 and a half feet high and 1 foot 3 inches thick. The main wing of the cottage contained 5 rooms. [Plan of cottage]: it measures from a to b 72 by 15 feet. The attached part in the rear, from c to d, is 55 by 6 and a half feet. It is situated in the midst of the lower island which is planted and covered with brushwood. The first planting was put down in these islands, commenced in 1807 and was finished in 1810, and consists of fir and ash chiefly, with a few evergreens at the cottage. From Rodger Glover, Patrick Boyle and John McCauley, near the islands. 28th April 1838.

Earl O'Neill's Donation to Poor

Earl O'Neill gives annually to the poor of the parish of Drummaul 40 guineas, which sum is distributed to 40 poor persons of the parish. Information obtained from [blank].

Randalstown Petty Sessions

Number of summonses issued in 1835 was 900: number of cases of theft 8, assault 45, disputes about wages 40, trespass 12, breach of excise of laws 3, breach of game laws 2, rescue 2, miscellaneous 150; sent to quarter sessions [blank], number of cases sent to assizes 262.

Number of summonses issued in 1836 700: number of cases of theft 6, assault 67, wages 50, trespass 20, breach of game laws 1, breach of excise laws 2, rescue 4, drunkenness 2, miscellaneous 120; sent to assizes and quarter sessions [blank].

Number of summonses issued in 1837 706: theft 14, trespass 40, assault 50, wages 25, rescue 3, drunkenness 10, [breaches of] game laws 2; number sent to assizes 1, number sent to quarter sessions 14, miscellaneous 130.

Manufactory for Linen Cloth

In the year 1812 Mr John Craig established a linen manufactory. The following are the number of pieces manufactured in each year, with the number of persons employed: in 1831 there was 1,812 pieces made by 120 men; in 1832 1,898 pieces by 130 men; in 1833 2,187 pieces by 142 men; in 1834 2,290 pieces by 147 men; in 1835 2,396 pieces by 159 men; in 1836 2,589 pieces by 173 men; in 1837 820 pieces by 60 men. Each piece 26 yards long by 38 inches wide, texture is from 1,400 to 2,500, and sold at from 1s 10d to 6s 6d per yard. One-fourth of the price of each is given to the weaver for his hire. The linen is all sold at the manufacturing house in the townland of [blank]. Information obtained from Mr John Craig, proprietor. 25th June 1838.

Mills

The cotton mills at Randalstown, in the townland of Ballygrooby, are all out of repair and almost in a state of dilapidation, and are the property of Mr James Black, now in America. Mr Charles McAuley was the former proprietor and manufactured cotton in them. Mr Dickey and others before McAuley used them as flour mills. About 6 years ago it ceased to be a cotton mill. The water wheels 3 in number: one is 14 feet in diameter by 12 and a half feet broad. There is a metal wheel, very narrow, outside the wooden rim. The other 2 water wheels are completely out of order. Each measures 15 feet in diameter by 4 and a half feet broad. Information obtained from Daniel Kenny, Bernard O'Neill and John French.

The corn mill at Aghanboy, Adam Davison proprietor, was originally a corn mill, afterwards a paper mill, and now a corn mill. Water wheel 16 feet in diameter by 5 feet 4 at the buckets; flax wheel 16 feet in diameter by 4 at the buckets.

The corn mill at the bridge at Randalstown, townland of Ballygrooby, John Cooper, proprietor: the water wheels 2 in number, viz. one is 14 feet in diameter and 3 and a half feet broad at buckets; the other is 12 feet in diameter by 5 and a half feet broad at buckets.

The corn mill in the townland of Killyfad has one water wheel which is 14 feet in diameter by 18 inches broad.

National and Sunday Schools

The Randalstown national school is situated a short distance south west of the village. Held in a good house, slated, 36 by 24 feet in the clear, built AD 1833 and cost 188 pounds 18s 7d. The income of the teacher is 24 pounds per annum, viz. 12 pounds from the scholars and 12 pounds from the National Board. The books used in the school are those published by the National Board only. The school is visited by the Reverend Daniel Curoe, parish priest. The average attendance for the last quarter was 70 scholars, viz. 54 males and 16 females; males above 15 years of age 5 and 20 from 10 to 15, and 29 under 10 years of age; females from 10 to 15, 6 and 10 under 10 years of age; Established Church none, Presbyterians of all denominations 38 and 32 Roman Catholics. James Gribben, a Roman Catholic, is the teacher.

There is a Sunday school held in the day schoolhouse. Established in 1826 and held in the chapel until the schoolhouse was built. Superintended by the Reverend Daniel Curoe, parish priest, taught on the monitorial system, same as the day school. The day school books are used. No school during the winter season. Total scholars during the last summer 202, viz. 101 males and 101 females. Hours of attendance from 3 till 5 o'clock p.m. Information obtained from the master of the day school.

Parish School

The parish school is situated near the church and held in a very bad house in a state of dilapidation. It measures 49 by 19 feet in the clear. Income of the master is 11 pounds 14s, viz. from the London Hibernian Society 3 pounds per annum, from Earl O'Neill 4 pounds 4s per annum and from the scholars 4 pounds per annum. Books published by the London Hibernian Society are used, with *Gough* and *Thompson's Arithmetic*, *Murray's English grammar* and *Thompson's Geography*. Authorised Version of Scripture is taught by the master. Visited by the Reverend Samuel Shenton Heatley, vicar of Randalstown, catechism on Saturday by the master. Total number of scholars for the last quarter 35, viz. 18 boys and 17 girls: 8 boys from 10 to 15 and 18 under 10 years of age; 7 girls from 10 to 15 and 10 under 10 years of age; Established Church 21, Presbyterians 14. Andrew

Parish of Drummaul

Moore, Established Church, is the teacher. NB From the dilapidated state of the schoolhouse, no Sunday school has been held since 1837, November.

Female School

Randalstown female school is held in the room of a small private house nearly opposite the church, established 19 years ago. Income of the mistress for last year, 1837, 6 pounds per annum, all paid by the scholars. The Kildare Place Society's books are used, with *Manson's Primer and spelling book* and the Authorised Version of Scripture. Total number of scholars for last quarter 10, viz. 2 above 15 and 8 under 10 years of age, Established Church 3, Presbyterians 6, Roman Catholics 1. Plain needlework is taught. Mary Clark, a Presbyterian, is the mistress.

Seminary

The Randalstown seminary for English and classics is held in an upper room in the new market house, established November 1836. Income of the teacher for the last year, 1837, 25 pounds, paid by the pupils. Total pupils 16, all boys, viz. 1 above 15 and 11 from 10 to 15, and 4 under 10 years of age. Books generally used in classical and English seminaries: English authors used, *Knowles' Elocutionist* as a reading book, *Murray's English grammar* by Davis, and dictionary, *Thompson's Arithmetic, Chamber's Mathematics* and *Bryce's Mathematics*. Classics are Virgil, Horace, Livy and the rudiments of the Latin grammar, *Nelson's Greek grammar and testament*. Established Church 1, Presbyterians 9, Seceders 3, Roman Catholics 3. Authorised Version of Scripture is taught by the Reverend Hugh Smyth, a Seceding minister. Information obtained from the Reverend Hugh Smyth, teacher.

Sunday School

Craigmore Sunday school is held in the Seceding meeting house in the townland of Craigmore. It was established in 1824, superintended by Thomas Butler, John Boyde and James McMullin, Presbyterian. 14 teachers, viz. 8 male and 6 female. Total scholars 100 in summer, viz. 50 boys and 50 girls, 8 of these Established Church, 8 Roman Catholic, 20 Seceders and 56 Presbyterians. Hours of attendance from 8 till 10 a.m. and from 5 till half past 7 p.m. during the summer, and in winter from 8 till 10 a.m. From the Reverend Hugh Smyth, Seceding minister.

Lenagh School

Lenagh private school is situated on the road leading from Sharvogues to the Milltown, and held in a small room attached to a dwelling house, 13 and a half by 11 feet, thatched, and rented at 1 pound 7s 6d per annum. Income for the last year 10 pounds. Books used are *Manson's Primer and spelling book,* with Authorised Version of Scripture and *Gough's Arithmetic*. Total scholars 30, viz. 20 boys and 10 girls, 15 Presbyterians and 15 Roman Catholics; 3 boys above 15, 2 from 10 to 15 and 10 under 10; 10 girls under 10 years of age and 5 girls from 10 to 15. Established 1831, John Dunlop, a Presbyterian, teacher.

Schools in Magheralane

Magheralane national school is situated nearly north of Randalstown and on the road leading from Randalstown to Ballymena. A good house, thatched, 28 by 13 feet. Income of the teacher 15 pounds per annum, viz. 10 pounds from National Board and 5 pounds from the scholars. Books published by the National Board only, and visited by the Reverend Daniel Curoe, parish priest. Total scholars for last quarter 96, viz. 64 boys and 32 girls; boys above 15, 4, from 10 to 15, 30, and 30 under 10 years of age; girls from 10 to 15, 12, under 10, 20; Established Church 3, Presbyterians 5 and 88 Roman Catholics. The teacher, James Martin, is a Roman Catholic.

A Sunday school is held in this schoolhouse from the 1st May till the 1st November.

Schools in Farnflough

Farnflough national school is in the townland of Drumough, on a by-road leading from the Randalstown road to the Antrim road, and held in a good house, slated, 30 by 16 feet. Built in 1834 and cost 101 pounds 18s 3d, viz. from the National Board 39 pounds 15s, from Reverend Daniel Curoe, parish priest, 62 pounds 3s 3d. Income of the teacher 8 pounds per annum from National Board and 4 pounds from the scholars, total 12 pounds per annum. Books published by the National Board only. Catechism on Saturday by the master, visited by the Reverend Daniel Curoe, parish priest. Total scholars for last quarter 50, viz. 30 boys and 20 girls; boys from 10 to 15, 20, and 10 under 10 years of age; girls from 10 to 15, 15, and 5 under 10; Presbyterians 4 and 46 Roman Catholics. John Martin, Roman Catholic, teacher.

There is a Sunday school held in this schoolhouse during the summer only, at which 120 scholars attend, viz. 64 boys and 56 girls, 8 Presbyterians and 112 Roman Catholics. About 30 of the total number used to attend day schools. 8 teachers, viz. 4 males and 4 females. Hours of attendance from 3 till 5 p.m. Superintendent John Martin, the schoolmaster.

Schools

Seymour's bridge school is in the townland of Ballytresna at Seymour's bridge, 1 mile nearly north of Randalstown on the road to Ahoghill. A good house, thatched, 22 and a half by 16 feet. Income of the teacher 5 pounds for the last quarter, paid by the children. The present master is only one quarter teaching. This school is one of the oldest in this district but was rebuilt 1837. Books used are *Manson's Primer and spelling book, Murray's Reader and English grammar, Gough's Arithmetic*. Authorised Version and catechism on Saturday by the master, visited by the Presbyterian clergy occasionally. Total scholars last quarter 55, viz. 30 boys and 25 girls, 49 Presbyterians, 6 Roman Catholics and 1 Established Church; boys from 10 to 15, 15, and 15 under 10; girls from 10 to 15, 15, and 10 under 10 years of age. William McCarroll, a Presbyterian, is the teacher.

Seymour's bridge Sunday schoolhouse, established the first in the county, but re-established in 1837. Total teachers 9, viz. 6 males and 3 females. Superintended by Mr George Jackson and James Reside, farmers. Total pupils 100, viz. 40 males and 60 females; Presbyterians 90, Roman Catholics 10; about 50 are exclusively Sunday school scholars. Books published by the Sunday School Society for Ireland. 19th and 20th April 1838.

Caddy school is on the road leading from Randalstown to Ballymena. Held in a tolerable house, thatched, 20 by 16 feet. Income of the teacher 15 pounds per annum, paid by the scholars. Books published by the Kildare Society, with *Gough's Arithmetic* and *Murray's English grammar*. Visited by the Reverend Samuel Shenton Heatley, Established Church minister. Authorised Version of Scripture is taught and catechism on Saturday by the master. Total scholars for last quarter 34, viz. 25 boys and 9 girls; 2 boys above 15 and 11 from 10 to 15, and 12 under 10 years of age; 6 girls from 10 to 15 and 3 under 10 years of age; 32 Presbyterians and 2 Roman Catholics. Thomas Birkby, Established Church, teacher. There is no Sunday school during the winter season, chiefly owing to the non-attendance of the teachers.

Cloghogue school is on the road leading from Toome to Ballymena, and held in a middling house, thatched, 21 and a half by 16 and a half feet. Income of the teacher is 15 pounds, paid by the children. Books published by the Kildare Place Society, with *Thompson* and *Gough's Arithmetic, Murray's English grammar*, Pinnock's *Catechism on geography* and *Manson's Primer and spelling book*. Visited by the Reverend Samuel Shenton Heatley, Established Church minister, occasionally. Total pupils 23, viz. 12 boys and 11 girls; 4 boys from 10 to 15 and 8 under 10 years of age; 3 girls from 10 to 15 and 8 under 10 years of age; 17 Presbyterians and 6 Moravians. School established 20 years ago. Samuel McCracken, a Moravian, is the teacher. No Sunday school is held here during the winter.

Terrygowan School

Terrygowan school is situated on the line from Randalstown to Ahoghill. A good house, thatched, 20 by 16 feet, established 30 years ago. Annual income of the teacher 12 pounds per annum, paid by the scholars. Books published by the Kildare Place Society, Sunday school books with *Gough's Arithmetic*. Visited by the Presbyterian clergy occasionally. Total scholars 45, viz. 30 boys and 15 girls; 5 boys above 10 and 25 under 10; girls from 10 to 15, 5 and 20 under 10; Established Church 1, Presbyterians 44. John Robinson, a Covenanter, teacher. No Sunday school during the last year from want of teachers.

Leitrim School

Leitrim school is on the by-road leading from Blackrock. A room attached to a dwelling house, thatched, 18 and a half by 15 and a half feet. Income of the teacher 12 pounds per annum, paid by the scholars. Books published by the Kildare Place Society, with *Thompson's* and *Gough's Arithmetic* and *Jackson's Book-keeping*, and *Bonnycastle's Mensuration, Murray's English grammar, Goldsmith's Geography*. Visited by the Reverend Samuel Shenton Heatley, Established Church minister, and by Reverend Alexander Crawford, Presbyterian; established 1825. Total scholars 36, viz. 24 boys and 12 girls; 6 boys above 15 years of age and 6 from 10 to 15, and 12 under 10; girls from 10 to 15, 5 and 7 under 10; Established Church 1, Roman Catholics 7 and 28 Presbyterians. Peter Aickin Black, a Seceder, [teacher]. Sunday school only held during the summer.

Parish of Drummaul

Ballydunmaul School

Ballydunmaul school, on the line between Toome and Randalstown, a good house, thatched, 20 and a half by 15 feet. Income of the teacher 12 pounds per annum, paid by the scholars. Books published by the Kildare Place Society, *Thompson's* and *Gough's Arithmetic*, *Murray* and *Lennie's English grammar*, *Thompson's Geography*, *Jackson's Book-keeping*, *Bonnycastle's Mensuration*. Not visited by any of the clergy, patron Mr Thomas Butler, farmer. Total scholars for last quarter 20, viz. 12 boys and 8 girls; 3 boys from 10 to 15 and 9 under 10; and 3 girls from 10 to 15 and 5 under 10; Presbyterians 20. Teacher Hamilton Dickson Malcom, a Seceder.

HISTORY AND ANCIENT TOPOGRAPHY

Legend of Banshee at Shane's Castle

It is confidently affirmed by persons of all denominations that the banshee follows or is attached to certain families, and is only heard to cry, in the tone of och-oh, och-oh, och-oh, previous to the death of some one of the family, or of some remarkable circumstance connected with some of the family or the house. The banshee which followed the O'Neill family was locally called Neane Roe or Catherine O'Neill, supposed to have [been a] beautiful virgin or young lady who was enchanted or taken away by the fairies. The banshee was never seen or heard after the castle was burned, but was heard and seen frequently before it by Bernard Moore, the second butler at Shane's Castle.

Traditions of O'Neill Family

Phelemy Roe O'Neill was a proprietor of Shane's Castle, at which he erected a wooden gallows on which several were hanged during his war.

The Marchioness O'Neill was first married to the Marquis of Antrim and secondly to her cousin, Henry O'Neill. At that time she consulted the Kings of Ulster how she might keep the 2 estates in their hands. In order to accomplish this, the kings desired her to have her remains interred a part in Carrickfergus and a part at Shane's Castle, which took place after her death. Her father, John O'Neill, had 7 sons, idiots who could never tell their own names. She was the only daughter and Protestant. Old Charles O'Neill, grandfather to the present Earl O'Neill, was married to Sarah Corethers, a Protestant. The late Lord O'Neill's father was married to Hariot Boyle, a Roman Catholic, who died at Portugal at the age of 37. She was neice to Lord Cork.

The present Earl O'Neill's father is said to have had in his possession an iron chest filled with gold, won chiefly by horse-racing, on which a song was composed which is still sung by the people about Tullamore and Shane's Castle. In order to try the disposition of his 2 sons (the present earl and the general) their father, during their vacation from school, one morning at the breakfast table gave each a 5 pound note and asked each how they would spend it. The general said he would put his into the poor box on the following Sunday, which he did, and the present Earl O'Neill said he would keep his to purchase a pony, which he did. Information obtained from [blank].

Inundation of Floating Moss

On the 22nd September 1835 an inundation took place in the flow bog of the townland of Ballylurgan and Farlough, and carried away a large portion of the bog, which covered upwards of 100 acres of land on Earl O'Neill's estate, for which his lordship did not charge rent to the tenants. The following are the principal sufferers: Hugh Magill of Farlough lost to the amount of 20 pounds; John Walker of Ballylurgan lost to the amount of 12 pounds; James Reid of the townland of Ballylurgan lost to the amount of 12 pounds; Peter Macrory, George McGill, John Boulton, Alexander Bell and Hugh Fisher. From Hugh McGill and Robert McDowell, farmers.

Ancient Graveyard and Church Ruins

The old graveyard in the townland of Drummaul is in the farm of Andrew Thompson. Nothing remains of the old church (which formerly stood in the centre of the graveyard, 40 by 25 feet) but a part of the east gable which stands 10 feet high by 9 feet broad and 3 feet thick. The graveyard is thickly covered with graves and tombstones. The oldest stone legible is dated 1721, to the memory of Jane King. There is a very curious stone about 55 feet west of the gable standing as a headstone, under which a quantity of gold was found many years ago by Robert Dickey. This stone is square with a cavity, very smooth cut and about 9 inches in diameter and 5 inches deep. The other stone which covered this is broken. The graveyard was much smaller, but about 9 years ago 1 perch was added to it all round at the expense of the parish. From Samuel Reaney and John Cooke, farmers.

Forts and Coves

There is a fort in the townland of Drumsough on the farm of Joseph Hill, which is circular and 135 feet in diameter, but not remarkable; and one on the farm of John Hannah; also one on the farm of Bernard Hannah, townland of Lenagh, 90 feet in diameter, but not remarkable.

There is a cove with rooms turning off at right angles on John Hannah's farm, same townland, but the entrance is obstructed by water.

Fort in Magheralane

A fort of earth is on the farm of Frank Martin, but all broken up except the trench which is circular. 18th April 1838.

Cove and Quern

Cove on the farm of Daniel Macauley, townland of Ballytresna, but the entrance is too small to describe the interior.

Biddy Magirle of Ballygrooby townland has a very ancient quern and very perfect, 6 inches in diameter inside the rim. The rim itself is 1 inch thick and 3 inches deep, supported by 3 feet, each 3 inches long. Found in a flow bog 6 feet under the surface in 1835 in the same townland.

Copper Rings

Adam Davison of Aghanboy townland about 6 years ago found 30 copper rings all linked together, each ring 1 and a half inches in diameter, found under a stone at the mills, but all lost. From Adam Davison, farmer and miller. 20th April 1838.

Forts and Coves

There is a fort of earth on the farm of Bernard Cullin in the townland of Ballylurgan, but part is dug away.

There was a cove on the farm of William Gallaway in the townland of Procklis, but dug away. 21st April 1838.

Forts and Coves

The fort in the townland of Downkillybegs, on the farm of John Christy, is very perfect but not remarkable.

There is a cove [on] Billy Mann's farm, townland of Caddy, containing 2 rooms, but too narrow to enter.

There is a fort in the townland of Killyknock, on Thomas Sloan's farm, but not remarkable; also one on the farm of Ambrose O'Roarke Esquire, Ballybollan, planted; also one in the townland of Grogan, on Thomas Rodger's farm.

Fort on Thomas Rodger's farm, townland of Grogan, but not remarkable; also one on Henry Smith's farm, Clonboy, part dug away; also one on William Craig's farm, but not remarkable; also one in the townland of Lisnagreggan, on Thomas Livingstone's farm.

Fort on Andrew Thompson's farm, townland of Artresnahan, but part dug away; also one in the townland of Lurgan West, on the farm of John Toole, but part dug away.

Standing Stone

There is a standing stone on the farm of Robert Agnew in the townland of Muckleramer, on a very conspicuous hill 30 perches north of the road from Randalstown to Toome. The stone is 4 feet high by 2 and a half feet broad and 2 feet thick. 23rd April 1838.

Ancient Clock at Shane's Castle

Lady Marchioness O'Neill was waiting maid to Queen Mary (wife to King William III), who presented the marchioness with a small clock in a black ebony case, which was to be handed down to the family of the O'Neills and is still to be seen at Shane's Castle. At the time the castle was burned this clock was preserved by the housekeeper Mrs Atkinson. From Mr David Moore.

Coin

The small ancient <antient> silver coin of 6d magnitude was obtained from Mr Davey Moore, watchmaker, Randalstown. 10th April 1838.

Ancient Coins

Thomas Davison of Maghereagh townland about 10 years ago found a large quantity of silver and copper coins carefully folded up in flannel and inside of a leathern bag, on his farm. The silver coins were of 2s 6d magnitude and of 1s magnitude and of 6d magnitude, of various kings' reigns, but are now all disposed of, some to Lord O'Neill. From Thomas Davison, farmer.

Quern and Brass Instrument

The Reverend Hugh Smyth of Craigmore has a very curious quern 1 foot 7 inches in diameter and 2 inches thick, with a hole in the centre 3 inches in diameter, with 6 smaller holes, and regularly

Parish of Drummaul

carved. It was found in clay soil near his house in 1837, but is broken in two. Also a curious brass instrument found by Jane [?] Inch in clay soil in the townland of Ballydrummaul.

Coin

The small silver coin of 6d magnitude was found in the parish of Drummaul and townland of Craigmore.

The Rock

[Drawing of 5 stones, numbered] The above is nearly an outline of the principal stones standing on a place locally called the Rock, supposed to be a giant's grave. It has all the appearance of such, as the stones appear to have been regularly placed, and measures in length from (a) to (b) 15 feet. No.1 is the stone at the foot of the grave; is 3 feet 8 inches high by 1 and a half feet thick. No.2 is 4 feet high by 1 foot thick. No.5 is the headstone; it measures 6 feet high by 4 and a half feet broad and 1 and a half feet thick. The bottom part is 2 feet wide and hollow. The grave becomes wider towards the head. It runs east and west, i.e. the head is at the east. The other stones are standing confusedly through the carn. There was another standing stone here which was 6 feet high by 3 feet broad and 1 and a half feet thick, but was tossed 20 years ago in search of money. Some are of opinion that a castle formerly stood here, or [of ?] some strength. It is on the farm of Mr William Davison in the townland of Barnish, about 50 perches off the road leading from the Milltown to Ballymena. From William and James Davison, farmers. 14th April 1838.

Coves and Forts

There was 2 coves in the townland of Barnish, on the farm of William Davison, with rooms turning off at right angles, but all demolished 19 years ago.
  2 forts on the farm of James Davison and William Davison, same townland but dug away. 17th April 1838.

Giant's Chair

A giant's chair, situated in the planting above the Seceding meeting house in Craigmore, but not remarkable as it is not artificial.

Coin

John French of Ballygrooby near Randalstown has a copper coin, ha'penny magnitude, of John of Gaunt <Guant>. 24th April 1838.

Skady Tower

Skady tower is situated in Lough Neagh. It is of octagonal form, each side 5 feet, total circumference 40 feet and 20 feet high from the pile to the top, and 34 feet from the foundation stone at the bottom to the top; 2-storey high. The walls are of brick, 1 foot 3 inches thick. It contains 7 oblong windows, each 3 feet 9 inches high by 1 foot 9 inches wide, and 1 oblong door on the north east side. It is 6 and a half feet high by 2 feet 9 inches wide, with 8 stone steps leading up to it from the water. The foundation pile is 30 feet in diameter on the top and wider at the bottom. It is 9 feet above the level of the water at low water mark and 6 feet at high water mark. It is about 18 years since the roof fell in and 34 years since it was built. No roof or platform on it. The south west side of the pile is nearly level with the water, the opposite part remains perfect. Lord O'Neill used it as a shooting lodge. It is now a resting place for daws and cormorants.

SOCIAL ECONOMY

Migration

List of persons who migrate annually from this parish. [Table gives name, age, religion, townland, port emigrated to].
  Bernard Keilty, 28, John Keilty, 24, Bernard Keilty Junior, 25, Roman Catholics, from Magheralane to Glasgow.
  Henry Young, 22, Roman Catholic, from Magheralane to Liverpool.
  Daniel Martin, 28, Roman Catholic, from Magheralane to Glasgow.
  John Cooper, 50, Presbyterian, from Ballytresna to Glasgow.
  James Watt, 22, Presbyterian, from Ballytresna to Glasgow.
  William Seymour, 22, Seceder, from Ballytresna to Glasgow.
  William McIlvenny, 35, Seceder, from Ballytresna to Glasgow.
  William Sandys, 40, Moravian, from Tamlaght to Glasgow.
  John Hindeman, 30, Presbyterian, from Tamlaght to Glasgow.
  Thomas O'Neill, 27, Roman Catholic, from Aghanboy to Liverpool.
  David Howard, 35, Presbyterian, from Coolsythe to Liverpool.
  Adam Harpur, 40, Presbyterian, from Coolsythe to Liverpool.

William Cameron, 32, Presbyterian, from Coolsythe to Liverpool.

Andrew Carson, 35, Presbyterian, from Coolsythe to Liverpool.

Harpur Brison, 40, Presbyterian, from Randalstown to Charlestown.

Henry Macrory, 34, Roman Catholic, from Magheralane to Glasgow.

Hugh Macrory, 20, Roman Catholic, from Farlough to Glasgow.

Patrick Macrory, 30, John Macrory, 26, Roman Catholics, from Magheralane to Glasgow.

John O'Neill, 32, Roman Catholic, from Magheralane to Glasgow.

Arthur O'Hara, 20, Roman Catholic, from Farlough to Glasgow.

John Cooper, 50, Presbyterian, from Ballytresna to Glasgow.

James Watt, 22, Presbyterian, from Ballytresna to Glasgow.

Edward Macurley, 27, Roman Catholic, from Tamlaght to Glasgow.

James Morgan, 21, Roman Catholic, from Tamlaght to Glasgow.

John Knox, 18, Roman Catholic, from Tamlaght to Glasgow.

William Armour, dealer, 39, Presbyterian, from Coolsythe to Glasgow.

Hugh Reaney, 30, Presbyterian, from Grogan to Glasgow.

Patrick Kennedy, 24, Owen Kennedy, 31, Roman Catholics, from Grogan to Glasgow.

James McDonald, 21, Roman Catholic, from Grogan to Glasgow.

Thomas Neily, 24, William John Neily, 26, Presbyterians, from Tannaghmore to Glasgow.

David McCarroll, 27, James McCarroll, 29, Thomas McCarroll, 22, Robert McCarroll, 25, Presbyterians, from Tannaghmore to Glasgow.

Hugh McCombs 25, Presbyterian, from Tannaghmore to Glasgow.

John Kincade, 23, Presbyterian, from Tannaghmore to Glasgow.

Henry Gilmour, 25, Roman Catholic, from Drumanaway to Glasgow.

Felix Melon, 33, Henry Melon, 24, Roman Catholics, from Kilknock to Glasgow.

Patrick McCann, 22, Roman Catholic, from Lurgan West to Glasgow.

William Pogue, 40, Presbyterian, from Ballynahany to Glasgow.

Felix McKowen, 30, Roman Catholic, from Ballynahany to Glasgow.

Henry McAnally, 24, Ephraim McAnally, 40, Roman Catholics, from Ballynahany to Glasgow.

David Howard, 35, Presbyterian, from Coolsythe to Glasgow.

Hugh Heaney, 26, Roman Catholic, from Leitrim to Glasgow.

Emigration in 1835

List of persons who have emigrated from the parish of Drummaul during the year 1835. [Table gives, name, age, religion, townland, port emigrated to].

Charles Neeson, 18, Established Church, from Randalstown to Charlestown, United States.

Elizabeth Baxter, 21, Edward Baxter, 25, Anne Baxter, three-quarters of a year, William Baxter, 27, [?] Bell Baxter, 24, Martha Baxter, 4, Roman Catholics, from Maghereagh to New York.

John Enniss, 2, Roman Catholic, from Maghereagh to New York.

Robert Thompson [blank].

Peter McClenaghan, 30, blacksmith, Roman Catholic, from Lenagh to New York.

George Thompson, 20, Robert Thompson, 20, Presbyterians, from Aghanboy to New York.

Jane Glover, 25, Presbyterian, from Aghanboy to New York.

William Hanan, 22, Roman Catholic, from Drumsough to New York.

John Henderson, 18, Presbyterian, from Tamlaght to Charlestown.

Hugh Nichol 20, Presbyterian, from Ballydunmaul to New Orleans.

Catherine Wright, 21, Presbyterian, from Ballydunmaul to New York.

James Wright, 19, Seceder, from Ballydunmaul to New Orleans.

William Hannah, 22, Roman Catholic, from Drumsough to New York.

John Walker, 55, Mary Walker, 25, Ann Walker, 21, Margaret Walker, 23, Presbyterians, from Terrygowan to New Orleans.

Thomas Carson, 21, Presbyterian, from Terrygowan to New Orleans.

Emigration in 1836

List of persons who have emigrated from the parish of Drummaul during the year 1836. [Table gives name, age, religion, townland, port emigrated to].

Samuel Courtney, 18, Presbyterian, from Randalstown to Charlestown.

Martha French, 22, Mary French, 19, Presbyterians, from Ballygrooby to New York.

James Gilliland, 24, Established Church, from Ballygrooby to Quebec.

Parish of Drummaul

Thomas Carlton, 18, John Carlton, 32, Margaret Carlton, 19, Established Church, from Clonboy to New York.

John Macrory, 30, Mary Macrory, 28, Roman Catholics, from Farlough to New Orleans.

John Walker, 30, Jane Walker, 32, Presbyterians, from Magherabeg to Glasgow.

Mary Jane Thompson, 13, Presbyterian, from Maghereagh to New York.

John Farrell, 25, Eliza Farrell, 20, Presbyterians, from Ballydunmaul to New York.

Martha Murray, 18, Presbyterian, from Ballydunmaul to New York.

John Grace, 26, Eliza Grace, 24, Established Church, from Ballealy to New York.

Bernard Kane, 36, Roman Catholic, from Ballealy to Quebec.

Daniel Morgan, 24, Roman Catholic, from Ballealy to Quebec.

Clara Craig, 24, Catherine Craig, 22, Roman Catholics, from Clonboy to New York.

John Robinson, 27, Presbyterian, from Clonboy to New York.

Emigration in 1837

List of persons who have emigrated from the parish of Drummaul during the year 1837. [Table gives name, age, religion, townland, port emigrated to].

William Taylor, 40, Presbyterian, from Randalstown to New York.

Sarah French, 17, Presbyterian, from Ballygrooby to New York.

Thomas Lyons, 22, Roman Catholic, from Maghereagh to Liverpool.

Catherine Craig, 19, Clara Craig, 17, Roman Catholics, from Clonboy to New York.

John Hannah, 60, Sarah Hannah, 58, John Hannah Junior, 40, Hugh Hannah, 38, James Hannah, 36, Thomas Hannah, 34, Margaret Hannah, 32, Sarah Hannah, 30, Anne Hannah, 28, Eliza Hannah, 26, Martha Hannah, 36, Presbyterians, from Lenagh to Quebec.

Hugh Keilty, 26, Roman Catholic, from Magheralane to New Orleans.

Charles Macrory, 27, Rose Macrory, 18, Roman Catholics, from Farlough to New Orleans.

Thomas McAuley, 25, Presbyterian, from Tamlaght to New York.

Martha Glover, 25, Presbyterian, from Aghanboy to New York.

John Watt, 65, Eliza Watt, 22, Mary Watt, 20, Rose Watt, 18, Alice Watt, 16, John Watt Junior, 14, James Watt, 12, Jane Watt, 10, Sarah Watt, 8, Presbyterians, from Coolsythe to Charlestown, United States.

William Irvine, 28, Presbyterian, from Coolsythe to Charlestown.

Eliza Loughlin, 26, Presbyterian, from Tamlaght to New York.

Samuel Howard, 38, Presbyterian, from Coolsythe to New York.

William Irvine, 25, Presbyterian, from Clare to New Orleans.

Eliza McCracken, 35, Presbyterian, from Clare to Quebec.

James Foster, 30, Presbyterian, from Clare to Quebec.

Robert Carson, 25, Seceder, from Procklis to New York.

John Small, 25, Anne Small, 20, Presbyterians, from Ballymackilroy to New York.

Mary Weir, 18, John Weir, 16, Presbyterians, from Ballymackilroy to New York.

John Allen, 25, Presbyterian, from Grogan to New York.

Eliza Toole, 40, Roman Catholic, from Lurgan West to Glasgow.

Martha Kelly, 20, Seceder, from Ballydunmaul to New Orleans.

Eliza Herrill, 27, John Herrill, 30, Stewart Herrill, 1 month, Roman Catholics, from Ballydunmaul to St John's.

Emigrants

Those who have emigrated for the last 3 years were chiefly labourers and small farmers, with a few tradesmen, who could command little or no capital, but emigrated to seek in a foreign land that comfort their own country no longer affords. All good characters.

School Statistics

Table of Schools

[Table contains the following headings: name of townland where held, name and religion of master or mistress, free or pay school, annual income of master or mistress, description and cost of schoolhouse, number of pupils subdivided by religion, sex and the Protestant and Roman Catholic returns, societies with which connected].

Randalstown, Dunmore, master Eugene Reilly, Protestant; pay school, annual income about 30 pounds; schoolhouse a substantial stone house, cost 200 pounds; fund raised by subscription with donations from lord lieutenant's fund and from Kildare Place Society; number of pupils by the Protestant return: 44 Established Church, 20 Presbyterians, 20 Roman Catholics, 60 males, 24 females; by the Roman Catholic return: 43 Established Church, 17 Presbyterians, 35 Roman Catholics, 56 males, 39 females; connected with Kildare Place Society, the parish school, the schoolhouse built by subscription, Lord O'Neill subscribes 4 guineas annually.

Randalstown, Dunmore, mistress Mary Clarke, Protestant; pay school, annual income about 10 pounds; schoolhouse a good house but bad internal accommodation, cost 60 pounds; number of pupils by the Protestant return: 7 Established Church, 7 Presbyterians, 3 other denominations, 3 Roman Catholics, 7 males, 13 females; by the Roman Catholic return: 6 Established Church, 8 Presbyterians, 3 other denominations, 3 Roman Catholics, 17 males, 13 females; associations none.

Randalstown, master John Getty, Presbyterian; pay school, annual income 50 pounds to 52 pounds; schoolhouse a hired room; number of pupils by the Protestant return: 12 Established Church, 22 Presbyterians, 5 Roman Catholics, 25 males, 14 females; by the Roman Catholics return: 10 Protestants, 22 Presbyterians, 7 Roman Catholics, 26 males, 13 females; associations none.

Randalstown barrack, master John Conningham, Protestant; pay school, annual income 8 pounds; schoolhouse a room in the barracks; number of pupils by the Protestant return: 4 Established Church, 13 Presbyterians, 3 Roman Catholics, 14 males, 6 females; by the Roman Catholic return: 4 Established Church, 13 Presbyterians, 3 Roman Catholics, 14 males, 6 females; associations none.

Ballygrooby, mistress, Agnes Finlay, Presbyterian; pay school, annual income about 8 pounds; schoolhouse a good apartment rented by mistress; number of pupils by the Protestant return: 4 Presbyterians, 4 Roman Catholics, 4 males, 4 females; by the Roman Catholic return: 5 Presbyterians, 4 Roman Catholics, 4 males, 5 females; associations none.

Seymour's bridge, Ballytresnaghan Lower, master H.D. Malcombe, Seceder; pay school, annual income 17 pounds 10s; schoolhouse a poor cabin, cost 30 pounds; number of pupils by the Protestant return: 4 Established Church, 8 Presbyterians, 8 other denominations, 10 Roman Catholics, 28 males, 12 females; by the Roman Catholic return: 3 Established Church, 15 Presbyterians, 8 other denominations, 4 Roman Catholics, 26 males, 14 females; connected with Kildare Place and London Hibernian Societies, the Reverend M.W. Henderson, Presbyterian minister, built the schoolhouse.

Terrygowan, master James McKellan, Seceder; pay school, annual income 16 pounds to 18 pounds; schoolhouse a good house, built by private subscription; number of pupils by the Protestant return: 35 Presbyterians, 5 Roman Catholics, 25 males, 15 females; by the Roman Catholic return: 40 Presbyterians, 3 Roman Catholics, 24 males, 19 females; connected with London Hibernian and Kildare Place Societies, the schoolhouse built by private subscription.

Tullycronaught, master John [?] Hawney, Roman Catholic; pay school, annual income 6 or 7 pounds; schoolhouse a barn; number of pupils by the Roman Catholic return: 7 Protestants, 23 other denominations, 24 males, 6 females; associations none.

Aughalish, master John Delap, Presbyterian; pay school, annual income 7 pounds 10s; schoolhouse in a wretched state of dilapidation; number of pupils by the Protestant return: 10 Presbyterians, 5 Roman Catholics, 8 males, 7 females; associations none.

Leitrim, master James McKillan, Presbyterian; pay school, annual income about 28 pounds; schoolhouse a new and substantial house, cost 40 pounds, built by subscription aided by the Kildare Place Society; number of pupils by the Protestant return: 3 Established Church, 40 Presbyterians, 13 Roman Catholics, 33 males, 23 females; by the Roman Catholic return: 4 Established Church, 15 Presbyterians, 5 other denominations, 13 Roman Catholics, 24 males, 13 females; connected with Kildare Place Society, the schoolhouse built partly by subscription.

Ballydunmaul, master Clotworthy Boyd, Presbyterian; pay school, annual income 20 pounds to 25 pounds; schoolhouse a good house, cost 40 pounds, built by subscription and aid from Kildare Place Society; number of pupils by the Protestant return: 34 Presbyterians, 16 Roman Catholics, 27 males, 23 females; by the Roman Catholic return: 30 Presbyterians, 6 other denominations, 14 Roman Catholics, 27 males, 23 females; connected with Kildare Place Society, the schoolhouse built partly by subscription.

Magheralane, master James Martin, Roman Catholic; pay school, annual income 20 pounds to 25 pounds; schoolhouse good, cost 40 pounds by subscription and from Kildare Place Society; number of pupils by the Protestant return: 3 Established Church, 37 Roman Catholics, 25 males, 15 females; by the Roman Catholic return: 3 Established Church, 47 Roman Catholics, 30 males, 20 females; connected with Kildare Place Society, the schoolhouse built partly by subscription.

Parish of Duneane, County Antrim

Statistical Account by Lieutenant C.H. Mallock, August 1830

NATURAL STATE

Name and Situation

Duneane, a vicarage in the diocese of Connor in the archdiocese of Armagh. It is situated in the south west corner of the half-barony of Upper Toome and on the south west borders of the county of Antrim, about 24 miles north west of Belfast and about 8 miles south south west of Ballymena. It is the property of Lord O'Neill, except a few townlands. I believe there are 4 townlands church property, namely Staffordstown, Lisknalisky, Gortgill and Dumbo. The townland of Moneyglass belongs to the Jones family. The farms throughout are generally held either at will or on very short leases, average rent from 25s to 30s Irish acre.

Boundaries, Extent and Divisions

It is bounded on the north by the grange of Ballyscullion <Ballyscullin>, on the north west by the parish of Ballyscullion, on the south by Lough Neagh, on the east by the parish of Drummaul, on the west by the River Bann, which separates Duneane from the parish of Artrea <Ardtrea> in county Derry. It extends from north to south about 6 miles and from east to west about 4. It contains within the boundaries of the parish 13,285 acres. Of this number, 1,063 acres belong to the parish of Drummaul and 834 to the parish of Cranfield. In Lough Neagh, a few hundred yards from the shore, are 3 small islands, which together are 4 acres in extent. These islands are not considered as belonging to any parish.

There are 53 divisions in the parish, namely 47 townlands and the parish of Cranfield. The other 5 divisions are subdivisions of townlands. 6 of the divisions within the parish are considered as forming a part of the parish of Drummaul, to which they pay tithes and other ecclesiastical dues. From the north point of the Creagh bog up to Toome Bridge one half of the River Bann belongs to Duneane parish but is not considered as belonging to any of the townlands within the parish.

NATURAL FEATURES

Surface and Soil

From the west and south boundaries the land rises gradually towards the centre of the parish from a level of 60 to about 250 or 300 feet, after which the surface presents a succession of low round-topped hills, a great number of which are covered with furze and stunted underwood, interspersed with large blocks of stone. All these, being the most conspicuous points, give to the parish an uncultivated and barren appearance, but in fact, such is not the case. Much of the land from the shores of Lough Neagh up to the centre of the parish is a very productive soil. This is particularly the case at the south east part, where is situated the parish of Cranfield, the whole of which is in a high state of cultivation. In the north west part of the parish is the townland of Moneyglass, Dunraymond Cottage, St Helena House and Creagh bog, all of which are covered or surmounted by plantations and present a pleasing appearance. The soil throughout the parish, though not particularly productive, yet affords to the farmer a fair return for his labour. One of the greatest drawbacks to the farmer is the want of lime, which cannot be procured except at a very great expense. Produce per Irish acre varies from 70 to 100 bushels of corn and from 200 to 250 of potatoes.

Produce and Turbary

From the centre of the parish to the north boundary potatoes and oats are the principal crops; flax and barley in small quantities. In the remainder of the parish oats, potatoes, flax and wheat are cultivated with success. In Cranfield wheat is grown. Turbary not very abundant in any part, but is quite sufficient for the supply required.

NATURAL HISTORY

Limestone and Minerals

Limestone: not any. Whatever is required is brought either from the parish of Carnmoney <Carmoney> or from Derry. Here again the toll on the Toome Bridge is felt as a great burthen.

Minerals: not any.

Parish of Duneane

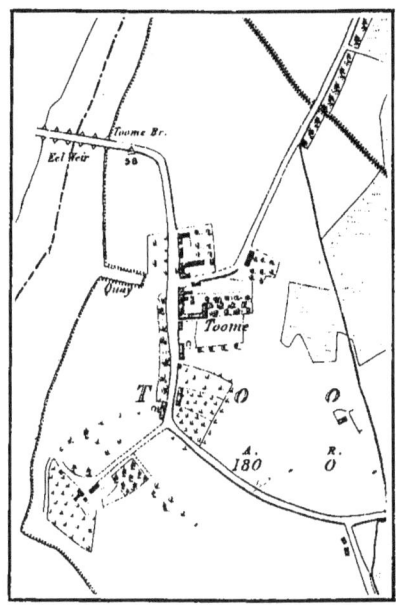

Map of Toome from the first 6" O.S. maps, 1830s

MODERN TOPOGRAPHY

Villages

There is not any town. The only villages are those of Toome and Staffordstown. The latter, which is situated near the centre of the south part, is a very small one hardly deserving the name, and appears to be gradually going to decay.

The village of Toome is also a very wretched one. It is situated in the townland of the same name on the banks of the River Bann and close to the Toome Bridge, and on the coach road from Belfast to Cookstown [and] Moneymore. Toome is famous for its eel fishery, the royalty of which belongs to the Donegall family. The right of fishery is at present with Lord O'Neill for which he pays a rent, said to be 400 [pounds] a year. In some seasons the profit has been 800 pounds.

Toome is a post village. There is a large inn at which post horses may be procured, but everything within the house is in a poor state. This house used to be much frequented during the season for eels, purposely for enjoying that fish in perfection. There are 2 fairs held here in the year, one on the 7th April and the other on the 4th December. There is little or no business transacted at either of them.

Manufactories

Linen weaving is still carried on in the farmers' houses. This branch of industry, which formerly used to enable the agriculturalists to pay enormous rents for their small holdings, at the present time hardly repays for the actual labour. Cotton weaving is now very general and bids fair entirely to supersede that of linen. The high rents still continue, although the means of paying them and at the same time retaining something beyond mere necessaries has passed away.

Roads

The roads, which are numerous, are generally kept in good repair. The coach road from Belfast to Moneymore passes through the centre of the parish. A coach passes twice a week.

NATURAL FEATURES

Rivers

The River Bann, on the boundary of the parish, is the only one. As before mentioned it is famous for its eel fishery, but does not in other ways contribute to the wealth of the district. The only advantage derived from Lough Neagh is that it enables a few individuals to gain a scanty livelihood by fishing. On the lough shore in the parish of Cranfield there were some small stone houses (they are now in ruins) and a quay. No use is now made of either.

Bogs and Woods

There are not any extensive bogs. The narrow strip of land situated between Lough Beg and the River Bann is generally known by the name of Creagh bog, but in fact it is not a bog. During the winter a great part of it is always flooded, but in the summer a great number of cattle are fed on it. There is not much wood except in the townlands of Moneyglass and Dunraymond and on the Creagh bog, but these are not of much extent. There is one plantation in the south west corner, but the general appearance of the parish is that of a country with little or no wood.

SOCIAL ECONOMY

Population

The inhabitants are mostly Catholics, Presbyterian the next in number, and a few of the Established Church. There are 2 Catholic chapels, one in the townland of Cargin, the other in that of

Ballymatoskerty. The Presbyterians have a meeting house in the townland of Ballynully and the church is situated in the townland of Lisknalisky. The markets generally frequented are those of Randalstown. The Jones family of Moneyglass are the only resident gentry. Lord O'Neill has a small cottage in the townland of Dunraymond, where he occasionally passes a few days.

ANCIENT TOPOGRAPHY

Antiquities

Several old forts <forths> but nothing else. In the parish of Cranfield, close to the lake shore, are ruins of a Catholic chapel and a holy well adjoining. The graveyard round the chapel is still used. The parish of Cranfield is united with that of Duneane and gives the title of vicar to the clergyman of Duneane, [signed] C.H. Mallock, Lieutenant Royal Artillery, August 12th 1830.

Memoir by James Boyle, May 1836, with additions from Office Copy and sections by G.W. Hemans

MEMOIR WRITING

Memoir Writing

[On covering page of Office Copy] Received 11 May 1835 from Mr Hannyngton [initialled] James McGann.

NATURAL FEATURES

Hills

This parish occupies a portion of the western side and southern extremity of the hilly ridge known by the name of the Killymurry's hills, which extends along the western side of this county from the parish of Finvoy, near its northern, to Lough Neagh at its southern extremity. The highest ground in the parish is near its north east boundary, where its elevation above the sea is 367 feet. From this it declines irregularly and slowly towards its southern extremity, where it terminates in a gravelling beach on the shore of Lough Neagh.

The descent eastward is irregular and undulating, being formed of successive ranges of little features, some of which are abrupt and steep, but declining in height as they approach its western boundary, where the slope terminates in a low and almost flat marshy tract extending along the eastern shore of Loughs Neagh and Beg and the River Bann.

The surface of this parish, except along its western boundary, presents great diversity, being a beautiful succession of hill [and] dale. The principal points are Ballydonnelly, 360 feet, Artlone, 357 feet, Four Towns, 292 feet and Killyfast, 254 feet above the level of the sea.

Lakes

Lough Neagh, which washes a considerable portion of the south western coast of this county, extends for 2 and a third miles along the southern and western coast of this parish, within the boundary of which 1,682 acres 1 rood 11 perches of its surface are included. There are 48,342 acres 3 roods 19 perches of its surface in this county. Its extreme length from north to south is 16 and a half miles and breadth from east to west 12 miles. Its bottom is sandy, its beach narrow and chiefly consists of a range of sandy banks of from 5 to 8 feet high; but in some places it is pebbly and shelving. Bog is found at a depth of from 2 to 3 feet under its bed near the shore at Toome. It is shallow immediately along its shore, but becomes suddenly deep. It rises in winter to an average elevation of 6 and a half feet and, as it requires a long time to retire, the cultivation of the ground along it is either totally or partially retarded, as ploughing or sowing cannot commence until it has wholly subsided; and in some parts where the ground is level and more subject to immersion, its cultivation is out of the question. The grass on the meadows is also soured. They are rendered "spritty" and their crops are uncertain.

Its waters possess a strong petrifying power and petrifactions of various substances, but particularly whin and holly, are found in the fields at a short distance from the shore. A beautiful pebble of a brownish yellow colour, precisely the form and size of a very large pea, was recently found near it. The gravel along some parts of its coast is much prized for garden walks and for studding the fronts of cottages. It is very clean and consists of pebbles of a small and similar size and of a golden or brownish colour. The coast of this parish is tame and uninteresting, and there is nothing immediately along it possessing any beauty.

Lough Beg

A portion of the south east extremity of Lough Beg, including 415 acres 3 roods 30 perches of surface, is situated at the north west side of this parish. It is connected with the northern extremity of Lough Neagh by the River Bann, which again issues from the northern extremity of this lake. It is said to be of comparatively modern formation and not noticed in Ptolemy's maps, and this is further supported by the fact of oak timber being sometime in summer found in its bed. It is shallow along its sides, but gradually deepens towards its centre, where its depth is from 18 to 20 feet. It rises to an average height of 7 feet in winter and does considerable mischief to the almost level ground along it, by its inundations. And as it requires a long time to subside, the ground either becomes soured and unfit for cultivation by its being so long in a state of immersion, or it does not fully retire in time to admit of its cultivation. The crops on the meadows are rendered uncertain and the grass rendered unfit for cattle.

[Insert addition by G.W. Hemans: Bann river at Toome. That part of the Bann river which joins the lakes Lough Neagh and Lough Beg always overflows its banks in winter and covers a large tract of land in its vicinity, which it converts into bog. It does not leave much deposit, but washes or spoils much ground, as the people cannot commence tillage until the water has completely retired, and consequently are very late in the season with their crops, which are never very good. See *Observations on the overflowing of Lough Neagh and its rivers in winter* by J.B. Woodhouse, [signed] G.W. Hemans]. Its bed is of a tough whitish clay except at Raymond Cottage, where there is some pretty planting. The scenery along it is dreary even in summer and in winter the adjacent lands are so covered as to present the appearance of a watery waste. It forms, however, a pretty object in the landscape, to which Church Island with its graceful spire gives a pleasing effect.

River Bann

The Bann, which, issuing from the northern extremity of Lough Neagh and entering the southern extremity of Lough Beg in this parish, flows along its western boundary for 2 and a quarter miles, forming a part of the boundary of this county, which it separates from that of Londonderry. Its course is for the first mile northerly. It then takes a sudden and angular turn to the west for a short distance and afterwards pursues a westerly course until it enters the centre of a fork formed by the southern extremities of Lough Beg, flowing through the centre of the very narrow and level tongue of land which extends for three-quarters of a mile into that lake. From the angle before mentioned, a cut was made about a century ago to the southern extremity of the eastern fork in order to facilitate the recession of the waters of the Bann and Lough Neagh, and since that time the Bann has, in its old natural course, been gradually decreasing in depth and width while the new cut is widening and deepening.

The depth of the Bann at Toome Bridge is 18 feet and it is thought there is little variation in the depth of its channel, except where it issues from Lough Neagh and enters Lough Beg, where it [is] crossed by a ford. At the former point the ford may be waded in summer; it is sandy and falls rapidly to each side. The water on this ford must at one time have been lower than at present, as there was a penalty against those crossing on it and thereby avoiding the toll on Toome Bridge.

The ford at the entrance of Lough Beg is clayey and also passable in summer. It is now navigable for lighters of 60 tons burthen, except in very dry weather. Its breadth varies from 31 to 99 yards and averages 71 yards. From an observation made at Toome Bridge it has been ascertained that the average rise of the Bann in winter is 7 feet, and that waters must not only rise higher but require more time to subside than formerly, as 30 years ago sowing along the shore of the parish commenced about the 20th March, while this year, 1836, but little has been sown up to the last week in April. Its trifling fall [is] insufficient for the drainage of the flooded country and the ground along it is therefore marshy and unfit for cultivation. Its deposits are trifling and immaterial. It is inapplicable to machinery or drainage.

It is said by the old people about Toome that their forefathers mention the increase of the Bann in breadth, and they say that though it is now narrowing, it must have at one time been much more so as the people used to cross it on a large oak tree which had fallen across it from the point where it grew, a little below Toome Bridge; and they further confirm this assertion by the fact of their finding oak trees in its bed and banks.

Its banks are almost on a level with its summer surface, and the scenery along [them] tame and cheerless.

Streams

The parish is amply supplied with water by the numerous little streams flowing down its sides, which, being confined in dams, afford a sufficient supply of water power for the small corn mills in the parish and also for domestic uses.

Bogs and Island

The most extensive tract of bog in this parish is situated in Ahaloughan and the adjoining townlands, and at an average elevation of 300 feet above the sea. This bog is but little known except about its edges. It was formerly the bed of a large lake which was drained only 5 years ago, and a short time previous to which small boats could sail on it. A number of little valleys terminating in it, it is hollow and lowest towards its centre. The bog is very deep and so soft towards the centre that it is nearly impossible to cut drains through it, as it is there covered with a tough and elastic sward, forming what is commonly termed a shaskin, or quaking bog. There is still a large quantity of water underneath this shaskin. The subsoil is a whitish clay, and timber occurs in the usual manner through the bog.

This bog is remarkable for an artificial island, constructed on piles, which it contains. The island is 68 feet in diameter and perfectly circular. A row of piles, mostly oak and of various dimensions but very long, are driven in all around it. Its summit was convex, rising in the centre about 4 feet above the level of the bog. The soil of which it is formed consists of alternate layers of bog and whitish and reddish clay, and is 6 feet deep. Underneath the clay is a strong platform of oak timbers, mortised and jointed. Any attempt to penetrate this has been frustrated by the water rising from underneath. [There is] a small portion of a stone wall in which no lime but some tough clay had been used.

This island was discovered or rather noticed about a year ago by a man drawing the bog. He found on the platform a steel helmet or cap, composed of several spherical-shaped leaves of iron. The pieces were riveted together and the joinings covered with thin stripes of iron. The ends of the leaves were connected at the top by a circular button also of iron. One of the leaves came off, but the rest, though much rusted, remains otherwise uninjured. Near the helmet he found a very fine brass pan or basin, similar in shape to a soup plate and perfectly free from corrosion or dinges. Its diameter at the bottom is 10 inches and depth 2 inches, breadth of the rim 1 and a half inches.

An iron spur, old-fashioned weaver's shuttle of alder, an iron skene, a small oak oar 5 feet 8 inches long and a cart-load of cows' horns (similar to those of the Kerry cows) with 1 deer horn, were the articles found in this island. It is said that it was the abode of Arthur Oge O'Neill, a celebrated marauder. Curraghs have also been found on the shores of this lake.

There is an immense quantity of oak stumps of enormous size in the bogs along the Bann, and some very large trunks are also found. They do not preserve any particular direction, but all bear marks of combustion. What is rather singular, oak and fir stumps are to be found in the same tracts of bog resting on the subsoil. This occurs in the partially cut out bog in the townland of Brecart, near the Bann. Very few trunks remain here, but oak stumps predominate.

Woods

The immense quantity of brushwood still remaining in this parish and the quantity of timber found in the bogs furnish ample proofs of the former existence of forests in it: but the only natural timber still existing is in the Creagh bog along the Bann, where there is a small marshy tract covered with alders. The most prevalent brushwood is hazel, alder, oak and holly, patches of which are to be found in almost every townland in the parish, but particularly on the summits of the rocky hills. The tradition that "a man could walk on the trees from one side of the parish to another" is almost borne out by the brushwood still remaining.

[Insert addition: There are no ancient woods in the parish].

Climate

The climate of this parish is rather moist along the Bann and Loughs Neagh and Beg, and the crops do not come to maturity in these districts so soon as in the higher parts of the parish, where they ripen about a week earlier than those in Drummaul. The most prevalent wind is the south west which blows sharply during three-quarters of the year, but the most stormy wind is from the north west. It is a singular fact that it is within memory since the south east was the prevailing wind and since the seasons were much earlier than they now are. Sowing used, within memory, [to] commence about the middle and be nearly completed by the 20th March, while now, in 1836, little has been sown up to the last week in April. The moisture of the climate along the shore, arising from its proximity to the water, the marshy state of the inundated ground and the numerous tracts of partially cut-out and unreclaimed bog tend to cause fever and rheumatic complaints.

Parish of Duneane

MODERN TOPOGRAPHY AND SOCIAL ECONOMY

Towns: Toome

There is no town in this parish and the only village is Toome, which is situated at its western side, at the point where the Bann issues from Lough Neagh and on the great leading road from the southern districts of Derry and the northern of Tyrone to Belfast. The fine bridge on this road and over the Bann is at the northern end of the village and Toome is therefore the great thoroughfare between the counties of Antrim and Derry. Its situation, in summer, is cheerful, but there is something dreary and desolate in the appearance of the village and the bare and bleak appearance of the adjacent country.

Toome in all probability owes its origin to its being the most important and at one time one of the 4 great passes between the county of Antrim and those of Tyrone and Derry. This pass here was by a ferry about 100 yards south of the village. Its direction was diagonal to the course of the stream and about half an English mile in length. It was the only means of communication here until the erection of the bridge in 1792, and previous to that time was let at an annual rent of 45 pounds; and 2 boats, a small and a large one, were then quite adequate to the business of the ferry. Some idea of the increased thoroughfare may be formed from the fact that 200 pounds per annum have until lately been paid as rent by the person holding the tolls of Toome Bridge from Lord O'Neill, and the sum of 400 pounds per annum is now offered for them.

At the end of the ferry on this side are some fragments of the walls of the old castle of Toome, which seems to have been the defence of the pass. Nothing is here known of the history of this castle, but it is said to have been built by the O'Neills and to have been only 1 month in erection. The late Lord Macartney was the last governor, but it being a sinecure situation, was abolished. It must evidently be of some antiquity, from the description of the masonry. Only a small portion of a foundation wall is standing, but there are some fragments of the walls lying about. One of these measures 6 feet in thickness. The stones are small and grouted, the grouting so hard as to be with much difficulty broken. A small portion of a doorway remains. The stones forming the jambs are of composition similar to those used in Cranfield old church. They do not seem cut, but rather cast in a mould (a small piece of one of them is sent with this Memoir). No person now living remembers more of the castle standing, but they say their forefathers did.

The eel fishery is another cause of support to Toome, as during the seasons (from June to March) several hands (generally 8) are employed at it, and eels, fresh or salted, with pike and trout constitutes the chief food of its inhabitants.

Buildings in Toome

Toome consists of 26 houses, 2 of which are 3-storey and 11 2-storey houses, and the remainder are 1-storey cabins and cottages. They extend in a single line southward from the bridge for a fifth of a mile along the Belfast road. The 2 and 3-storey houses are tolerably good and slated, but not neatly kept. The 1-storey cottages are small, poor and comfortless, and mostly thatched. The houses mostly front the river, along which there is a row of trees. There is a large and good-looking 2-storey house used as an inn, near the centre of the town, but it is extremely dirty and comfortless, though much frequented in summer by persons who come from a distance to enjoy the fly-fishing here, which is reckoned equal to any in Ireland.

Conveyances

The coaches from Belfast to Derry and Cookstown change horses here. The former goes to Derry on Tuesdays, Thursdays and Saturdays and returns on Mondays, Wednesdays and Fridays. The latter goes and returns every day except Sunday. The mail from Dublin is conveyed on horseback from Randalstown and arrives at 20 minutes before 12 at noon, and is dispatched at 7 p.m.

Bridge at Toome

The only public building is the very fine bridge over the Bann. It is a plain and substantial structure, well finished but by no means heavy in its appearance. It consists of 9 semicircular arches, gradually lessening in span as they approach each end. Its extreme length over the waterway is 314 feet and between the extremities of the piers 451 feet, its breadth 21 feet. It is protected at the sides by a low parapet and neat iron railing. At the county Derry end is an iron gate and the toll gatherer's house. This bridge rises rather rapidly from either end to the centre. In 1798 one of the arches was broken down by the rebels to retard the pursuit of the king's troops.

This bridge was built in 1792 at the sole expense of the late Lord O'Neill, who obtained a grant from parliament, by letters patent, to build this bridge and to set a toll on it, of which he and his heirs were to be the proprietors. The first architect employed commenced building the bridge a little further down the river but, not finding a solid foundation and being otherwise unskilful, he was dismissed, a new architect employed and the present site chosen. This failure cost Lord O'Neill 3,000 pounds. For a list of the tolls, see appendix.

Remarks on People

The people of Toome are of the middle or lower class and are not opulent. They are engaged as petty dealers and hold small farms or as labourers. They are not an industrious class of persons.

Local Government

A manor court for the manor of Mullaghane is held monthly in Toome, for the recovery of sums not exceeding 20 pounds Irish, Peter Aickin Esquire, seneschal. Petty sessions are held on every alternate Wednesday, when 2 magistrates form the bench. There are 4 constabulary stationed in Toome.

Fairs

An annual fair is held on Easter Monday, more for amusement than any other purpose, as no cattle are exposed for sale in it. Crockery and pedlar's goods are almost the only articles except whiskey and cakes sold in it.

Toome is not increasing or improving, nor is there anything in it worthy of further notice.

MODERN TOPOGRAPHY

Public Buildings in the Parish

The public buildings in the parish consist of: the church, situated in the townland of Lismacloskey, near the centre of the parish and about a quarter of a mile south of the road from Randalstown to Magherafelt; is a simple little building 50 feet long and 19 feet wide, and containing accommodation for 227 persons. It was erected in 1729. It is perfectly plain. On its western gable is a little arch, from which is suspended a bell. It is not in good order. Tradition affirms that St Patrick commenced a church on or near the site of this one.

The Presbyterian meeting house is prettily situated in the townland of Ballylenully, on the southern side of the road from Randalstown to Magherafelt. It is said to have been originally built of mud, afterwards of stone and rebuilt by the congregation in 1815. It is a plain but substantially finished house, well fitted up inside and containing accommodation for 360 persons. Its dimensions are 60 feet long and 24 feet wide.

There is a Roman Catholic chapel in the townland of Ballymatoskerty, towards the northern side of the parish and on the southern side of the road from Ballymena to Toome. It was built by subscription in 1793 and was newly roofed and improved in 1835 by the congregation at a cost of 200 pounds. It is 60 feet long and 20 feet wide, commodiously fitted and has a large gallery. It contains accommodation for 1,800 persons. A bell was erected in 1835 on its northern gable and was the first bell erected on a Roman Catholic chapel in the province of Ulster, since the passing of the Relief Bill.

The second Roman Catholic chapel is situated in the townland of Cargin, towards the south of the parish. It is a plain substantial building 54 feet long and 22 feet wide, and containing accommodation for 500 persons. It was erected by subscription in 1821 and cost 600 pounds.

Gentlemen's Seats

Raymond Cottage, a seat of the Right Honourable Earl O'Neill, lieutenant of the county, is prettily situated in the townland of Drumraymond and on the shore of Lough Beg. It is said the cottage was originally built of wood by the late Lord O'Neill. It is quite rustic in its style, 1-storey, thatched, the windows octagonal and the walls studded with the beautiful pebbles of Lough Neagh. The cottage is small but kept in the nicest order. The grounds are tolerably extensive, tastefully laid out and thickly planted. It is 2 miles north of Toome.

Moneyglass House, the residence of Mrs Jones and the old family residence of the Jones, of whom "Bumper Squire Jones" or "Six-Bottle Jones" was not the least celebrated of its proprietors. It is a large family mansion situated in the centre of a well wooded and tolerably large demesne. The offices are at a distance from the house. The garden is very large, well stocked and walled and contains a very fine hothouse.

St Helena, the residence of the Reverend William Boyes, curate of the parish, is very prettily situated on an eminence in the townland of Moneyglass and [blank] miles north of Toome. The house is 2-storey and modern in its appearance.

Parish of Duneane

Brecart, in the townland of the same name, and about a half-mile north of Toome, is prettily seated on the shore of Lough Beg. It is the residence of Captain O'Neill.

Mills

The machinery of the parish consists of 2 corn and 2 flax mills. One corn mill is situated in the townland of Ballymatoskerty. The machinery is propelled by an overshot water wheel 16 feet in diameter and 3 feet 3 inches broad, [insert addition: fall of water 9 feet].

The other corn mill is in the townland of Derrysolough. The machinery is propelled by a breast water wheel 14 feet diameter and 3 feet broad, [insert addition: fall of water 10 feet].

The flax mill in the townland of Creggan is propelled by an undershot water wheel 14 feet 8 inches in diameter and 2 feet broad, [insert addition: fall of water 8 feet].

The flax mill in Killyfad is propelled by an undershot water wheel 15 feet in diameter and 2 feet broad, [insert addition: fall of water 17 feet].

Communications

This parish is amply supplied with main and by-roads, all of which are repaired at the expense of the barony. The principal road is that from Belfast to Magherafelt, which traverses the centre of the parish for 3 and a half miles. Its average breadth is 24 feet. It is very hilly and might be easily rendered much less so by conducting it round the hills and through the little valleys on the side of the ridge it passes over. It is in tolerable repair.

The road from Magherafelt to Ballymena through Toome passes through the parish for [blank] miles. It is in tolerable order and rather level. Its breadth is 23 feet.

The by-roads are in general good and sufficient in every respect.

The only bridge is that over the Bann at Toome. For a description of it, see under Bridge at Toome.

Scenery

Except in the diversity of its surface, this parish cannot in itself boast of anything striking or interesting. From the higher grounds in it there is one of the finest views in the north of Ireland: Lough Neagh with its shores in Derry, Antrim, Tyrone and Armagh [and] Lough Beg. The western side of the county Derry, with its numerous towns and villages, lie stretched beneath. The lofty mountain range in Derry and Tyrone on the west and that in Down and Antrim on the south and east form a magnificent boundary to the prospect.

SOCIAL ECONOMY

Early Improvements

The march of improvement has been less rapid in this parish than in the neighbouring one of Drummaul, the inhabitants of which are in general a more independent, orderly and civilised class than those of this parish. This is perhaps to be attributed to its having been less generally colonised by Scottish or English settlers and to its being a more retired district, little frequented by strangers, and those districts of it along its coast inhabited by people who are said to have almost wholly subsisted upon fish and to have neglected the cultivation of the ground. This is particularly borne out by the fact of there being still much uncultivated ground, either in the scraggy hills or numerous tracts of bog with both of which it abounds, and it would almost seem as if the increase of population had alone rendered the cultivation of the ground necessary.

There are a few very numerous clans or families, who constitute the majority of the population, and the dispositions and habits of these would imply their being of Irish descent. Among these are the McErlanes, who are very numerous and live chiefly along the River Bann and Lough Neagh, the McAteers, McAuleys and McCanns and McOwens. These families are said to be the descendants of the native Irish. The other numerous families are the Kennedys, Hannas and Fentons who, though exclusively Roman Catholic, are probably of English or Scottish extraction and live almost in colonies together, persons of the same names in some instances forming almost the entire population of a townland. [Insert marginal note: "Mayble" is a female Christian name not uncommon in this parish].

The principal causes of improvement seem to have been the establishment of schools and the exertions of the more active clergy of the present day.

Settlement of Scots

A small or partial settlement of Scots took place in this parish here at a very early date, as the present meeting house in the townland of [blank] is said to have been originally built of mud, as was also the church. The Presbyterians inhabit the interior of the parish, the Roman Catholics being chiefly found along its coast.

Calico and Linen Manufacture

The introduction of the manufacture of calico, union and linen into this parish has been a matter of great importance to it, and in the manufacture of some of these articles, but principally calico, the majority of the population are employed. Calico weaving has not been so profitable of late, and the elder branches of the family have latterly engaged more in the manufacture of linen while the younger members, including children of both sexes of from 12 years upwards, are engaged in weaving calico. This is here particularly advantageous, as since the introduction of mill-spun yarn, the women cannot earn a support by spinning and they can now earn from 2s 6d to 3s 6d by weaving calico. Their intercourse with strangers, which is now becoming more general, has also tended towards their civilisation, and though they certainly are improving, still they are in most respects considerably behind their neighbours in Drummaul and hold rather a low rank in the scale of civilisation.

Obstruction to Improvement

There are no legal obstructions to improvements, but this parish suffers from the want of some resident gentleman of influence, either as a landed proprietor or a magistrate, who by his example or influence could command the respect of the people. It is true there are several parishes in this county where the people are particularly orderly and where there is not a resident gentleman, for instance Kilraghts, but there they are educated and are of a more independent description of people, but here they are chiefly of the lower class, poor in their circumstances. Few except the rising generation are educated. Impatient of control and very turbulent, they have been wholly left to themselves until latterly, when they have been brought round a little by the exertions of their clergy.

Local Government

There is no magistrate resident in the parish, but there are several within short distance of it. There are 4 constabulary stationed in Toome, where petty sessions are held on every alternate Wednesday. A manor court and courts leet for the manor of Mullaghane are held in Toome, the former monthly and the latter twice a year, Peter Aickin Esquire, seneschal. Sums not exceeding 20 pounds are recoverable at these courts by civil bill process. The only outrages are riots and assaults which, though numerous, are of but a trivial description and are on the decrease. Illicit distillation was until a few years carried on very extensively in this parish, particularly along its coast, but it has latterly from a variety of causes declined considerably. There are few, if any, insurances.

Dispensary

This parish is included in the district of Randalstown dispensary, which was established in 1813. It has been attended with very beneficial results in this parish, where there are so many who could not otherwise obtain the assistance it affords. Smallpox is on the decrease, but fever is increasing, owing probably to the inferior quality of their food and the increased wetness of the seasons. It is of a very malignant nature and often proves fatal; but the most prevalent disease is scrofula, from which few of the lower class (the native Irish) along the coast are free. This is probably caused by the practice of intermarrying in the same family, for instance the McErlanes seldom intermarrying out of their own clan. This is also customary with several other families and it may be remarked there are more idiots or half-idiots along the shore, but particularly near Toome, than in any other rural parish in the county.

The dispensary has also promoted cleanliness in their persons and cabins, which are in general still far from being as much so as they ought. For a detailed account of this dispensary, see parish of Drummaul.

Schools

The general introduction of schools into this parish has been of comparatively recent date. Few of the passing generation of the poorer class have received any education, but they gladly send their children to school, though they take them from it at an early age, generally by 12, when they are able to earn something by weaving calico. The females receive but a very imperfect education, as their being instructed is not deemed a matter of consequence. The results of the introduction of schools is very perceptible in the rising generation. The children are remarkably quick of apprehension and it is not unusual to find children of 6 years old able to read the Scriptures and several of a year older who are learning writing. It is only from want of means that any children are kept from school.

Parish of Duneane

Poor

There are few strolling poor in this parish and, there being few who could assist them, they generally move to another; and, except the trifling collections at the places of worship on Sundays, there is no other funds for their support. There is such an equality among the people as to circumstances, or rather there being but few farmers or resident gentry in this parish, that the relieving of objects of charity falls heavily on the few who can afford to do so. The introduction of a system of poor laws would therefore in this parish be desirable.

Religion

By the revised census of 1834 there are in this parish 309 Protestants, 1,548 Presbyterians, 4,947 Roman Catholics and 80 of other sects. The vicar is non-resident, but pays his curate 80 pounds per annum. The Presbyterian and Roman Catholic clergy are supported in the usual manner by their flock and the former receives 75 pounds per annum regium donum.

Habits of the People

The inhabitants of this parish, particularly its districts along the shore, are far behind those of the neighbouring parish of Drummaul in civilisation. The Presbyterians chiefly occupy its interior or eastern districts and are a more peaceable, industrious and comfortable class of persons than its other inhabitants. The holdings or farms are much smaller and the people of a much poorer description than those in Drummaul. Their houses also are less comfortable and cleanly, the state of agriculture less improved and the general aspect of the parish as regards its artificial appearance, arising from the industry or neatness of its inhabitants, much inferior to the former.

In those districts inhabited by the Irish the appearance of their cottages and farms is characteristic of their own habits and dispositions. The houses are slovenly and comfortless and the ground partially cultivated, the fields being enclosed with crooked and insecure ditches, while the people are dirty and careless in their persons, unsettled and irregular in their dispositions, and the passing generation ignorant and unenlightened. It is true that there are many exceptions to these and the improvement in the rising generation, in the style of their cottages, their own persons and conduct, is striking.

Employment and Wages

The majority of the population are employed in the manufacture of either linen, union or calico, but chiefly the latter. The yarn is given out to them to be woven and they are paid according to the quality of their work. The men are now turning more to the weaving of linen, as calico does not afford such good wages as formerly, at which they can earn from 9s to 13s per week. Children of both sexes from 14 years upwards, and also a good many men, weave union, at which they can earn from 4s to 5s 6d per week, and at calico children of 12 years old are employed. They can earn from 2s 6d to 3s 6d per week, according to the age and ability of the person. The younger children are usually employed at winding bobbins or preparing the yarn for the shuttle. The members of a family being thus regularly employed and supported, very little attention has been paid to farming, and hence probably the cause of its neglected state.

Character and Houses

Along the western district of the parish the people are idle, ignorant and turbulent, prone to whiskey drinking and riotous, very impatient of control, careless in their persons and habitations, poor in their circumstances and manner of living and litigious and refractory. Their houses are small, damp and comfortless, many built of mud and all thatched, smoky and dirty. They seldom consist of more than 1 apartment, are lit by 1 or 2 small lead windows and but scantily furnished. They are generally in clusters of from 3 to 5 but are built without the least regard to regularity. Towards the interior of the parish the houses are of a better and neater description and the people of a more respectable class, gradually approximating in character and circumstances to those in Drummaul as they approach the confines of that parish.

Food and Dress

The people of this parish live but poorly and their food is of an inferior and less nutritive quality than formerly. Few of them possess a cow. They are therefore obliged to buy milk, chiefly buttermilk, and this with potatoes constitutes the food of the major proportion of the population. Fish, particularly eels which are caught in such quantities at Toome, formerly formed their chief subsistence, but now they are taken to the neighbouring markets, where a higher price than they can pay is obtained for them. Pike and trout are not near so plentiful as formerly. A fourth of the meal is not now consumed that was 10 years ago, the corn being now brought to market. Salt herrings are much used and baker's bread is now substituted for oaten by those who were in the habit of using the latter. They generally kill their pigs at home and send them to Belfast or Ballymena market.

They are much improved in their style of dressing and in the quality of their clothes, which they now procure at a much cheaper rate than formerly. On Sundays they appear cleanly and tolerably well dressed, but they are still behind the inhabitants of the more eastern parishes, not only in neatness but also in the quality of their attire. The women do not generally wear bonnets, though they are otherwise comfortably dressed. During the week their clothes, particularly those of their children, are ragged and squalid.

Turf, which is everywhere abundant, is their only fuel.

Longevity and Poverty

They are not so long-lived or healthy as formerly, owing, it is supposed, to their want of nourishment and the early age at which the children are put to work.

They marry early, particularly the Roman Catholics and the poorest class of them. They are poor and they think they cannot be worse, and that any change in their circumstances must be for the better. Many females are married at 16. This is another cause of their poverty, for a man who has got 6 acres of land and 5 sons will, on their marriage, allot an acre to each, on which he erects a hut. The father is liable for the rent of all, but this he seldom can procure from them. The land is inadequate for their support and all are reduced to poverty.

Amusements and Traditions

Their amusements are now but few. Dancing and cock-fighting used to be their favourite ones, but they are denounced by their clergy and partially given up. A fair, or rather a pattern, at Toome on Easter Monday is well attended by both sexes, but it has frequently been the scene of riots and sometimes of bloodshed. Wakes are much frequented as places of amusement, but less so than formerly; and now on their holy days or idle days about Easter or Christmas they generally loiter about the public houses and indulge in whiskey drinking.

They sometimes burn fires on St John's Eve and the Ribbonmen occasionally observe Patrick's Day by walking in procession. Secret societies prevail and it is said that nocturnal meetings are not infrequent. All sects, but particularly the Roman Catholics, are superstitious and place implicit belief in fairies [and] the cures performed by the water of Cranfield holy well. Their traditions concerning it, St Patrick, ghosts, banshees are still innumerable, but too absurd to be worthy of notice, as they neither tend to corroborate or throw light on any historical incident.

Hymns have taken the place of the Irish cry at funerals and wakes, as the former are encouraged by the clergy; but still, when the head or eldest person in any of the families before mentioned dies, the Irish cry is yelled at his funeral. Instruments of music such as clarionettes and flutes are used at Duneane chapel and have been once used at a recent funeral. At their wakes in the remote districts several low games are enacted and also playing on the "trump" or "jew's harp", but smoking and drinking and telling stories, particularly the former, are the chief amusement at these places.

Physical Appearance

There is not anything particularly remarkable in their features or appearance. The men are mostly of low stature. This is perhaps to be attributed to their being put to work at so early an age, their being confined almost entirely to the house and their being bent over the loom from morning to night.

Emigration and Migration

From 20 to 25 farmers' sons or labourers annually emigrate in spring to the British settlements in America and generally afterwards find their way on to the United States. Few return. This custom is rather on the decrease within the last 2 years, as the linen trade is taking the place of the manufacture of cotton in this parish and at present holds out good encouragement.

About 30 young men go annually to the Scottish harvests and return immediately they are over. This practice also is decreasing from the bad encouragement the Irish labourers have received in the last 2 seasons.

There is no record of this parish having been the scene of any remarkable events nor of its having given birth to any remarkable person.

Parish of Duneane

PRODUCTIVE ECONOMY

Table of Trades and Occupations

Blacksmith 1, constabulary 4, grocers 2, innkeepers 1, lodging houses for the poor 3, postmaster 1, schoolmaster 1, spirit shops 2, total 15.

Tolls

A schedule of the tolls paid on Toome Bridge: for each wagon 5s; for each coach 2s 6d; for each chaise 1s 6d; 1-horse gig or chaise 1s; 1 cart 1s; travelling cars loaded 6d, unloaded 3d; lime cars loaded 6d; a horseback load 3d; a person on horseback 2d, on foot 1d; bullock, cow, sheep or pig 1d; a person on horse running away 10s, a person on foot running away 5s; "sconcin" a car 5s.

Toome Fisheries

[Insert addition by G.W. Hemans: The right of eel fishing in the River Bann at Toome belongs to the Donegall family, to whom it was granted by charter in the year [blank] by [blank]. The salmon and trout caught here do not belong to them, but to the Coleraine Company. The mode of fishing for eels is by means of weirs or rows of stakes driven into the bed of the river in shallow parts, which conduct the eels in their passage down the river into narrow mouths or openings to which the stakes tend, where they are received into a long net, called here the "cochill net", and are taken up in the morning. Lord O'Neill at present rents the eel fishery from the Donegall family, for which he pays [blank]. By act of parliament the fishing is allowed to commence from 1st June and to continue until 1st March, but the best months are August, September and October. The establishments kept up for the fishing consist in cots, weirs and boats. 8 men are kept in constant employment during [no further information].

Table of Schools

[Table contains the following headings: name, situation and description, when established, income and expenditure, physical, intellectual and moral education, number of pupils subdivided by age, sex and religion, name and religious persuasion of master or mistress].

National school, in a house which is rather small, bought for the purpose in the townland of Moneynick, established 1833; income: from the Board of National Education annually 8 pounds, from pupils 12 pounds; intellectual education: spelling, reading, writing, arithmetic, books of the Board of National Education; moral education: the Scriptures and catechisms of all versions on Saturdays and hours set apart, visits from the priest; number of pupils: males, 22 under 10 years of age, 10 from 10 to 15, 8 above 15, 40 total males; females, 11 under 10 years of age, 3 from 10 to 15, 7 above 15, 20 total females; total number of pupils 60, 1 Protestant, 3 Presbyterians, 56 Roman Catholics; master Francis Grant, Roman Catholic.

National school, in a suitable house built for the purpose in the townland of Gallagh; intellectual education: spelling, reading, writing, arithmetic, books of the Board of National Education; moral education: the Scriptures and catechisms of all versions on Saturdays and hours set apart, visits from the priest; number of pupils: males, 9 under 10 years of age, 13 from 10 to 15, 3 above 15, 25 total males; females, 11 above 10 years of age, 14 from 10 to 15, 25 total females; total number of pupils 50, 3 Protestants, 7 Presbyterians, 40 Roman Catholics; master James Treanor, Roman Catholic.

London Hibernian Society's school, in a house the property of the teacher in the townland of Lisnaclusk, established 1832; income: from the London Hibernian Society annually 4 pounds, from pupils 8 pounds; intellectual education: spelling, reading, writing, sewing, books of the London Hibernian Society; moral education: visits from the clergy, Authorised Version of Scriptures daily, catechism on Saturdays; number of pupils: males, 5 under 10 years of age, 2 from 10 to 15, 7 total males; females, 11 under 10 years of age, 12 from 10 to 15, 23 total females; total number of pupils 30, 6 Protestants, 10 Presbyterians, 14 Roman Catholics; mistress Mary McCully, Protestant.

London Hibernian Society's school, in a house (now in a ruinous state) built for the purpose by subscription in the townland Creeve, established 1821; income: from the London Hibernian Society annually 8 pounds, from pupils 12 pounds; intellectual education: spelling, reading, writing, sewing, books of the London Hibernian Society; moral education: visits from the clergy, Authorised Version of Scriptures daily, catechism on Saturday; number of pupils: males, 26 under 10 years of age, 12 from 10 to 15, 38 total males; females, 25 under 10 years of age, 7 from 10 to 15, 32 total females; total number of pupils 70, 13 Protestants, 4 Presbyterians, 53 Roman Catholics; master James McLornan, Roman Catholic.

London Hibernian Society's school, in the kitchen of the teacher's father's house (an unsuitable place) in the townland of Moneyglass, established 1824; income: the London Hibernian Society pay the teacher on an annual average 10 pounds, from pupils 7 pounds; intellectual education: spelling, reading, writing, books of the London Hibernian Society; moral education: visits from the Protestant curate, Authorised Version of Scriptures daily, catechisms on Saturdays; number of pupils: males, 17 under 10 years of age, 2 from 10 to 15, 6 above 15, 25 total males; females, 8 under 10 years of age, 7 from 10 to 15, 15 total females; total number of pupils 40, all Roman Catholics; master Patrick Brady, Roman Catholic.

London Hibernian Society's school, in a suitable house rented by the teacher in the village of Toome, established 1833; income: the London Hibernian Society pay the teacher on an annual average 6 pounds 10s, from pupils 8 pounds; expenditure: the teacher pays for the house annually 2 pounds 12s; intellectual education: spelling, reading, writing, books of the London Hibernian Society; moral education: visits from the Protestant curate, Authorised Version of Scriptures daily, catechisms on Saturdays; number of pupils: males, 3 under 10 years of age, 14 from 10 to 15, 4 above 15, 21 total males; females, 5 under 10 years of age, 19 from 10 to 15, 24 total females; total number of pupils 45, 6 Protestants, 39 Roman Catholics; master Thomas Berry, Roman Catholic.

London Hibernian Society's school, in a house built by subscription in the townland of Staffordstown, established 1822; income: from the London Hibernian Society annually 4 pounds, from pupils 12 pounds; intellectual education: spelling, reading, writing, arithmetic, books of the London Hibernian Society; moral education: Sunday school, Authorised Version of Scriptures daily and catechisms on Saturdays; number of pupils: males, 13 under 10 years of age, 16 from 10 to 15, 29 total males; females, 22 under 10 years of age, 17 from 10 to 15, 39 total females; total number of pupils 68, 8 Protestants, 30 Presbyterians, 30 Roman Catholics; master James Glover, Presbyterian.

London Hibernian Society's school, in a small cabin the property of the teacher in the townland of Killyfad, established 1832; income: from the London Hibernian Society on an annual average 2 pounds 5s, from pupils 3 pounds; intellectual education: spelling, reading, writing, arithmetic, books of the London Hibernian Society; moral education: Authorised Version of Scriptures daily and catechisms on Saturdays; number of pupils: males, 9 under 10 years of age, 5 from 10 to 15, 14 total males; females, 11 under 10 years of age, 5 from 10 to 15, 16 total females; total number of pupils 30, 5 Protestants, 6 Presbyterians, 19 Roman Catholics; mistress Susan Gallagher, Roman Catholic.

[Totals]: income: 42 pounds 5s from public societies and benevolent individuals, from pupils 62 pounds; expenditure: house rent 2 pounds 12s; number of pupils: males, 104 under 10 years of age, 74 from 10 to 15, 21 above 15, 299 total males; females, 104 under 10 years of age, 83 from 10 to 15, 7 above 15, 194 total females; total number of pupils 393, 42 Protestants, 60 Presbyterians, 291 Roman Catholics.

Memoir on Ancient Topography by J. Stokes, [before] July 1837

ANCIENT TOPOGRAPHY

Ecclesiastical: Duneane Church

The parish church in Duneane townland is 50 feet by 22 feet in the inside. It is lit by 3 square windows in the side, and the east window. The portion of a thick ancient wall upon which the eastern gable has been erected evidently shows it to have been patched up out of an old one. This is corroborated by the circumstance of one gable being thicker than the other. The eastern gable is 3 feet 3 inches and the western gable 2 feet 9 inches thick. The walls are 3 feet. The more ancient wall protrudes from the bottom of the east gable thus: [small drawing]. The door is evidently modern, being of the adjacent form: [small drawing]. The roof is very high pitched thus: [small drawing].

According to tradition the old wall at the east gable and the 2 present side walls belonged to a monastic building that extended to 4 times the present length of the church. The entrance gate of the yard was then close to the door. At it there are still 2 large blocks of stone laid down like an unfinished cromlech. They were used as a horseblock by the monks and by their successors ever since.

It was originally an appanage and chapel of ease to Kells monastery. As for the foundation of the chapel, the tradition is obscure, some attributing it to St Patrick, others claiming that honour for St Bridget. After the siege of Derry, Major

Parish of Duneane

Dobbin, the then landlord, finding it much too large for the number of Protestants remaining in the parish, pulled down three-quarters of it, rebuilt the eastern gable and repaired the side walls. All is covered with a thick coat of plaster <plaister>, so that the character of the masonry cannot be seen. It may be mentioned that the side walls are completely decayed. They will not stand much longer.

Graveyard

There is no stone in the yard older than the siege of Derry. The tombstones are comparatively few and scattered. They are inscribed with the Scotch and Irish names usual to the parishes of Ballyscullion and Ahoghill.

In many parts there is such an unusual and thick growth of nettles reaching to the average height of 3 feet that the tombstones could not be examined. Nearly one-half the area of the yard was covered with that weed. This circumstance seems to show that under the graves are concealed the foundations of ancient buildings: at least that they are probably so, for it does not usually grow in any but dry strong grounds, very different from the soft material of the graveyard. If this one had been once covered with fragments and ruins of masonry, there is from thence at least a plausible explanation of the circumstance above mentioned. It is rendered more probable by the circumstance of its being said that the ancient graveyard stood apart from the present one. It lay in what is now a small cornfield at the foot of the hill on which the modern one is situated. The latter is about half an acre in extent. No wall surrounds it. The piers at the gate are cylindrical with conical tops, apparently not older than Queen Anne's age.

Mass Altar and Graveyard

In the townland of Moneynick there was formerly a fort on a hill (now altogether destroyed) at which there stood a Roman Catholic altar for the purpose of mass during the Penal Laws. Immediately adjacent to it there stood, covering about half a rood, a graveyard now altogether dug away. No standing stones or wall is remembered to have been at it or around it. Many human bones were found below the surface, but no coffin boards. The graves had been smoothed over to produce a good pasture field before the present tenant came to hold the farm in which it is situated. No coins of any kind were found in the immediate neighbourhood.

If there had ever been a holy well or cross near this graveyard or that of the parish church, it is long destroyed. There are none in any part of Duneane.

Military: Toome Castle

The foundations of Toome Castle extend over a space measuring 25 yards by 12. They stand on the summit of a small headland called Old Castle Point and are elevated to the height of 18 feet above the summer level of Lough Neagh. The waters flow up to the foot of the point. In the centre, there are the traces of a small cellar. The rest of it is very much overgrown with long grass and weeds, so much so as to conceal entirely the original arrangement of the foundations. At the side next the lake there was originally a very strongly built wall 12 yards long. This has been undermined by the beating of the winter floods of the lough and has fallen down in 3 great unbroken masses, thus showing the great strength of ancient masonry. See drawing[s]. They are composed of undressed stones grouted together.

The greater part of the stones of this castle were taken away to build the bridge of Toome. For its history, see the general Memoir. The erection of this bridge was the cause of its final destruction. A great many silver coins, very thin and of the modern sixpenny magnitude, were found about their foundations, as well as 2 cannon-balls, one a 24-pounder and the other an 18-pounder. It is said to have been burned in 1641.

Staffordstown Castle and Guardhouse

At the back of the hamlet called Staffordstown, at the distance of 4 miles from Toome, there was formerly a military building. All traces of it have long since been destroyed, leaving only to mark its site a great quantity of brick and mortar mixed up with the clay of the field. Its form and dimensions are not remembered.

It was a guardhouse to a castle that formerly stood 60 perches to the south east and of which considerable traces still remain. It was destroyed under the following circumstances. It was commanded in the year 1641 by a Sir Moses Hill, who had stationed a considerable body of troopers at it and at the guardhouse, for the purpose of protecting any Protestants who fled here for refuge from the adjacent counties. He posted the greater part of his force at the guardhouse.

Accordingly, many Protestants quickly took shelter, locating themselves within the area of the castle which, with the surrounding ditch, covered the space of 2 and a half Irish acres (or Cunningham). Their number continually increased till at length it amounted to more than 10,000 men, women and children, who pitched themselves within and without the entrenchment in huts and wigwams. Their retreat was quickly betrayed to the Irish by one Hill, the natural son of a Protestant and Catholic. They were suddenly surprised. The soldiers in the guardhouse were cut off from the main body. Sir Moses Hill was killed and all massacred. The former made an attempt to succour their friends by endeavouring to cut a way through the Irish to join them, but on seeing their desperate condition, fell back and fled to Randalstown. There they found the betrayer Hill in a house, sitting over a fire warming himself. He was immediately dragged out and hung *on the top of a slide car*.

It is more than probable that the quarter from which they were surprised was from the top of a hill rising suddenly from the west side of the castle and completely commanding it. In less than 3 minutes a large body of men could have rushed down the slope and surrounded the entrenchment. It rises to the height of 50 feet, commencing in the very next field. The remains of this entrenchment is 20 perches long by 18 wide. The western ditch is still perfect, being 18 perches long and 20 feet broad. It is at present 6 feet deep at an average but, being greatly filled with mud, that is evidently less than its original depth. The other 3 sides are partly dilapidated, filled up and occupied with a stream of water running along the bottom of the ditch. The corners, however, still remain, the ditch being everywhere 20 feet broad and the sides of the enclosed space all at right angles to one another.

That enclosed space never was cultivated until the father of the present occupying tenant built his farmhouse directly on the foundations of the keep or castle itself. The gable stands on part of Sir Moses Hill's cellar. The present farmer made an orchard and began to cultivate that enclosed space. In doing so he found the beginnings of 15 different pits of human bones. He immediately closed them up again. He also found, in working a ditch, many bones mixed with trooper's spurs, greatly decayed. Near every spur the bones of the leg always appeared. He also distinguished the fine teeth of women and the small bones of children in the pits which he closed up. More than half of the tract has been cultivated and broken up. The remainder is still in its original condition. The tenant is unwilling to disturb it, believing that it contains the principal deposit of bones.

It is more than probable that this castle was originally built by the Stafford family of Portglenone. They were the founders of Staffordstown, the adjacent hamlet, at first intended to be of much more considerable dimensions than it has at present. This entrenchment seems never to have had any outworks or bastions about the corners. There is a very large and copious spring in the interior. Several brass scales and iron wedges were found in it.

Pagan: Forts and Coves

The forts of Duneane are of the usual form, i.e. a circular platform encompassed by a ditch and rampart. [Insert footnote: It contains no cromlechs or giant's graves].

In James Lyle's fort, townland of Ballyclaghan, there were found in the bottom of the ditch a great number of wooden staves, hoops and mutton bones. In the interior much cinders and scoriae, like those of a smith's forge but larger, were picked up. Also some coins, two of which, still in the possession of the occupying tenant, appear to be ha'pennies of George I's reign. The impressions are very nearly effaced. There is a cove too, now choked up, but showing its roof above the surface. See the margin for a plan of the whole: [plan and section, with dimensions, inner trench 10 feet deep, scale quarter of an inch to a chain]. The outer rim of the ditch had once a parapet on it as high as the interior platform. It is now dug away. The outer edge of the parapet was strengthened by a neatly fitted row of stones laid side by side, each square and containing at an average a cubic foot. They were upon the whole circumference. A few remain still at "a." It appears probable that this fort and cove was inhabited in George I's reign by either a smith or a cooper? The tenant is about to level the whole of it.

There is a cove in John Edgar's fort, townland of Tamnyderry. The cave runs north and south through the centre of the fort. It is entirely choked up. The fort is now a circular garden 100 feet in diameter.

In Hugh McClarnan's fort, townland of Derrygowan, there was a cove, now demolished. It formerly extended from the parapet towards the centre of the fort.

In a cove in the townland of Moneynick there is, at the farthest end, a squared cavity about 2 feet wide similar in form and appearance and evidently intended for the same purpose as that described in the Ancient Topography of the

Parish of Duneane

parish of Banagher, county Londonderry. In the longest room there is a good floor of earth, but all the others are covered with loose stones. There is usually a great proportion of loose stones in every cove.

[Insert footnote: In each of the coves represented in drawing[s] nothing interesting was presented by any section. As usual the ceiling was always a little narrower than the floor, so as to make the side walls incline inwards].

Miscellaneous Discoveries

There are many flint arrowheads in the parish, but none of unusual form.

A very large quern-stone of freestone was found in the townland of Mullaghgawn, in a turf bog. It was 11 and a half feet in diameter and 2 and a half feet thick. It was circular and had no peculiarity in its form. No coins can at present be procured.

An ancient stone is said to have been removed about 30 years ago from Church Island to the house of Thomas Buttle Esquire of Toome, which house is now held by Mr David Weir. Under the influence of superstitious feelings, Mr Buttle soon brought it back to its original situation.

Artificial Island

In the townland of Derryhollagh there is, in a small flow bog known by the name of Lough Revel, a dried-up lake and artificial island in the centre of it. About 20 years ago there was a little water here and some wildfowl. The artificial island is circular, 75 feet in diameter. It was formed by a circle of stakes 73 feet in diameter, each 20 feet long at an average and set down perpendicularly. They are of white oak. 12 is the number of those that remain. 3 feet only of each appear above the surface of the island or rather, the surface of the excavations made by the tenant for the purpose of searching for ancient articles and drawing away the island for manure. He found a quantity of decomposed straw and heather. The last substance is still visible pressed down in flakes. They were all thrown upon a framework resting upon beams that connected the great stakes at the circumference with one another. It should be mentioned that the tops of these stakes are on a level with the top of the island and when pulled out are found pointed at the lowest end. Their greatest length therefore, 24 feet, shows that the lake was at time 20 feet deep.

At the island and in the bog round about the tenant found, in the harvest and summer of 1836, the following articles, viz. the remains of a boat with paddles and oars of oak, a brazen dish see drawing, some iron tools supposed to have been used in coining, 2 long knives, a brass instrument pointed like a pin, a Danes' pipe, a fragment of an ancient wooden dish, a pair of shears and old iron candlesticks, with beads and bullets, an ancient crock curiously carved see drawing, a dirk, a helmet and finally a cart-load of bones with cows' horns.

[Insert footnote: On the 22nd July Mr Boyle, having been the first to hear of the discovery by the tenant of some more ancient articles in this island, proceeded from Antrim to Derryhollagh to take drawings, dimensions etc. See his Mer. oirs for particulars of them.

It is not known with certainty in whose hands this helmet is at present. See drawing, however, for a representation of it according to description].

This island was inhabited by a robber called Art Ogue. He preyed upon the surrounding country and always found in his island a safe refuge, possessing as he did the only boat for many miles. At length the inhabitants succeeded in letting off the water by boring the side of the lake, but not without great loss of life to themselves from the attacks of the robber. It, however, had ultimately the effect of dislodging him. Some years ago, Lord O'Neill completed the drainage by ordering drains and cross-drains to be cut. It is probable from the modern character of many of the remains that this robber did not live at an earlier [period] than that of Queen Anne.

Moulds and Amber Beads

3 ancient moulds of slate for casting crucifixes in were dug up in a field of upland in the townland of Derryhollagh about 20 years ago.

A large string of amber beads, 58 in number, the largest about the size of a handball, the smallest about the size of a large pea, were discovered 12 years ago in a flow bog in the townland of Toome, at the depth of 1 foot from the surface.

Shoe

An ancient leather shoe, all in one piece except having a back seam, which was sewed with horse hair and of leather not well tanned or dressed but in a good state of preservation, was discovered in 1834 under the surface of a flow bog in the townland of Gallagh.

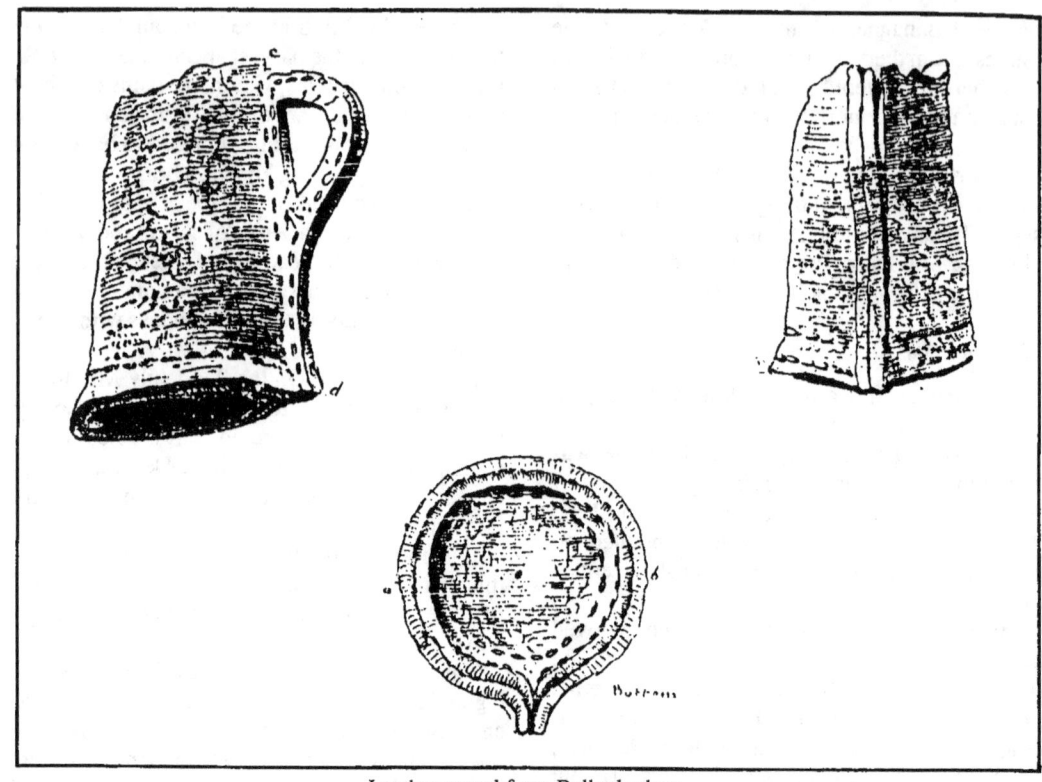
Leather vessel from Ballycloghan

Mether

A very ancient mether of the usual form is in the townland of Moneyglass and in the possession of Michael McErlane. There is nothing remarkable in its appearance. He had formerly an oak lossett or dish and an ancient churn. The former was 1 foot in diameter, circular and with no rim. The latter was made from one solid piece of timber and was dug from the edge of the bog in Moneyglass, at the depth of 3 feet from the surface.

Leather Vessel

An ancient vessel of leather, said to have [been] dug out of the parapet of a Danish fort in the townland of Ballycloghan, is represented in drawing. However, from the state of preservation presented by the stitching, it is not probable that it is very old.

Appendix of Drawings by J. Stokes

Drawings of Antiquities

Fragments of Toome Castle masonry on the beach of Lough Neagh, giving dimensions of 3 main sections and individual stone.

Cove in Mullaghgawn, "L"-shaped plan with dimensions, height of roof 3 feet, passages 16 feet; cove in Moneynick, "L"-shaped plan with dimensions, height of roof 3 to 6 feet, passages 18 feet and 18 feet plus 12 feet; helmet from Derryhollagh bog.

Brazen dish-like object found in Derryhollagh bog with section, 11 and half inches on base.

Fragment of rim of decorated pottery crock from Derryhollagh with side view and dimensions, rim 4 inches long, 2 and half inches deep, half an inch thick.

Leather drinking vessel, 2 side views and bottom.

Map showing relative position of standing stones.

Notes on Social Economy by J. Stokes

SOCIAL ECONOMY

Relief of Poor

The poorest townland in the parish of Duneane is that of Derryhollagh. It contains 32 cottier houses with sod gables and in very bad repair. There are 22 farmers. There are no regular

Parish of Duneane

paupers as yet resident in it, but many of the cottiers are on the eve of going out as paupers. On an average about 12 of them are relieved each week by each farmer. They give about 2 stone of potatoes in the week which, at 3d per stone, would amount to 6d from each or 11s a week from them all.

The richest townland is Carmain. It contains 12 cottier houses, all of stone and in good repair. There are 20 farmers. On an average about 24 paupers are relieved weekly by each farmer. The value of the charity given amounts to 1 pound a week, each farmer giving in that time victuals to the amount of 1s. On the church list there are the names of but 3 persons, namely 2 Protestants and 1 Catholic. In 1829 the annual amount of the collection from which they receive relief was 7 pounds 13s 7d ha'penny. In 1836 it was 6 pounds 19s 9d ha'penny, including a collection at a charity sermon of 2 pounds 15s 3d.

Clergy

The annual income of the Reverend Denis Magreevy is 150 pounds. He is the parish priest. The congregation of the Established Church consists of persons from the parish of Duneane and the grange of Ballyscullion. The curate gives a lecture in a farmhouse in the grange every Sunday evening.

Traditions

Fires on St John's Eve are still continued. Nothing more than cheering and running with lighted torches takes place.

Remarkable Events

About 80 years ago a murder was committed on a woman called Gallagher. The dead body was found in Derryhollagh bog and then laid at the chapel on the ensuing Sunday. All the congregation were commanded by the priest to touch the body, it being supposed that it would bleed afresh on coming into contact with the murderer. To their disappointment, however, no such phenomenon <phaenomenon> took place.

Drinking

The quantity of permit spirit supplied by the excise man to the publicans in his district, i.e. from Antrim to Toome, in the 3 months ending 1st April 1837 was 4,522 gallons.

Fair Sheets by J. Bleakly, March to July 1837

NATURAL FEATURES

Planting

There are 4 or 5 rows of trees planted along the road from Toome to Brecart, chiefly fir, birch and alder, along the road to Samuel Fineston's house, planted by Lord O'Neill about 40 years.

The planting at the edge of the lake at John O'Neill's house in the townland of Anaghmore is chiefly fir, planted 28 years ago by John O'Neill. From John Stafford.

Bogs

Brecart flow bog is at present about 5 feet deep. The imbedded timber consists of black oak. The largest found is about 3 feet in diameter across the face. No other imbedded timber is found in this bog. From Robert Berry and Alick McCullagh.

Toome flow bog: its average depth is about 5 feet. The imbedded timber consists chiefly of black oak, very small, only fit for roofing small cabins. There have also been small pieces of yew found in this bog. All the above bogs are said to have been cut away. The original depth in the deepest parts is said to have been about 15 feet.

The flow bog in the townland of Galliagh: its average depth is about 8 feet. The only imbedded timber consists of oak about 18 inches in diameter and found on the clay with the top eastward. From Andrew Wilson and Nicholas McIntyre, farmers. 8 March 1837.

Annaghmore flow bog is about 10 feet deep in the deepest part. Oak is the only imbedded timber worth notice, and that only 18 inches in diameter across the face and found near the clay with the top eastward. From Edward Walsh.

The flow bog near Lough Beg in the townland of Drumraymond: its depth is not well known, but at the edge it is about 10 feet deep. Oak is the only imbedded timber but very little of it is found. The largest is said to have been about 2 feet across the face in diameter and found with the top eastward. From Sergeant Pelan.

Natural Wood

There are about 3 acres of natural wood in the townland of Moneyglass, but all cut down and replanted 3 years ago with all kinds of forest trees, Irish growth, by Mrs Jones, proprietor.

Modern Topography

Toome Bridge

The following tolls are to be paid at the bridge, which has been erected at private expense according to act of parliament. Founded on the site of a ferry granted to the proprietor by letter patent from the Crown.

A wagon 5s, a coach 2s 6d, a chaise 1s 6d, an horse chair or gig 1s, a cart 1s, travelling car loaded 6d, travelling car not loaded 3d, lime cars loaded 6d, a horseback loaded 3d, a person on horseback 2d, a person on foot 1d, bullock and cow each 1d, sheep and pigs each 1d, a person on horseback running away 10s, a foot person running away 5s, for sconcin on a car 5s.

The bridge was built in the year 1787 by the late Lord O'Neill and cost [blank]. The present Lord O'Neill is the proprietor, who receives the benefit of it. Edward Neeson holds it in contract for the year ending 1837. Proposals were given to Lord O'Neill for the bridge by John Sheil Esquire of Blackpark, county Derry, at 400 pounds. 200 pounds is the sum usually paid for the bridge, although 500 pounds was offered by 2 persons for it last year. The bridge was formerly begun to be built about 10 perches farther down on the Bann and the foundation laid but, the bottom being bad, it failed and about the sum of 3,000 pounds is said to have been lost by the failure.

The bridge is 21 feet broad on the top. The wall at the centre part of the bridge is 1 and a half feet thick and 2 feet high. The paling is of iron on the top of the wall and is 3 and a half feet high. The iron paling is 4 and a half feet high. The timber of the bridge is of forest oak and is said to have grown at St Helena in townland Moneyglass. The bridge spans the River Bann with 9 arches: no.1, or the arch next Toome, is 21 feet in the span; no.2 25 feet in span; no.3 34 feet in span; no.4 37 feet in span; no.5 43 feet in span; no.6 34 feet in span; no.7 38 feet in span; no.8 34 feet in span; no.9 21 feet in span. The toll-house is at the county Derry end of the bridge. Information obtained from Edward Neeson, John Crawford and David Weir. 14 July 1837.

Natural Features

River Bann

The average depth of the river where the ferry was is about 10 feet at low water mark with a gravel bottom. The River Bann deposits useful soil upon the lands which are flooded and the meadow is generally enriched by it.

Modern Topography and Social and Productive Economy

Toome Village

Toome is a small village situated on the banks of the Bann near the bridge and contains 22 houses, 6 of which are 2-storey high and slated, and 2 are 1-storey high, slated, and 14 are 1-storey high, thatched. The oldest house in the village is a thatched house or rather a cabin occupied by John Crawford and is about 120 years built, but now in a state of dilapidation. The hotel, which is now unoccupied, is the oldest 2-storey house in the village. This house, with the market house and police barracks, were all built in 1786, all slated. 3 houses are uninhabited. The houses are nearly all in very bad repair, chiefly owing to the bad encouragement given by the proprietor.

Fairs and Markets

There is a fair for pleasure held on every Easter Monday, and many who have had previous disputes assemble on that day in the fair to take revenge with the stick. About 12 years ago a man named Michael Richey was killed at this fair. 15 July 1837.

There is also a monthly market held. It was established the year which the bridge was built, but it is now almost reduced to nothing. A cloth market was also held in the village, but ceased [blank] years ago. There is nothing sold in the fair but crocks, gingerbread and soft goods and hardware, nothing in the market but crocks and delf. The inhabitants chiefly live on fish, no meat nearer than Randalstown <Ranaldstown> and Ballymena.

Trades and Occupations in Toome

The following are the trades and occupations: post office 1, publicans 1, grocers 4, weavers of linen and union 4, lodging houses 5, cottiers 1, labourers 1, farmers and blacksmith 1, constabulary 4. The stones to build the houses were procured at the Carn rock, a short distance from the town, lime from the neighbourhood of Magherafelt, slates from Ballyronan and Belfast, and the timber (chiefly fir) from Belfast.

Constabulary

Toome became a station for constabulary about 10 years ago and has, since the commencement, been a station for 4 men. 16th and 17th July 1837.

Parish of Duneane

Fisheries

The fishery was established by the Marquis of Donegall, who obtained it by letters patent from the Crown about 10 years ago. Lord O'Neill gave the sum of 8,000 pounds of an input and 400 pounds per annum to the Marquis of Donegall. The amount of the Bann fishery in 1800 was about 300 pounds.

The eel fishery commences in March and ends in June. The eel fishery is said to be on the decrease (as to the quantity of fish taken) since Lord O'Neill became proprietor. Information obtained from Sergeant Phelan, keeper of the fishery, John Crawford and David Weir.

Ferry

The right of ferry belongs to the Marquis of Donegall. The ferry was about 5 perches above the upper side of the bridge, on which was 2 boats, viz. 1 large one and 1 small one, the large boat for cattle and the small boat for foot passengers. A foot passenger paid 1d, a horse and man 2d, a horse with back load 3d, horned cattle 1d each, sheep 1d each, pigs 1d each, loaded car 6d, empty car 3d. 18 July 1837.

Communications

The leading road from Toome to Belfast is 21 feet clear of drains and fences, and in middling repair, made by contract for 5 years at 7d 3 farthings per perch from Toome to Randalstown, 2,050 perches, by Robert Berry of Brecart townland. Also the road leading from Toome to Ballymena is kept in repair by contract for 5 years at 4d ha'penny per perch, by Andrew Quinn of Moneyglass townland. These are the only roads made or kept in repair by contract in the parish. This road is also 21 feet wide clear of drains and fences, and in good repair.

The road leading from Randalstown to the lake is 21 feet broad clear of drains and fences, and in good repair by presentment. Also the by-road leading from this road to Toome is 16 feet broad, kept in repair by presentment and in middling repair.

The Staffordstown by-road leading from the Gallows Corner to Staffordstown is 21 feet clear of drains and fences, and in good repair, kept in repair by presentment of the grand jury. Also the by-road leading from the Ballymena <Ballymenna> road to the Belfast road is 16 feet clear of drains and fences, also by presentment and in middling repair. Information obtained from Robert Berry and Andrew Quinn, contractors. 20 July 1837.

Mills

Ballymatuskerty corn mill is on the leading road from Portglenone to Randalstown. Lord O'Neill is the proprietor. The machinery is contained in one house, which is built of stone and lime, slated. The roof is in bad repair. There is only 1 water wheel, by which the machinery is worked, and is 16 feet in diameter. The breadth across the paddles is 2 feet. The fall of water, or height above the part of the circumference which first comes in contact with the stream, is 12 feet, but is idle from want of water from March till November. Information obtained from William Dobbin, miller.

There is also a corn mill in the townland of Duneane, near the church, but in a state of dilapidation and has not worked any for the last year. The water wheel is all broken. James Courtney is the proprietor. Information obtained from the proprietor.

Established Church Congregation

The Established Church congregation consists of persons from the parish of Duneane and the grange [of Ballyscullion ?]. The curate gives a lecture in a farmhouse in the grange on every Sunday evening after divine service in the church. 21 July 1837.

Parish Census

The following is a copy of the census taken from the enumerator's book in 1834 by the Reverend William Boyes, curate of the parish of Duneane: Established Church 306, Roman Catholics 4,988, Presbyterians 1,518, total 6,812.

Income of Rector and Curate

The rector is the Reverend George McCartney, whose annual income from the parish of Duneane is 230 pounds tithe composition. His residence is at Killead parish.

The Reverend William Boyes is the curate, whose annual income is 75 pounds, paid by the rector.

Poor

There are only 3 poor persons whose names are on the church list receiving poor box money, viz. 2 of the Established Church and 1 Roman Catholic. In 1829, the year after the curate came to the parish, the collection amounted to 7 pounds 13s 7d ha'penny, and in 1836 it amounted to 6 pounds 19s 9d ha'penny, including a collection at a charity sermon which amounted to 2 pounds 15s 3d. The average attendance at Duneane church on each Sunday throughout the year amounts to about 60 persons. From the Reverend William Boyes, curate, and the churchwarden Edward Rice. 22 July 1837.

Residence of Curate

The residence of the curate, the Reverend William Boyes, is a 2-storey house situated on the top of a hill in the townland of Moneyglass, called St Helena, built about 35 years ago by David Babington Esquire. Mrs Jones of Moneyglass is the head proprietor. The curate is only a lodger. Henry River Birch Esquire is the proprietor or tenant. The house is insured. Information obtained from Reverend William Boyes, curate, and Henry River Birch Esquire.

Union Hall

Union Hall is the residence of Mr Robert Davison. The house is 2-storey high, slated, and was commenced in 1834 and finished in 1837, and cost 1,000 pounds. It is situated near the corn mill in the townland of Ballymatuskerty, on Lord O'Neill's estate. The above appropriate name was given to it by the proprietor Mr Davison, as it was from the benefit of the union linen Mr Davison made his money. From Mr Robert Davison, proprietor.

Cotton Bank

The Cotton Bank is the residence of Mrs McMullan. The house was built about 24 years ago by Mr James McMullan. The house is 2-storey high, slated. The planting consists of fir, larch, beech, alder and birch planted about 20 years ago, situated in the townland of Ballymatuskerty. From Mrs McMullan, proprietor. 23 July 1837.

SOCIAL ECONOMY AND MODERN TOPOGRAPHY

Gallows Corner

The Gallows Corner is at the second crossroads leading from Toome to Randalstown and is so called from 2 men who were hanged at this corner about 27 years ago for the murder of Alexander McCullagh of the townland of Toome. The names of the men hanged were John Chambers and Robert Montgomery, natives of the county Derry. From Mr David Weir, Robert Berry and John Crawford.

Income of Presbyterian Clergy

The income of the Reverend Archabald Hutchinson, Presbyterian minister of the parish of Duneane, is 50 pounds per annum regium donum and 50 pounds per annum stipend. His residence is in the townland of Drumderg.

Meeting House: Collection and Congregation

The average collection in the meeting house amounts to 4s 6d each Sunday. During the last 15 years the repairs of the meeting house amounted to 180 pounds, by subscription of the inhabitants. The average attendance on each Sunday amounts to about 250 families; about 50 of those families are nominal and not hearers in communion. The meeting house was rebuilt about 25 years ago. Nearly 1 acre of land is attached to the meeting house.

Meeting House

The Presbyterian meeting house was formerly a thatched house but was rebuilt about 25 years ago and slated. The total dimension inside is 57 by 30 feet. It contains 30 pews, 2 of which are double pews, each 10 by 5 feet and 28 single pews, each 10 by 3 feet. The floor is of earth except 2 double pews which are boarded. The aisle is 6 and a half feet wide. There are 10 windows, oval shaped, viz. 4 on each side, and 1 on each end, each 3 feet wide, of glass. There are 2 doors on the side or front of the meeting house, each 6 and a half by 4 feet. There is nearly 1 acre of land attached. The border round the yard is planted with 3 rows of Scotch fir and ash trees planted about 15 years ago. The oldest tombstone is erected to the memory of Margaret Baily, who died August 20th 1816. The pews are in very good repair. The meeting house is in the townland of Ballyglenullar.

Original Presbyterian Clergy

The first in the memory of the oldest inhabitant was the Reverend Robert Scott, the second was the Reverend Henry Cook, the third was the Reverend [blank] Elder, the fourth is the Reverend Archabald Hutchinson who still continues. From the Reverend Archabald Hutchinson, minister. 28 July 1837.

Parish of Duneane

Mills

There is a flax mill in the townland of Ballyglenullar, near the leading road from Toome to Randalstown. The machinery is contained in 1 house which is 1-storey high. There is 1 water wheel which is 16 feet in diameter and 2 feet 1 inch across the buckets. The fall of water is 8 feet. This mill is idle during the summer from want of water, the house and machinery in very good repair. Information obtained from Robert Chesney, proprietor.

Roman Catholic Chapel at Cargin

There are 2 Roman Catholic chapels in the parish. The one in the townland of Cargin was built 13 years ago, chiefly at the expense of the congregation. The ground floor is of earth. There are only 1 row of single pews around the wall of the lower part, 34 in number, each pew 74 by 2 feet 4 inches. The gallery contains 60 pews single, each 8 and a half by 2 feet 4 inches. The space occupied by the altar is 18 by 12 feet. The same span is unoccupied on the gallery. The total dimensions of the chapel inside is 70 by 30 feet. There are 2 doors on the ground floor viz. 1 on each end, each 4 and a half feet broad, arched at the top. The door leading to the gallery is at the back of the chapel outside. There are 6 windows, Gothic style, on the front, the one half of each window showing light to the gallery and the other half showing light to the lower part. There are also 1 large window and 2 smaller windows on each end of the gallery, all in excellent repair. There are 3 rows of Scotch fir trees planted round the yard, planted about 13 years. Lord O'Neill gave 10 guineas towards its erection and General O'Neill gave 5 guineas.

The following are the original Roman Catholic clergy, as far back as can be ascertained from the oldest inhabitant. About 127 years ago the Reverend Henry McCorrey was the priest of this parish and he was succeeded by the Reverend [blank] McVey. The third was the Reverend Paul McCarton, the fourth was the Reverend Felix Cunningham, the fifth was the Reverend Hugh Devlin, the sixth was the Reverend [blank] Murray, the seventh was the Reverend John McMullan, the eighth was the Reverend Dennis Magreevy, who is the present and came to this parish 12 years ago. This is the first Roman Catholic chapel which was erected in this part of this parish. Previous to the erection of this, mass was celebrated in a church of wood where the present chapel stands. Residence of the parish priest is at lodgings near the church of Duneane. From the Reverend Dennis Magreevy, parish priest, and Hugh McMullan, farmer. 1 March 1837.

The Roman Catholic chapel at Cargin was built by subscription and cost 600 pounds. From Hugh McIntyre and Henry McCrudden of Moneynick townland.

Moneyglass Roman Catholic Chapel

The Roman Catholic chapel in the townland of Moneyglass was built in the year 1792 at the expense of the congregation, and in 1835 it was raised 4 feet higher and a new roof, with 16 single pews at the lower part and 16 Gothic windows, with an iron gate and wall at front. Total cost of all the above repairs in 1835 165 pounds, all by subscription of the congregation.

The gallery was erected 12 years ago. The wall in front at the gate is 5 and a half feet high. The chapel inside is 71 by 30 feet. The floor is of earth. There are only 16 single pews on the floor, each 10 and a half by 2 and a half feet, and 1 pew on the gallery, double, for the singers. There [is] nothing more than steps on the gallery, no pews nor forms, and is the full extent of the chapel, except 15 by 3 feet which is occupied by the altar. There are 6 Gothic windows on the front and 1 Gothic window on each end, and 1 at the altar, each 3 feet wide, and 2 square windows on the back side, small. There are 2 doors, 1 on each end, each 4 feet wide, square, and 1 door on the gallery which is outside and is 3 and a half feet. There are 2 crosses, 1 on each end, and a good bell. There are 6 small bells hung above the altar.

The oldest tombstone is dated 1815. There are 2 rows of fir trees round the graveyard. From the Reverend Dennis McGreevy, parish priest, and Patrick McCort. 4 March 1837.

Remarkable Circumstance: Triplets

About 18 years ago Mary Gormley of Toome brought forth 3 children at one birth. All lived for some short time.

Post Office

The post office at Toome was established the year after the bridge was built.

Superstitions of the People

Daniel Mellon, who resided in the townland of Artlone some short time ago, built his house near the Danish fort. On Thursday the 2nd March this year, 1837, he died of paralysis at the age of 54 years. His superstitious neighbours affirm that he was shot by the fairies. From Moses Mays.

Scripture Reader

The schoolmaster of the Staffordstown school is a Scripture reader and itinerates through the parish. Appointed by the London Hibernian Society, income is 4 pounds 10s per annum; merely teaches the Scriptures' grammatical meaning. From James Glover and Reverend William Boyes. 6 March 1837.

Sunday School

There is a Sunday school held in the day schoolhouse at Staffordstown during the whole year, except the winter, and is said to be well attended. From James Glover, schoolmaster.

Fires at St John's Eve

Fires at St John's Eve are still continued in this part. Nothing more than cheering and running with lighted torches takes place.

Superstitions

The same superstition prevails through this parish also with respect to fairy or gentle bushes and the veneration for them, the same as in county Derry, as many of them are to be seen standing alone in the midst of cultivated fields. From the Reverend William Boyes and John Stafford.

Sunday School and Night School

There is a Sunday school held in the national schoolhouse in the townland of Gallagh and which is said to be well attended, but is not held during the winter quarter. A night school is also held in the same schoolhouse during the winter, but none this winter from want of fire. From the parish priest and Lawrence Trayner, schoolmaster.

Brecart Tower

Brecart Tower is the residence of Captain Daniel O'Neill. It was in 1818 the house was commenced and almost every year since that time additions have been built to it by Captain O'Neill. Previous to the above date, it was a thatched cottage. Information obtained from Captain O'Neill and Mr David Weir, postmaster. 9 March 1837.

Local Government

About 3 years ago the magisterial bench was established in Toome and was held in a [room] below the hotel, but is now held in a large parlour of Mr David Weir's in the 2-storey house above the village. Bench days are on every second Tuesday. John Sheil Esquire of Blackpark, county Derry and John Hill Esquire of Bellaghy, county Derry were the first magistrates, but now only Mr Sheil attends. From Mr Sheil and David Weir.

Market House

The market house at Toome was erected at the expense of Lord O'Neill and the manor of Mullaghgawn. Lord O'Neill discharged one-half of the expense. The manor court is held in the market house once a month, seneschal Major Higgison.

Barrack

Toome was a military station for many years for both horse and foot. The barrack was the first house on the left turning the Moneyglass road, now occupied by Sergeant Pelan, clerk to the fishery.

Markets

The main body of the people of the parish of Duneane go to Ballymena, about 10 miles distant Irish, to fairs and markets. A few go to Randalstown and Magherafelt. From Mr William Birch and the Reverend Archy Hutchinson. 14th March 1837.

Gentlemen's Seats

About 12 years since, a gentleman's house stood near the church of Duneane and was at that time occupied by cottiers. The last gentleman who occupied it was Harkness Ellis Esquire. The house was built by one O'Roarke before King William's war. Nothing remains of the house at present standing. From William Carey and Rigby Barry, farmers.

Poorest Townland

The poorest townland in the parish of Duneane is Derryhollagh. It contains 32 cottiers' houses, built of stone with sod gables, thatched and in very bad repair, mere cabins. There are no regular paupers in this townland but many of the cottiers are on the eve of going out as paupers. On an average, about 12 paupers are relieved each week by each farmer, of 22 in the townland, each giving about 2 stones of potatoes in the week at 3d per stone, which would amount to 6d from each farmer per week

Parish of Duneane

in the above townland. Total amount of the charity thus given, 11s per week.

The greatest poverty exists in the cabins at Art Ogue's mill. The cause of their poverty is chiefly owing to the very great failure in the cotton and linen trade, as the greater portion of the inhabitants (chiefly females) are weavers and live by it. Many of the females, particulary those at Art Ogue's mill, have been brought to their poverty by misconduct. Lord O'Neill is the proprietor of the above townland. Information obtained from John Wilkinson, Charles McClean, farmers in the townland, 14 March 1837.

Richest Townland

Carmain is the richest townland in the parish. It contains 12 cottiers' houses, all built of stone, thatched and in tolerable repair. There are 20 farmers in this townland, each paying from 32s 6d to 34s 2d per acre. On an average, about 24 paupers are relieved weekly by each farmer. The value of the charity given would amount to 1 pound per week, each farmer giving to the value of 1s each per week. The worst time for the poor is from spring till harvest, as many of the poor householders are compelled from want to go as paupers during the summer season. From John McKowen and John Thompson, farmers. 15 March 1837.

Superstition

The Roman Catholics and also many of the Established Church will not keep a tobacco pipe in the house after the corpse is interred, lest they should have further use for them by the deaths of some other of the family.

Muckrim Rocks

Mass is said to have been celebrated on Muckrim rocks near the Roman Catholic chapel at Moneyglass, before the chapel was built. From Mr William Birch and the priest.

Cottage at Brecart

Brecart Cottage is situated on the north east side of the Bann in the townland of Brecart, near the tower. The house was erected about 50 years ago by John O'Neill Esquire, who was succeeded by Mr Samuel Finiston. The present proprietor is Mr Finiston's son, Mr Samuel Finiston. The planting consists of all sorts of forest trees of Irish growth, about 7 acres Irish plantation measure. From Mr Samuel Finiston, proprietor.

Bann Fishery

About 10 years ago the Bann fishery was held by Mr Samuel Finiston for 25 years. The gross amount of its value was 1,600 pounds per annum, the net amount was 1,000 pounds per annum. Information obtained from Mr Samuel Finiston of Brecart Cottage. 17 March 1837.

Bridge at Toome

The toll of the bridge at Toome is undoubtedly one of the greatest obstacles to the improvements of the country, as it prevents a greater intercourse between the 2 counties. From David Weir and Samuel Finiston.

Tower at Brecart

The tower at Brecart is nearly square and 11 feet by 10 feet outside. The door is square and on the west side of the tower, 5 and a half by 2 feet broad.

Raymond Cottage

Raymond Cottage is about 60 years erected; was originally a frame of wood erected at Shane's Castle and brought down by water, and placed in the townland of Drumraymond, where it has been considerably improved year after year by Lord O'Neill. The walls are all of wood, plastered and pebble-dashed outside. The roof is thatched. The planting consists of all sorts of forest trees, Irish growth, and evergreens of all sorts, about 12 acres 2 roods and some perches. The last was planted in 1835. From Sergeant Pelan and James Crawford.

Sunday Schools

There is not a Sunday school at present in existence in the parish, chiefly owing to the want of teachers [and] of zeal in the people to send out the children. There are no Sunday schools held in this neighbourhood during the winter season. From the Reverend William Boyes, curate. 18th March 1837.

Income of Roman Catholic Clergy

The annual income of the Reverend Dennis McGreevy, parish priest of Duneane, is about 150 pounds paid by the congregation. From the Reverend Dennis McGreevy.

Moneyglass House

Moneyglass House is 3-storey high with 2 pillars in front, on the top of which is a balcony on each, built in 1787 by Thomas Morris Jones Esquire.

The ancient beech tree at the old lawn at Moneyglass House is said to have been a hiding place for many persons during the rebellion of '98.

Market House in Toome

The market house in Toome is 50 by 20 feet inside. The room where the manor court is held upstairs is 31 by 2 [20?] feet inside. The jury room is 10 by 20 feet inside. From Patrick McLorinan, courtkeeper.

By-roads

The by-roads of this parish are all 16 feet clear of drains and fences and only in tolerable repair, made by presentment and kept in repair by the same at the expense of the county.

Toome Village: Houses

[Table lists house number, occupation of owner, number of storeys, whether slated or thatched].

No.1, post office, grocer and farmer, 1-storey, thatched.
No.2, fish-seller, grocer and farmer, 1-storey, thatched.
No.3, fish-seller, grocer and farmer, 1-storey, thatched.
No.4, grocer, 1-storey, thatched.
No.5, farmer, 1-storey, thatched.
No.6, lodging house, 1-storey, thatched.
No.7, blacksmith, 1-storey, thatched.
No.8, farmer and lodger, 2-storey, thatched.
No.9, publican and grocer, 3-storey, slated.
No.10, labourer, 2-storey, slated.
No.11, farmer, 2-storey, slated.
No.12, market and court house, 2-storey, slated.
No.13, hotelkeeper, 2-storey, slated.
No.14, publican, 2-storey, slated.
No.15, lodging house and [publican ?], 2-storey, slated.
No.16, police barrack, 2-storey, slated.
No.17, empty (late a grocer), 2-storey, slated.
No.18, widow, 1-storey, slated.
No.19, labourer, 1-storey, thatched.
No.20, labourer, 1-storey, thatched. 2nd May 1837.

Insurances

There are 3 houses insured in the parish of Duneane. From Mr Samuel Finiston and David Weir. 20 March 1837.

Permit for Spirits

The quantity of permit spirits supplied by the excise man to the publicans in his district, i.e. from Antrim to Toome, for the last 3 months from the 1st January to 1st April 1837, amounts to 4,522 gallons. Information obtained from Mr Edward Skinner, excise man, Antrim.

ANCIENT TOPOGRAPHY

Church at Duneane

The church is situated in the townland of Duneane. Tradition says it [was] founded about 1,400 years ago by St Bridget and was rebuilt about 100 years ago at the expense of the parish, and is 50 by 22 feet inside in the clear. It contains 15 pews, viz. 8 are double pews, 2 are 8 by 9 feet and 6 are 8 by 6 feet; and 7 single pews each 8 by 3 feet. 1 double pew is unoccupied except by a baptismal font of stone. The aisle is 6 feet wide, flagged and covered with a mat carpet. There are 3 windows viz. 2 on the south side, square, each 4 by 5 and a half feet. The east window is 6 feet 2 inches by 10 feet high. One door [is] on the west end, square, and is 5 by 7 feet. The roof is cove ceiled and in bad repair. The pews are in pretty good repair, newly repaired and painted about 10 years since, at the expense of the parish. The walls are 2 feet 2 inches thick.

There is no steeple or tower on the church. The only ornament is a bell which is on the west end of the church, put up about 10 years ago at the expense of the parish and cost 7 pounds. The graveyard contains about 1 Irish acre, churchland property. From the curate and churchwarden, Henry River Birch and Edward Rice.

Remarkable Circumstance

The year after the Irish rebellion, Rodger McCorley was hanged and buried on the bridge of Toome for being a United Irishman.

Raymond Cottage

Raymond Cottage was brought from Shane's Castle down the lake and was a frame of wood and is pebble-dashed. The walls are all studded and plastered. The roof is thatched. The planting consists of fir, oak, ash, elm, alder, beech and sycamore with a variety of evergreen, and was erected about 60 years ago, about 10 acres of ornamental planting. The latest planting was about 5 years planted and is in the townland of Drumraymond. Lord O'Neill takes a title from this cottage. A large quantity of natural wood is round this cottage, oak and ash. From William Phelan, keeper in the cottage. 24 July 1837.

Old Castle at Mr Weir's House

The old castle which formerly stood at the rear of Mr Weir's house is said to have been built by Colonel Gee about 120 years ago. Nothing remains of this old edifice but 3 lumps of the walls at the edge of the lake. The stones are small and nearly round and like other old buildings appear to have been cemented together with hot mortar called grouting. Several pieces of old coins of gold, silver and brass have been dug up in the ruins of the castle. It is commonly reported that a cellar or vault is under the surface of the garden. Bottles of wine and beer, with cannon-balls, have been dug up in the ruins and Danes' pipes have been dug up. Many of the stones of this old building was taken to build the bridge. Some of the old coins were as passes to cross over the ferry.

Mr Weir's House

The 2-storey house occupied by Mr David Weir, a little above the village of Toome, is said to have been connected with the old castle and was occupied by [blank] Buttle Esquire about the year '98. From Mr David Weir and John Crawford. 25 July 1837.

Flint Arrowheads

This flint arrowhead [drawing] was found by Bernard O'Neill in the townland of Aughacarnaghan upwards of 30 years ago. His son states that his father found it stuck in the handle of his spade when he came out from his dinner. It is affirmed by the superstitious of the parish also that these elf stones are thrown by the fairies and have the effect of curing cattle that are said to be elfshot, by giving them a drink of oatmeal and water in which the elf stone is put. From Bernard O'Neill.

Ancient Querns

The under part of ancient querns was found by John Malone in digging the land in the townland of Mullaghgawn: 2 and a half feet in diameter and 2 and a half inches thick, of freestone. [Insert marginal query: by J. Boyle: 2 and a half feet or 4 and a half feet?]. Also an ancient pair of querns may be seen in the house of StJohn Glover in the townland of Ballynamullan, 8 inches in diameter with a verge or hoop round it 2 and a half inches deep. From John Malone and StJohn Glover. 2 March 1837.

Ancient Furniture

There is an ancient cupboard in the house of StJohn Glover of Ballynamullan, of oak, 6 and a half feet high and 5 and a half feet broad, on which is the following inscription: "Andrew Hum Iohn Hum 1679." The carving on the front is very curiously executed. Several antiquarians is said to have called to see it. From the owner, StJohn Glover.

Brass Hatchet

The ancient brass hatchet represented in the margin [drawing] is the property of John Costello, a farmer in the townland of Gortgarron, and was discovered by him 5 years ago under a block of black oak, on the clay about 3 feet under the surface of Gortgarron moss. Information obtained from John Costello.

Caves

[L-shaped plan with dimension, 10 feet long and annotation]. There is a cave in the townland of Mullaghgawn, on a bank about 100 yards from the road and nearly opposite the Roman Catholic chapel, on the farm of John Malone. One branch of it runs east and the other runs north. The entrance into the east branch is obstructed by water at present. The north branch is 10 feet long, 3 and a half feet broad and 2 feet high, the entrance at the north end 1 and a half feet high by 2 feet broad, all rudely built of large undressed stones.

There is another cave in the townland of Mullaghgawn, a short distance from the Roman Catholic chapel in the townland of Corgan and on John Malone's farm. This cave runs north and is 11 feet long, 3 feet wide and 3 feet high.

[L-shaped plan of cave]. There is also a cave in the townland of Moneynick, on the farm of Henry McKinstry near the Moneynick national school, a few perches from the road leading to Art Ogue's corn mill. This cave runs east 30 feet, viz. 18 feet from the entrance and 12 feet above the entrance. "A" is the part above the entrance; "b" is the entrance or space to descend to the smaller entrance; "c" is the first entrance and is 2 feet broad by 1 foot high; from "c" to "d" [is] 18 feet long and 4 feet wide, with a descent from 3 feet to 6 feet high; "d" is the entrance into the second apartment and is 2 by 1 foot; from "e" to "f" is 18 feet long and near "e" is 3 and a half feet high by 3 feet wide; near "f" is 5 feet high by 3 feet wide and 2 feet wide at the top; "f" is a small fixture like a fireplace, 2 feet in length and at the end of the cave. At this end or branch of the cave for about 12 feet there is a good floor of earth and at all the other parts of the cave the bottom is all stones thrown together. The above caves are like those of the county Derry, artificial, rudely built of stones without mortar. 3 March 1837.

Stone Hatchet

The large stone hatchet discovered in 1819 by Moses Mays, and on his farm in the townland of Moneyrod, is 9 inches long by 3 inches broad at broadest end, 2 inches broad at narrowest end (see specimen) with 2 other smaller ones. These hatchets are commonly called thunderbolts, artificial.

Caves

There is an artificial cave in a fort at John Edgar's house in the townland of Tamnyderry. This cave runs north through the centre of the fort, but is closed up at the mouth long since. The fort is a garden 100 feet in diameter, which is said to be the length of the cave. The fort is 10 feet high. John Edgar last winter commenced digging round the parapet but was forced to quit it for fear of the fairies. His wife states, with many of her neighbours, that the flax on her [?] rack, which was left by the fire at night, would be found very nicely plaited in the morning and tied at the end in 2 hard knots, and frequently the hank tied and the band off. This was done for many nights until he ceased to dig the fort. From John Edgar, James Lyle and William Stewart.

There is also an artificial cave on the farm of William Stewart in same townland which contained 2 apartments, but long since closed up. This cave is also in a fort.

Old Fairs at Staffordstown

It is stated that 2 fairs have been held at the large oak tree in the cluster of houses at Staffordstown and a patent granted for fairs at Staffordstown, but from fighting at those fairs the patent was removed. Information obtained from David Pearson and William French.

Caves

There is an artificial cave in the fort on James Lyle's farm in the townland of Ballycloghan. This cave commences on the parapet and runs along it about 32 feet and then turns into the centre of the fort. The total length of the cave is 64 feet. The mouth is closed up. The stones of the roof are all nearly visible [plan]. From James Lyle and John Edgar.

Meader

A very ancient meader of [?] ben leather, all in one piece stitched together round the handle, bottom and side, and 5 inches long and 2 and a half inches across the mouth, and 3 and a half inches in diameter at the bottom, is in the possession of Rose French of Staffordstown for the last 20 years. It is said to have been dug up at the parapet of the fort on the farm of James Lyle of Ballycloghan [marginal drawing]. From John Edgar.

Old Castles

There was an old castle at David Pearson's of Tamnyderry, but all demolished long since. From David Pearson and James French.

An ancient castle formerly stood at Staffordstown and is said to have been occupied by a gentleman named Stafford. The ruins many years ago have been demolished and about 2 years ago part of the foundation was dug up. 7 March 1837.

Caves

There is a cave, artificial, in a fort on Hugh McClarnan's farm, in his garden, and runs north from the parapet into the centre of the fort, but is long since closed up. From the proprietor.

There is also an artificial cave on the farm of Samuel Hives on a hill in a potato field in the townland of Derrygowan, which also runs north but was closed up last November, 1836, lest the cattle should fall into it. Samuel Hives states that he went into it about 10 yards. It runs much farther, but is obstructed by water. From the proprietor and James Glover.

Ancient Coins

A quantity of ancient silver coins of shilling magnitude was dug up in the townland of Greenan and sold for old silver by Hugh Gilmore.

Lough Revel and Island

This is a dried-up lake in which is an artificial island, situated in the townland of Derryhollagh in the flow bog. The inhabitants affirm that about 20 years ago this was covered with water. The

Parish of Duneane

island is artificial and circular, 75 feet in diameter and appears to have been formed by means of a frame of white oak stakes regularly pointed and stuck in the bog, each about 20 feet long, mortised together. 12 of these stakes at present presents the appearance of pinnacles about 3 feet above the surface of the island, or rather above the holes which have been made by James McGrogan in search of ancient articles, many of which have been discovered by him in this island. The island is composed of clay, moss, gravel and a quantity of decomposed straw and bracken, which may seen on the island, pressed together in flakes. Some of the stakes may be seen in James McGrogan's house at the bog, each 18 feet long, 18 inches in circumference at the mortised end and smaller to the top.

Ancient Articles found in Bog

The following are the ancient articles found by James McGrogan during the summer and harvest of 1836.

Old boats, paddles and 5 oars of oak, an old dish nearly the colour and sound of bell-metal, 1 foot in diameter at the mouth, 1 and a half inches broad at the rim, 2 and a half inches deep, 10 inches in diameter at the bottom and much thinner than the pewter plates now in use, and in a very good state of preservation except a little crack at the bottom rim. Also a piece of very thin, silver-coloured hoop, an iron cam or gusset 21 inches long by 5 inches broad in the centre, oval shape and very thin. The handle is of iron, 2 and a half feet long, carved and supposed to have been used in coining. 2 old knives, a curious carved piece of wood with a hole in the end of it, a piece of brass wire, a curious brass instrument pointed like a hackle pin, 6 inches long, a Danes' pipe, a piece of an old wooden dish carved, a pair of old shears, old candlesticks of iron, beads and bullets, an old crock curiously carved, old dirk, an old helmet of steel, in quarters riveted at the top. The helmet was taken to Lord O'Neill's, but the peak was not found with it [marginal drawing]. A cart-load of horns, chiefly cows, and a quantity of human bones, many of which may be seen on the bank in the island.

The deepest part of Derryhollagh flow bog is about 20 feet. Near the lake the average depth is about 10 feet. The imbedded timber consists of oak chiefly, some of which is about 3 feet in diameter. This is the thickest and found near the clay or bottom, with the top towards the east. [Insert marginal note: Those marked thus [ticked] are to be had in the house of John Magrogan of Derryhollagh [all but boats, paddles and the helmet are ticked].

Art Ogue

Tradition says that the island in Lough Revel was formerly the residence of a celebrated robber called Art Ogue. Information obtained from James Magrogan and Bernard Kennedy. 10th March 1837.

Stone Hatchet

A stone hatchet found by Felix Mackerlain about 7 years ago in digging a potato field in the townland of Lismacloskey, see specimen procured by JB [Boyle].

Old Castle at Toome

Nothing remains of this ancient fortress but 3 large lumps of the wall, which appear to have rolled down from their former situation to the edge of the lake. The walls are 6 feet thick and, like other similar old buildings, composed of small stones undressed and cemented together with hot lime and water cast among them in building, called grouting. Part of the stones of this old castle were taken to build the bridge. In one or two places of Mr Weir's garden, where the ruins formerly stood, openings have been made and arched passages discovered, but are now entirely closed up. It is stated that a large quantity of human bones and pieces of silver, chiefly of sixpenny magnitude and very thin, have been at different times discovered about the place. Cannon-balls have been also discovered, 2 of which are to be seen at Mr Weir's house, one a 24-pounder and one an 18-pounder.

Colonel Gee is said to have been the last proprietor of the old castle and is said to have been killed in his own room by one Hagan of the county Tyrone. From John Crawford and David Weir. 11 March 1837.

Hatchet and Spear of Brass

An ancient brass hatchet and spear was found in a fort in townland Moneynick about 10 years ago by Hugh McIntyre, but long since lost. From the owner.

Fort at Moneynick

Mass is said to have been celebrated in a fort in which are 2 stones in the townland of Moneynick. One of the stones has a small hole in it, on the farm of Hugh McIntyre, a little above his house. The fort is almost demolished. From Hugh McIntyre and Henry McCrudden.

Ancient Moulds for Casting Crosses

3 ancient moulds of slate for casting crucifixes was dug up in a field of upland in the townland of Derryhollagh, on the farm of John Wilson and by him, about 20 years ago. Hugh McIntyre of Moneynick cast a few lead crosses in this mould, which is long since lost.

Arrowheads

Hugh McIntyre of Moneynick has got in his possession 3 flint arrowheads but will not part with them, as they are used by him in curing cattle that are elfshot. From Hugh McIntyre and John Wilson. 13 March 1837.

Ancient Shoe

An ancient leather shoe, all in one piece except the back seam which was sewed with horse hair, with 3 holes at each side of the upper part of the vamp, of very strong leather, not well tanned or dressed, but in a good state of preservation, discovered about 3 years ago by James McAstocker of Ballydugennan, 10 feet under the surface of Gallagh flow bog, but is not to be had at present. From James McAstocker, farmer.

Ancient Tree

There is an ancient hawthorn or gentle bush about a quarter of a mile from the Roman Catholic chapel at Cargin and on the side of the by-road leading from the chapel to Staffordstown. Mass is said to have been celebrated at this bush before the chapel was built. From Henry Kennedy and John Logan, near the chapel.

Brass Hatchet

[Marginal drawing] Found by Hugh Grant in March last, 1837, in digging a clay ditch in the townland of Aghacarnahan and is now in his possession. 16 March 1837.

Cave

[Plan of cave, "L" shape]. There is an artificial cave in the townland of Mullaghgawn on the farm of John Malone, in which is an excellent spring at present 2 feet deep of water. This cave runs north with a chamber at right angles west. Mouth at "A" is 2 by 2 feet; mouth at "b" is 2 by 1 and a half feet; total length of cave north and south 16 feet; total length east and west 16 feet; height 4 feet by 3 and a half feet wide; height north and south [of] chamber 3 feet by 3 feet wide. 3 May 1837.

Ancient Beads

A large string of beads, amber colour, 58 in number, the largest about the size of a handball, smallest about the size of a large pea, discovered 12 years ago in Grogan flow bog, 1 foot under the surface, parish of Drummaul, by Catherine McCudden, and now in the possession of Bernard Maddigan in the townland of Toome. From Bernard Maddigan. 3rd April 1837.

Miscellaneous Discoveries

Ancient mether, the property of James Brannan of the townland of Toome, with 4 handles (see specimen) was handed down from his ancestors. There is also a very ancient mether in Michael McErlane's of Moneyglass townland, of a similar shape, four-square; also an ancient trencher 1 foot in diameter, of oak, no rim and quite flat; also an ancient churn made from one piece was dug 3 feet deep near the edge of the bog in Moneyglass townland. The churn was at Moneyglass House, but now lost. Giltha Ruskin was the name of the person who made the methers, churn and trencher and the old vessels like the bark of a tree in which the ancient butter was deposited. Ruskin is the name of the vessels which contained the butter. A tax of 1d was paid by Giltha Ruskin for liberty to make them, as well as all other tradesmen.

Superstition about Stone

About 30 years ago Thomas Buttle Esquire removed the ancient stone, grey colour, shaped like a greyhound, and placed it at the entrance of the avenue to David Weir's house, Toome. He never did any good after removing the stone from the Church Island. It is now in the Church Island. From McErlane. 3rd April 1837.

SOCIAL ECONOMY

Emigration in 1835

List of persons who have emigrated from the parish of Duneane during the year 1835. [Table gives name, age, townland in which resided, religion, port emigrated to].

James McClarnan, 30, Catherine McClarnan, 30, from Moneyglass, Roman Catholics, to Quebec.

Parish of Duneane

Patrick McCoart, 25, from Moneyglass, Roman Catholic, to Quebec.

William Ferguson, 25, Margaret Ferguson, 23, Jane Ferguson, 70, from Ballymatuskerty, Presbyterians, to Quebec.

Mary Mulholland, 50, from Ballymatuskerty, Roman Catholic, to Quebec.

John Neil, 23, Jane Neil, 20, from Tamlaghtmore to New York, returned October 1836.

Henry Mitchell, 65, Margaret Mitchell, 64, Mary Mitchell, 25, Margaret Jane Mitchell, 20, William Mitchell, 22, from Ballydonelly, Presbyterians, to New York.

Esther Cooke, 16, from Ballyglenullar, Presbyterian, to New York.

Robert Mitchell, 30, from Ballyglenullar, Presbyterian, to New York.

Elisabeth Berry, 20, from Lismacloskey, Roman Catholic, to Quebec.

John Cunning, 23, from Ranaghan, Roman Catholic, to Quebec.

George Connolly, 21, from Ballynafey, Roman Catholic, to Quebec.

Sally Cooke, 40, William John Cooke, 23, Sally Cooke Junior, 6, William John Cooke Junior, 4, from Ballydonelly, Presbyterians, to Quebec.

Mary Reaney, 22, from Moneyrod, Presbyterian, to New York.

Mary Wilson, 20, from Moneyrod, Presbyterian, to New York.

Isabella Mundle, 18, from Moneyrod, Presbyterian, to New York, died.

John McIntyre, 18, Ellen McIntyre, 16, Margaret McIntyre, 20, from Moneynick, Roman Catholics, to Boston.

George Murphy, 25, John Murphy, 20, from Derryhollagh, Roman Catholics, to New York.

John Neill, 25, Peggy Jane Neill, 23, from Gortgill, Established Church, to New York.

Henry Costello, 30, from Brecart, Roman Catholic, to Glasgow.

Patrick McAstocker, 38, Catherine McAstocker, 40, David McAstocker, 12, Bridget McAstocker, 10, Mary Anne McAstocker, 8, Charles McAstocker, 6, from Gortgill, Roman Catholics, to Glasgow.

Emigration in 1836

List of persons who have emigrated from the parish of Duneane during the year 1836.

Hugh McKowen, 20, from Carlane, Roman Catholic, to New York.

William Murphy, 45, Mary Murphy, 34, George Murphy, 16, Robert Murphy, 18, Thomas Murphy, 14, James Murphy, 12, Mary Anne Murphy, 10, Jane Murphy, 8, Samuel Murphy, 6, Robinson Murphy, 4, from Derryhollagh, Presbyterians, to New York.

Abram Livingstone, 20, from Derryhollagh, Presbyterian, to New York.

Margaret McCord, 20, Robert McCord, 24, from Derryhollagh, Presbyterians, to New York.

John McCullagh, 22, Anne McCullagh, 45, James McCullagh, 18, Levina McCullagh, 20, Eliza McCullagh, 16, from Killyfast, Presbyterians, to Quebec.

David Irwin, 45, from Moneyglass, Established Church, to Glasgow.

William McKane, 22, Martha McKane, 20, Martha McKane Junior, 1, from Ballymatuskerty, Presbyterians, to New York.

Patrick Devlin, 31, from Ballynamullan, Roman Catholic, to New York.

Neil Grant, 40, from Carlane, Roman Catholic, to Philadelphia.

George Conolly, 21, from Ballynafie, Roman Catholic, to Philadelphia.

William Baily, 21, from Tamnyderry, Presbyterian, to New York.

Sally Glover, 20, from Drumboe, Presbyterian, to New York.

William Murphy, 50, Mary Murphy, 35, Robert Murphy, 18, Margaret Murphy, 20, George Murphy, 13, Thomas Murphy, 11, James Murphy, 9, Mary Anne Murphy, 7, Thomas Robinson Murphy, 4, from Derryhollagh, Presbyterians, to New York.

William John King, 32, Hannah King, 24, Margaret Jane King, 2 and a half, from Derrygowan, Presbyterians, to Quebec.

Migration

List of persons who migrate annually from the parish of Duneane. [Table gives name, age, townland in which resided, religion, port emigrated to].

John Costello, 20, from Brecart, Roman Catholic, to Glasgow.

John McCloskey, 25, from Brecart, Roman Catholic, to Glasgow.

Patrick McBride, 20, from Brecart, Roman Catholic, to Glasgow.

Hugh O'Neil, 25, from Gloverstown, Roman Catholic, to Liverpool.

Robert McFarland, 30, from Gloverstown, Presbyterian, to Liverpool.

Hugh Boyle, 20, from Gloverstown, Roman Catholic, to Liverpool.
Andrew Malowney, 20, from Gloverstown, Roman Catholic, to Liverpool.
Daniel Malowney, 22, from Gloverstown, Roman Catholic, to Liverpool.
William Pollock, 26, from Ballynaleaney, Established Church, to Glasgow.
Felix McKowen, 28, from Ballynaleany, Roman Catholic, to Glasgow.
Henry McAnally, 22, Abram McAnally, 34, from Ballynaleany, Roman Catholics, to Glasgow.
Neal McCue, 35, from Ballynaleany, Roman Catholic, to Glasgow.
Edward Boyle, 35, from Gallagh, Roman Catholic, to Glasgow.
Hugh O'Neil, 28, Henry O'Neil, 35, from Aughnacarnaghan, Roman Catholics, to Glasgow.
John Murray, 28, from Aughnacarnaghan, Roman Catholic, to Glasgow.
Daniel Devlin, 35, from Aughnacarnaghan, Roman Catholic, to Glasgow.
William McMullan, 32, Charles McMullan, 36, from Cargin, Roman Catholics, to Glasgow.
William McCann, 38, from Ballynamullan, Roman Catholic, to Glasgow.
John McCorley, 36, from Tullaghbeg, Roman Catholic, to Glasgow.
Henry O'Donell, 45, from Tullaghbeg, Roman Catholic, to Glasgow.
Henry Kennedy, 38, from Ballylurgan, Roman Catholic, to Merryport.
John O'Neill, 28, from Carmorn, Roman Catholic, to Glasgow.
James Duncan, 25, from Moneynick, Roman Catholic, to Glasgow.
James Glasco, 30, from Annaghmore, Roman Catholic, to Glasgow.
William Pogue, 40, from Ballynamullan, Roman Catholic, to Glasgow.
Patt Macue, 35, from Ballynamullan, Roman Catholic, to Glasgow.
Felix McKowen, 30, from Ballynamullan, Roman Catholic, to Glasgow.
Rodger Fury, 24, from Gortgill, Roman Catholic, to Glasgow.
Patt McBride, 20, from Gortgill, Roman Catholic, to Glasgow.
John Magill, 22, from Gortgill, Roman Catholic, to Glasgow.
Frank O'Neill, 21, from Gortgill, Roman Catholic, to Glasgow.
Frank Cudden, 30, from Gortgill, Roman Catholic, to Glasgow.
James McErlaine, 37, from Gortgill, Roman Catholic, to Glasgow.
Henry Shivers, 23, from Gortgill, Roman Catholic, to Glasgow.
John McCann, 40, John McCann Junior, 30, from Gallagh, Roman Catholics, to Glasgow.
Edward Shea, 40, from Gallagh, Roman Catholic, to Glasgow.
William McMullian, 29, from Gallagh, Roman Catholic, to Glasgow.
Henry Kennedy (dealer), 53, from Ballydugenan, Roman Catholic, to Glasgow.
Neal McAstocker, 21, from Ballydugenan, Roman Catholic, to Glasgow.
Hugh Boyle, 18, from Lismacloskey, Roman Catholic, to Liverpool.

School Statistics, 1837

Table of Schools

[Table contains the following headings: name of townland where held, name and religion of master or mistress, free or pay school, annual income of master or mistress, description and cost of schoolhouse, number of pupils subdivided by religion, sex and by the Protestant and Roman Catholic returns, societies with which connected. All are pay schools].

Mill Quarter, master Sampson McCallin, Protestant; salary uncertain, receives gratuities from the London Hibernian and Kildare Place Societies; schoolhouse stone and lime, cost 40 pounds, altogether unsuitable for the purpose; number of pupils by the Protestant return: 24 Protestants of the Established Church, 14 Presbyterians, 4 other denominations, 67 Roman Catholics, 60 males, 49 females; connected with London Hibernian and Kildare Place Societies.

Taylorstown Park, master John Boyd, Presbyterian; salary 5 pounds 10s; schoolhouse stone and lime, cost 550 pounds, built by Moravian Society; number of pupils by the Protestant return: 61 Presbyterians, 2 other denominations, 20 Roman Catholics, 51 males, 32 females; connected with London Hibernian and Kildare Place Societies.

Dunean Cloughog, master Patrick Talbot, Protestant; salary 14 pounds; schoolhouse stone and lime, cost 45 pounds, fitted up by the Kildare Place Society; number of pupils by the Protestant return: 5 Protestants of the Established Church, 10 Presbyterians, 27 Roman Catholics, 30 males, 12 females; by the Roman Catholic return: 18

Protestants of the Established Church, 24 Roman Catholics, 30 males, 12 females; connected with Kildare Place Society and the parish school, the incumbent gives 2 pounds per annum.

Killyslaven Moneyglass, master John O'Neil, Roman Catholic; salary 14 pounds to 16 pounds, inclusive of gratuities from London Hibernian and Kildare Place Societies; schoolhouse: porter's lodge of J.S. Smyth Esquire; number of pupils by the Protestant return: 2 Protestants of the Established Church, 2 Presbyterians, 56 Roman Catholics, 34 males, 26 females; by the Roman Catholic return: 5 Protestants of the Established Church, 3 Presbyterians, 55 Roman Catholics, 34 males, 26 females; connected with London Hibernian and Kildare Place Societies.

Cargin, master Joseph McCann, Roman Catholic; salary uncertain, 2s 6d to 5s 5d rates of payment; schoolhouse large and well built house of lime and stone; number of pupils by the Protestant return: 4 Protestants of the Established Church, 6 Presbyterians, 3 other denominations, 39 Roman Catholics, 32 males, 20 females; by the Roman Catholic return: 6 Protestants of the Established Church, 2 Presbyterians, 3 other denominations, 41 Roman Catholics, 32 males, 22 females.

Gallagh, master Samuel Trainer, Roman Catholic; salary 2s 6d per 6 months from each pupil; schoolhouse well built; number of pupils by the Protestant return: 3 Presbyterians, 19 Roman Catholics, 12 males, 10 females; connected with the Kildare Place Society.

Staffordstown, master David Browne, Presbyterian; salary 2s 6d to 5s 5d per quarter; schoolhouse a new house just finishing at the expense of the parishioners, aided by the Kildare Place Society; number of pupils by the Protestant return: 2 Protestants of the Established Church, 30 Presbyterians, 26 Roman Catholics, 35 males, 23 females; by the Roman Catholic return: 2 Protestants of the Established Church, 12 Presbyterians, 13 Roman Catholics, 19 males, 13 females; connected with Kildare Place Society.

Ballymatuskerty, master James Reid, Roman Catholic; salary 2s per week, badly paid; schoolhouse part of an old wretched dwelling house; number of pupils by the Protestant return: 20 Presbyterians, 12 males, 8 females.

Public Schools by J. Bleakly

[Table contains the following headings: name, situation and description, when established, income and expenditure, physical, intellectual and moral education, number of pupils subdivided by age, sex and religion, name and religion of master or mistress. No physical education].

Duneane parish school, situated near the church in the townland of Duneane, a house built of stone and lime, thatched, 30 by 14 feet inside and in bad repair, established in 1811; income: the present master is not a quarter teaching yet; intellectual education: books published by the London Hibernian Society, *Gough's Arithmetic, Jackson's Book-keeping;* moral education: visited by the curate of the parish, the Presbyterian minister and the priest; the Authorised Version of Scripture is taught, but no catechism; number of pupils: males, 9 under 10 years of age, 27 from 10 to 15, 3 over 15, total 39; females, 10 under 10 years of age, total 10; total number of pupils 49, 5 Protestants, 21 Presbyterians, 23 Roman Catholics; master Thomas Barry, Roman Catholic.

Moneyglass, held in a private house in the townland of Moneyglass, established in 1825; income: from the London Hibernian Society 8 pounds per annum, 15s from pupils; intellectual education: books published by the London Hibernian Society, *Gough's* and *Vostin's Arithmetic;* moral education: visited by the curate the Reverend William Boyes, and the priest the Reverend Denis Magreevy; Authorised Version of Scriptures is taught; number of pupils: males, 20 under 10 years of age, 20 from 10 to 15, total 40; females, 10 under 10 years of age, 10 from 10 to 15, total 20; total number of pupils 60, 3 Protestants, 57 Roman Catholics; master Patrick Brady, Roman Catholic.

Moneynick national school, on the by-road leading from Toome to Randalstown; the house is built of stone and lime, thatched by subscription and is 21 by 16 feet inside; the National Board gave 10 pounds towards its repairs, established in 1833; income: from the National Board 8 pounds per annum, 16 pounds from pupils; expenditure: house rent per annum 5s; intellectual education: books published by the National Board only; moral education: visited by the Roman Catholic clergy; number of pupils: males, 71 under 10 years of age, 5 from 10 to 15, 5 over 15, total 81; females, 30 under 10 years of age, 10 from 10 to 15, total 40; total number of pupils 121, 2 Protestants, 6 Presbyterians, 113 Roman Catholics; master Francis Grant, Roman Catholic. Report for February 1837.

Staffordstown, on the by-road leading from the Toome and Randalstown road; a good house, slated, 21 by 15 feet inside, established under the Kildare Place Society in 1815 and under the

London Hibernian Society in 1826; established 1815; income: from the London Hibernian Society 9 pounds, 7 pounds 10s from pupils; intellectual education: books published by the London Hibernian Society with *Gough's Arithmetic;* moral education: visited by the Reverend William Boyes, curate of the parish, Authorised Version of Scripture is taught; number of pupils: males, 27 under 10 years of age, 5 from 10 to 15, 3 over 15, total 35; females, 22 under 10 years of age, 3 from 10 to 15, total 25; total number of pupils 60, 15 Protestants, 21 Presbyterians, 24 Roman Catholics; master James Glover, Established Church.

Gallagh national school, near the flow bog in the townland of Gallagh, a good house of stone, thatched, 30 by 14 feet inside; under the National Board since 1833, previous to this it was under the Kildare Place Society; established 1822; income: from the National Board 8 pounds, 5 pounds from pupils; intellectual education: books published by the National Board only; moral education: visited by the Roman Catholic clergy only; number of pupils: males, 6 under 10 years of age, 6 from 10 to 15, total 12; females, 4 under 10 years of age, 6 from 10 to 15, total 10; total number of pupils 22, 2 Presbyterians, 20 Roman Catholics; master Lawrence Trayner, Roman Catholic. Report for March 1837.

Notes on Cranfield and Drummaul

Schools

[Table contains the following headings: name of townland, number of pupils subdivided by religion and sex, remarks as to how supported, date of erection].

Leitrim, 3 Protestants, 9 Catholics, 21 Presbyterians, 23 males, 10 females, 33 total; supported solely by the scholars who pay a 1d a week, date of erection 1820.

Cranfield, 4 Protestants, 60 Catholics, 61 Presbyterians, 94 males, 30 females, 124 total; the greater part of these scholars attend only in summer; the school is supported partly by the scholars, partly by the London Hibernian Society, date of erection 1822.

Tamnaderry, 8 Protestants, 40 Catholics, 30 Presbyterians, 48 males, 30 females, 78 total; attendance and support as above.

Killyfad, 3 Protestants, 40 Catholics, 7 Presbyterians, 25 males, 25 females, 50 total; supported as above, date of erection 1831.

Grange of Shilvodan, County Antrim

Statistical Report by Lieutenant C.H. Mallock, August and October 1830

NATURAL STATE AND NATURAL FEATURES

Name and Situation

Name: Shilvodan <Shilvoden> grange. It is situated in the north east side of the half barony of Upper Toome, on the south west side of the county of Antrim, about 5 miles north of the town of Antrim, about 16 miles north west of Belfast and about 6 miles south east of Ballymena. It is not annexed to any parish. The inhabitants attend the meeting house of Connor. Marriages and baptisms are performed by the minister of Connor, the inhabitants of which parish have at different periods endeavoured to prove that Shilvodan belongs to the parish of Connor, and was liable to pay tithes. It was decided in a recent lawsuit that they were not liable. Lord O'Neill is the proprietor, and the farms are with few exceptions held either at will or on short leases.

Boundaries, Extent and Divisions

It is bounded on the north and east by the parish of Connor, on the west by that of Drummaul and on the south by that of Antrim. It extends from north to south about 2 miles and from east to west about 3 miles and a half. It contains 3,542 acres. It is divided into 7 townlands.

Surface, Soil, Produce and Turbary

It presents no very marked features, but gradually rises from the west, where the level of the ground is between 160 and 200 feet, to the east, where it is 860 feet. The western side for about half a mile from the boundary is bog land. From the extreme point east, and as far west as the road from Antrim to Connor, [it] has the appearance of a district lately enclosed, and from the state of cultivation it is in, can not be classed much higher than mountain pasturage; but every year there is a very perceptible improvement. The remaining part of the parish has a thriving appearance: the soil light, rather sandy, but tolerably productive, yielding good crops of oats, barley, flax, potatoes and some wheat. Turbary is abundant in the west side of the grange and of a good quality, and as there are good roads in every part, fuel is easily procured throughout.

Geology

Limestone, minerals, sandstone: not any. The only stone is greenstone, of which there is great quantity throughout the grange. The nearest point from which lime is procured is from the parish of Carnmoney, about 12 miles distant.

MODERN TOPOGRAPHY

Towns and Villages

Towns: not any; villages: not any, but there are a great number of comfortable cottages in every part. A Catholic chapel has lately been commenced in the townland of Tavnaghmore.

Manufactories

[Crossed out: That of linen is the only one, and this to a very small extent at any time, and most probably is now entirely knocked up].

[Insert additional note: Linen weaving still employs a few hands. It is generally of a fine quality, about 6 hanks to the pound, but this trade is gradually failing and bids fair in a very few years to be entirely superseded by cotton, which branch now employs a considerable number of hands. [Signed] C.H. Mallock, October 25th 1830].

Roads

The whole of this district is well opened by roads in every part, and all of them tolerably good. A daily coach passes through the east end of the grange from Ballymena to Belfast.

NATURAL FEATURES

Rivers, Bogs and Woods

Rivers: not any, and but a few streams, all of which are very small ones. On the west side there is a considerable tract of bog, but very little in any other part. There is not any wood, but on some of the hills there is a sort of stunted underwood.

SOCIAL ECONOMY

Population

Are almost all Presbyterians and appear to be a quiet industrious class. The nearest markets are those of Antrim, Ballymena and Randalstown <Randlestown>. To this last the greater part of the grain that is grown in the grange is taken.

ANCIENT TOPOGRAPHY

Antiquities

There are 5 or 6 of the mounds so common in this part of Antrim, but nothing remarkable about any of them. There are not any antiquities other than the mounds above mentioned. [Signed] C.H. Mallock, Lieutenant Royal Artillery, August 11th 1830.

Memoir by James Boyle, August 1838, with insertions from Draft Memoir, April 1835

MEMOIR WRITING

Memoir Writing

This Memoir is complete up to 25th August 1838. It was originally commenced on 28th April 1836, and was completed on 20th August 1838. Total time employed at it: 126 hours, or 14 days. [Signed] James Boyle, 20th August 1838.

    [Draft Memoir] Received April 25 1835 by J. McG[ann]. Refer to Mr Boyle, [signed] R.K. D[awson], 18 September 1835.

NATURAL FEATURES

Hills

The grange of Shilvodan includes a portion of the western side of Carnearny mountain (1,060 feet above the level of the sea) in the adjoining and easterly parish of Connor. The highest point in the grange, 896 feet above the sea, is at its eastern extremity, and from this it descends westward by a succession of undulations, until it declines to an average level of 180 feet above the sea at its western side. The little ridges or undulations forming the descent of the mountain are at first rather abrupt in their declivity, but become less so as they approach its base. They are frequently intersected by little valleys, which give considerable variety to the surface of the grange. The higher grounds are under pasture. The lower contain some small patches of bog and are cultivated, but from the total want of planting and hedgerows the appearance of all is bare and uninteresting.

    The highest or principal points in the grange are Lady hill, 875 feet, Bruce's hill, 407 and Stable hill, 278 feet above the level of the sea.

Rivers

There is no river in the grange. There are numerous little rivulets which trickle down the sides of the hills and which, after making their way into the adjoining parishes and uniting into others, are there turned to some account; but here they are not applicable to any other purpose than that of drainage. Besides, their inclination is so rapid that they are in general dry in summer. The higher districts of the grange are well supplied with water for domestic purposes from wells and rivulets, but in the lower districts the inhabitants are obliged to sink pumps or draw-wells to obtain a sufficient supply of water.

Bogs

In the townland of Drumkeeran, at the western side of the grange, is a tract of about 42 acres of flow bog, being about one half the entire tract, the remainder of which is in the adjoining parish of Drummaul. The form of this bog is somewhat convex. Its mean elevation above the sea is 170 feet and above Lough Neagh (from which it is distant about 3 and a quarter miles) 122 feet. There is no river or stream of any consequence immediately in its vicinity, but there are several little rivulets issuing from it and which, by being deepened and widened, might without much cost or difficulty be rendered available in draining it. Its depth, so far as it is known, does not exceed 12 feet, but it is little cut or known except along the edges. Its surface consists of an unprofitable flow, which towards the centre of the bog is very soft. Its subsoil is a reddish clay, in which a considerable quantity of oak stumps are embedded as they grew. They are most numerous about the edges of the bog. The trunks seem to have been broken or rather burnt off very closely, as they all bear marks of combustion.

    A layer of fir blocks or stumps pervades this bog at a little distance from its bottom. They also bear marks of fire and seem to have been burnt off very close. They are of considerable growth and size. But few trunks of firs, and still fewer of oak, are found. They do not preserve any particular direction or position but lie indiscriminately. As the bed of this bog seems to be convex it may have originally been that of a lake which, having been naturally drained to a partial extent, originated the present bog; or it may be that its hollow form rendered it liable to a lodgement of water, on which vegetable matter may have accumulated.

    There are several small patches of bog in the other townlands in the grange. Most of these have

Grange of Shilvodan

been partially cut for fuel and are found to contain stumps of fir timber, with, however, but few trunks; and all of them have oak stumps embedded in the clay forming their beds. Few oak trunks are found and those discovered are generally small and do not preserve any particular position. These bogs usually occupy little hollows where water may have lodged. Occasionally trifling patches are to be found on the acclivity of a hill where a spring oozes forth.

The bog in this grange is chiefly confined to its lower districts, there being scarcely any in its higher grounds.

[Insert addition: The western side for about half a mile from the boundary is bog land. Note on separate sheet: This is in Mr Hannyngton's district].

Woods

The grange, with the exception of the high ground along its eastern border, is said to have been formerly densely wooded. The only remains of these woods are now to be found in that discovered in the bogs and in the small patches of low hazel brushwood occasionally to be met with in unreclaimed spots. In the townland of Tavnaghmore there is a good deal of this brushwood. Hawthorns, a little holly [and] a few oak shoots are the only other description of natural wood in the grange.

[Insert addition: There is not any wood, but on some of the hills there is a sort of stunted underwood].

Climate

The climate of this grange is, from [its] situation on the western side of Carneany mountain, mild, but it is very moist and subject to rain. This is owing to several causes, the principal of which are: its situation between the summit of the mountain and Lough Neagh, the rains and mists being attracted to and condensed by the former; the prevalence of westerly and south westerly winds which, with the north west, blow for 9 months in the year and which waft the mists and showers from the lake to the mountain, where they are quickly condensed, renders the grange very subject to rain. The north west wind is very squally and stormy and, there being neither planting nor hedgerows, the higher grounds are much exposed to it. The lower districts are more free from rain and of course less exposed. The seasons in them are from a fortnight to 3 weeks later than in the others.

The moisture of the ground and of the climate and the backward state of cultivation renders the grange unsuited for the growth of wheat. Oats are sown chiefly during the month of April and reaped during the months of September and October. Potato planting takes place during the month of May and the general raising of the crop from the beginning of November until the middle of December.

[Insert addition: Wheat, oats, potatoes and flax are the usual crops. Wheat is reaped at the latter end of August, oats in September, potatoes are dug in November and flax is pulled in August].

Modern Topography

Towns and Public Buildings

There is neither town nor village in the grange. The only public building is the Roman Catholic chapel in the townland of Tavnaghmore, towards the north west side of the grange and near the road from Antrim to Ballymena. It is [a] plain but neat building, built of stone and roughcast, and measuring externally 61 by 32 feet. It does not contain a gallery and [is] fitted up with merely a few temporary seats. It was erected by subscription in 1830 and cost 300 pounds. It would in its present state accommodate 300 persons.

[Insert addition: There is a Roman Catholic chapel in the townland of Tannaghmore. There is nothing remarkable in its appearance or architecture. It was built in 1829. The expense was defrayed by subscription. It will accommodate 250 persons. It is about 60 feet long and 26 broad].

There are neither gentlemen's seats, manufactories nor machinery of any description in the grange.

Communications

The grange possesses every facility of communication with the neighbouring districts, by means of the numerous main and by-roads which traverse its surface. There are 3 miles 6 furlongs of the former and 9 miles 6 furlongs of the latter. Both are too numerous and they are also, with a few trifling exceptions, badly laid out and kept in but middling repair. These roads have been made by the county and are kept in repair at the expense of the barony of Upper Toome.

The main roads are: that leading from Antrim to Ballymena, of which there are in this grange 2 miles traversing its centre from north to south. The portion of this road in this grange is level and so far pretty well laid out, and kept in pretty good repair. Its average breadth is 26 feet. A new line of turnpike mail coach road from Belfast to Coleraine and Derry through Antrim and Ballymena is just being constructed. It passes near to and will supersede the road in this grange.

From the northern end of the above road another strikes off in a north easterly direction to Kells and Connor. There are only 2 furlongs of this road in the grange. Its average breadth is 23 feet. It is in pretty good repair.

About 1 mile to the eastward of and parallel to that of Antrim to Ballymena a road runs from Antrim to Kells and Connor. There is 1 and a half miles of it in the grange. Its average breadth is 21 feet. It is very badly laid out, being carried too high up the hill and running in an almost right line without regard to the numerous hills and hollows over which it passes. It is consequently very hilly and some of its inclinations average 1 in 9 feet. It would be difficult to keep such a road on the side of a mountain in repair, on account of the heavy rains in such situations which, flowing down declivities, acquire increased velocity and force in their course, and necessarily cut up and tear the road and carry off the metalling from its surface. This road is rarely used by conveyances, the former one being that commonly used.

The lower road which leads from Antrim to Ballymena, Kells and Connor is joined near its northern end by one from Randalstown to the latter villages. There is 1 mile 2 furlongs of this road in the grange. Its average breadth is 22 feet. It is tolerably level and is kept in tolerable repair. Its direction is also pretty good.

[Insert addition: The principal is that from Ballymena to Belfast, 2 miles of which is in the parish. Its average breadth is 28 feet. It was made at the expense of the county and is kept in repair by the barony. It is kept in good order. The high road from Kells to Antrim crosses the parish. At the northern boundary a branch strikes off from it to Randalstown. There is 2 miles of each in the parish. Their average breadth is 28 feet and they were made and repaired as the first mentioned and are kept in good order].

In this grange, which extends over but 3,456 acres, of which nearly a third is uncultivated, there are 12 different by-roads or portions of by-roads, the united length of which is 9 miles 6 furlongs. They are unnecessarily numerous and generally injudiciously laid out, running frequently in direct lines without any regard to the inequality of the ground and thereby, where hills intervene, expensive to keep in repair and generally out of order. A few of these have been made at the expense of the tenantry, and under the direction of Lord O'Neill and his surveyor, but the majority have been made at the expense of the county. They certainly afford great facility of intercourse, but literally one half the number of judiciously laid out roads would afford equal convenience as to communication, with less wear and tear <tare> of horses and conveyances, at less expense to the public.

There are not any bridges, but merely a few pipes across the rivulets over which the roads pass.

General Appearance and Scenery

In the grange of Shilvodan, a traveller proceeding from the fertile districts of the south of the county first encounters the dreary and uninteresting scenery with which his eye will have become more familiar before he shall have reached its northern limits. It is here that, in travelling northwards, dreary tracts of unreclaimed bog, small and badly cultivated fields, without the rich bushy hedgerows which give the southern parishes all the effect of planting, are to be first seen. There is no planting, and only occasionally a few trees are to be found about a farmhouse. The cottages of the peasantry are much less comfortable and neat looking. Lime is rarely used in ornamenting their exterior. The features of the higher grounds are tame, and their broad smooth slopes under pasture are not all varied or relieved by the dry stone fences which chequer them.

Agriculture, though improving, is still in a very backward state. The farms are so small that a snug farmhouse and its well stocked stackyard are rarely to be seen. The view from the lower grounds is confined and limited, and seldom reaches beyond the mountain on the eastern and the boggy districts along the western side of the grange.

[Insert addition: The grange is well cultivated and appears to be fertile, but presents nothing remarkable or picturesque to the traveller. This is occasioned by the want of planting and gentlemen's residences].

Social Economy

Early Improvements

The inhabitants of the grange of Shilvodan are, with a few exceptions, the descendants of the Scottish settlers of the 16th and 17th centuries. There are still to be found in the grange a few whose habits, religion and names would infer their being of a different descent, probably Irish, among whom the name of Madigan is the most prevalent. The townland of Tavnaghmore at the western side of the grange is peopled almost exclusively by Roman Catholics, apparently of Irish extraction, while the other districts of the grange are principally inhabited by Presbyterians whose religion, names, accent and habits are strongly indicative of their being of Scottish descent.

The grange of Shilvodan still forms a portion of the estates of the O'Neill family, and is held directly (with a trifling exception) under Lord O'Neill. This may perhaps account for its not being on a par as to improvements in any respect with the adjoining southerly parishes. It would appear from the manner from which the grange is colonised that, on the invasion of it by the Scotch, the original inhabitants retreated to the boggy fastnesses along its western side, which they subsequently settled themselves in and cultivated. These districts are still inhabited by Roman Catholics and are the best cultivated and most improved portion of the grange; and the people are among the most comfortable in their circumstances and habits of living. In this respect this grange forms an exception to almost all the districts similarly colonised, for here the descendants of the aboriginal inhabitants have, speaking generally, the advantage of those of the settlers as to civilisation.

There are few districts which possess fewer advantages except as to situation, as there has not been any event, social or political, which might be looked on as a likely cause of improvement, further than those generally affecting the country, by which the inhabitants of this grange have benefitted. Their situation with respect to markets, where a demand for every description of farm produce and manufacture is always to be had, is advantageous. The great weekly market at Ballymena is only 6 miles distant from the centre of the grange, and that for the sale of grain at Antrim is but 3 and three-quarter miles distant. To the grange of Shilvodan this is not so important an advantage as might be imagined. Merely one half the adult male population had until within the last 7 years been engaged in the manufacture of linen, and as agriculture had therefore been but little attended to, it is now in a very backward state except in a few instances in the lower grounds.

The upper districts are but partially cultivated, and are principally under pasture. As many have been thrown out of employment by the decline of the linen trade, farming is now resorted to as their only alternative, and the cultivation of the grange is now, as their only means of their earning of livelihood, becoming more general. The present Roman Catholic priest (the Revd Daniel Curoe), who resides at Randalstown, has been unremitting in his exertions among the members of his flock, and has by his endeavours, particularly in the course of education, produced a considerable change for the better in their morals.

Obstructions to Improvement

Though there may not be any actual obstruction to improvement, still there is an almost total absence of those causes to which, in most districts, beneficial effects produced upon either the morals, habits or circumstances of the people are usually attributed. There are but few leaseholders, nor freeholders. The lands are let as highly as when the linen trade, upon which the bulk of the population depended for their support, was most flourishing. Lord O'Neill, their landlord, takes no interest whatever in the welfare or comforts of his tenants, either by holding out inducements for good conduct, giving premiums for improvements in agriculture, encouraging education by giving his support or countenance to schools, or by contributing anything towards any one charitable or useful purpose or institution. On the contrary, his tenantry are worse than neglected, for the land is so highly let that they are always in difficulties and he is unpaid.

There is not a single resident gentleman or clergyman and the only place of worship is the Roman Catholic chapel. Nor is there anyone to interest himself in the welfare of the people other than the priest, or the clergy of other persuasions, who pay but little attention to this district. The linen trade, which had in some of its branches been almost the entire support of the majority of the population of both sexes, now affords but partial employment and low wages to a small proportion of the males. All the females and many of the males are therefore almost unemployed and, as there is neither a manufactory nor a large landed proprietor nor extensive farmer, they are likely to remain so. Lime at the nearest is 16 miles distant and is therefore within the reach of few.

Local Government

There are neither magistrates nor police in the grange. The nearest magistrates are those in the parish of Antrim, whose residences are situated within 3 miles of the centre of the grange. A portion of the grange is included in the district of the Antrim petty sessions and a portion in the district of those held at Randalstown; the former on every second Thursday and the latter on every alternate Tuesday. The grange is free from outrage of any description, and the most serious case rarely exceeds a private quarrel. The grange of Shilvodan is included in the manor of Edenduffcarrick, the manor courts of which are held at Randalstown once a month and courts leet twice a year. Sums not exceeding 20 pounds are recoverable at these courts. Smuggling is confined to the sale of spirits by unlicensed persons. This practice was formerly carried to a considerable extent, but has latterly been greatly diminished, there being at present but 2 "shebeen" houses in the grange. There are not any fire or life assurances.

Dispensary

There is no dispensary in the grange. There is one at Connor, 2 and a quarter miles, and another at Randalstown, 3 and a half miles distant from the centre of the grange, to which patients from it are admissible; but owing to the distance they are not frequently applied to, and their benefits and effects are here consequently imperceptible. The grange is comparatively free from infectious and contagious diseases, and the people are healthy and rather hardy. Fever is less frequent than in any of the adjoining districts. Scorbutic diseases are less prevalent than formerly, owing perhaps to the less frequent use of meal, while consumption is considered to be on the increase here as well as in the neighbouring districts.

Schools

There is 1 day and 1 Sunday school in the grange. At the former 70 children, being one-sixteenth of the entire population, are receiving education, and at the Sunday school 53 children, who from various causes are unable to attend the day school, receive instruction.

The proportion of pupils to the population is unusually low. Schools, however, are here of but comparatively recent introduction and, until within a few years, and since by the aid they receive from public bodies, which enables them [to] afford education at a lower rate, they had been only attended by the children of weavers and farmers, the cottiers and most of the agricultural labourers rarely having availed themselves of their advantages. There is not the same taste or anxiety to obtain information and acquire knowledge as among the inhabitants of the more southerly districts. There are still many who are unable to afford the trifling expense at which education may now be obtained. In this therefore, as in many other respects, the benefits of Sunday schools are evident.

The effects of education upon the rising generation are already perceptible here in many instances, and it is probable that nothing has tended more towards improving their morals and habits.

Table of Schools

[Insert addition: table gives townland, numbers of pupils by religion and sex, support, when established].

Tannaghmore, Protestants 25, Catholics 77, males 72, females 30, total 102; supported by scholars and an allowance from National Board, established 1832.

Creavery, Protestants 39, Catholics 3, males 30, females 12, total 42; 1d a week from scholars, established 1828.

The attendance at these schools is very irregular. The parents do not enforce it, and all who are old enough to do any work are taken away during the spring and autumn for the purpose of setting or gathering potatoes].

Poor

Though there are few actual paupers or strolling beggars, still there are many objects of compassion to be found, in old couples or individuals who either from age or sickness, or perhaps both, are unable to support themselves. These poor creatures are usually to be found inhabiting a ruinous and scantily furnished hut and depending upon the charity of neighbours, who may perhaps be little better off than themselves, and no doubt some of them perish from want of nourishment or attention to their distress. The people are generally humane and charitable and very rarely withhold their assistance when solicited, not from the terrors of the "beggar's curse", so much and so commonly dreaded in Ireland, but from a better motive, which indeed is not always unaccompanied with the little vanity they feel in receiving the "beggar's benison."

The ancient Scottish custom of "lifting", which is not unfrequently practised in the adjoining parish of Connor, is here occasionally, though rarely, adopted. A few farmers carrying a bag perambulate the parish and, calling at each house, receive a contribution, chiefly consisting of meal or potatoes, which they deliver to the object for whom they have undertaken the mission.

The average weekly collection at the Roman Catholic [chapel] amounts to 3s. This is distributed among the poor of the congregation. It is almost unnecessary to remark that a regular legal provision for the aged, helpless and infirm is here much required.

Religion

There are not more than 36 members of the Established Church residing in the grange. About three-quarters of the remaining population are Presbyterians and the rest Roman Catholics. The grange of Shilvodan (in the Church of England) is episcopally united to the prebend of Connor, which consists of the adjoining vicarage or parish of Connor, the parish of Killagan and the granges of Killyglen and Solar, and of which the Revd Richard Jones Hobson is prebend. The living is in the gift of the Bishop of Down and Connor. The vicarial tithes amount to about 4 pounds per annum and are paid by an individual who has some property in the grange, and to whom the rectorial tithes amounting to about 40 pounds per annum are paid. The church is situated in the adjoining parish of Connor and is [blank] miles distant from the centre of the grange.

The Presbyterians are not confined to any particular parish but are members of different congregations, but chiefly of those in Antrim and Connor. In the Roman Catholic church this grange is united to the parishes of Drummaul, Donegore, Antrim and Connor, of which the Revd Daniel Curoe, who resides at Randalstown, is parish priest. He is supported by his flock, from whom he jointly receives (according to his own statement) 150 pounds per annum but, according to the general opinion, from 500 to 600 pounds per annum. He keeps a curate whose salary is paid by himself. There is a Roman Catholic chapel in this grange, one in Antrim and one in Randalstown in the parish of Drummaul.

Habits of the People

By the enumeration returns of 1831 the population of this grange amounts to 220 families, consisting of 1,124 individuals, which would give an average of 5 and one-ninth individuals to a family and 8 and one-sixth to the acre. Of the families, 165 are chiefly engaged in agriculture and 36 in trade, manufacture or handicraft. 32 occupiers of land employ labourers and 92 do not. 57 individuals are employed in retail trade or handicraft. There are 94 agricultural labourers and 33 female servants. It has been shown by the foregoing statement that this grange is almost exclusively an agricultural district. The manufacture of linen, which had at one time been extensively carried on here, is now, owing to the decline in that trade, almost abandoned, and spinning is now resorted to more as an alternative to being idle than to any profit which it can yield. There are but 2 grades in the grange, namely the farmers and the cottiers and labourers.

Farmers

The farmers are with a few exceptions much inferior in circumstances, style of living and general habits and civilisation to those of the more highly cultivated and faintly populated districts south of the grange. Their system of farming is much less advanced, their farming implements of less improved description; their farms are also much smaller and their general appearance, as also that of their houses, indicative of an inferiority in neatness, comfort, affluence and ideas of economy.

With a few exceptions, their houses are 1-storey high and thatched, all built of stone and lime, and are generally roomy and substantial, consisting of from 2 to 4 but chiefly of 3 apartments, which are well lit, usually by leaden windows. They are pretty comfortable but at the same time evince but little regard for cleanliness or neatness, their approaches being generally obstructed by manure heaps or cesspools. Their outoffices are not kept in good order, and their gardens seldom contain any vegetables except potatoes, cabbages and leeks.

The farmers live chiefly upon potatoes, some salt or dried pork or beef, eggs, milk, butter and salt herrings. Oatmeal is much less frequently used than formerly, less meal being made and more raw corn being taken to market. Baker's bread, which is now hawked about the country in bread carts, is much more commonly used. Tea also is in more general use, owing to its being more easily procured, both as to price and the facility afforded by the numerous petty grocery shops throughout the country. By the farmers it is no longer looked on as a luxury, but is used at least once a day.

There is not much taste for acquiring knowledge or information among this class. They seem to prefer pursuing the same beaten track of their fathers to altering their habits or system of living by adopting any recent improvement, which they look on rather as an innovation and to which custom alone could reconcile them. In their circumstances they are rather comfortable than otherwise. The district being rather retired, their wants are but few and easily supplied, and they are not exposed to the temptation of purchasing what to those in the neighbourhood of towns and villages would appear but necessaries, but which to themselves in their present state are little thought of and would be considered superfluities or luxuries.

With the exception of being prone to whiskey drinking, they are rather a moral class, that is, there is no actual crime or outrage, there is not much profligacy and they are rather punctual in fulfilling their engagements; but at the same time they are avaricious and fond of litigation.

Labourers

Under this head may be included the cottiers and poor tenants along the bogs and who, holding at the most not more than 2 or 3 acres, are obliged to seek employment to obtain a support. These families jointly amount to about 100 which, when contrasted with the number that employ labourers (32), is a large proportion; and now that the females cannot earn anything by spinning, and that almost all these are dependent solely on the agricultural employment they may receive, it may be inferred that their comforts are but few. Those in the neighbourhood of the bogs are in most respects better off than the cottiers in the higher grounds. The former, besides having fuel for the trouble of cutting it, can also in spring and summer obtain pretty regular employment in cutting and preparing turf for the neighbouring farmers, while with those in the higher grounds at the east side of the grange, fuel is scarce and dear, and employment much less constant. Still, the latter live quite as well and much more comfortable, cleanly and regular in their circumstances and habits than the former, who are in general slovenly, dirty and comfortless in their abodes, their persons and their habits.

Except along the western side of the grange the cottages are all built of stone and lime, thatched, pretty substantial, dry and warm. They usually consist of 2, but frequently of but 1 small apartment, each of which receives light by a small lead window. The smoke finds its exit alternately by a wide chimney and the door. The floors are of clay and generally damp, and the doorway is approached generally by a narrow causeway extending between the house and a range of cesspools in front of it. The furniture is but scanty and many cottages cannot boast of more than a single bed.

In the eastern side of the grange the cottages are of a much better description, more cleanly and roomy than in the west. This is chiefly owing to the inhabitants of the former having been more generally engaged in the manufacture of linen than in agriculture. In the western side of the grange the cabins are less cleanly and comfortable, of smaller size and not so dry or warm. There are a few miserable sod huts tenanted by families supported by charity. Their distance from lime renders that article scarce and dear. It is therefore but rarely used either in ornamenting the exterior or in cleansing and purifying the interior of their dwellings, and in many instances they want merely the outward appearance of neatness which it can give and which in reality they may possess.

The quantity of vegetables consumed by this class is, with the exception of potatoes which constitute their almost entire support, but trifling. Their little gardens contain, besides potatoes, seldom more than a few cabbages or curled kale. Potatoes with salt herrings and some milk, which, owing to the extent of pasture, is rather more plentiful, constitute their food. Very little animal food is consumed by them.

They are in general industrious and peaceable, but prone to whiskey drinking, and when intoxicated are quarrelsome and unruly, evincing a great deal of obstinacy and bad temper, without any of their redeeming spirit for fun and mirth so characteristic of the Irish. There is also much profligacy among them. There had been much party spirit and some party quarrels had taken place among the inhabitants of this and the neighbouring districts, but these have almost wholly subsided. They are otherwise amenable to the laws and nowhere is life or property in greater security.

All classes are civil and obliging, but at the same time they are neither frank nor communicative, and their disagreeable Scottish manners would, to a stranger, stamp them as rude and uncourteous, when in reality they may mean to be otherwise.

In the eastern side of the grange their habits and ideas are Scottish and their accent peculiarly so, while in the western side of the grange their manners partake somewhat of the Irish character and their dialect and accent are much less strong.

Fuel

Turf is their only fuel. Along the western side of this grange it is convenient and abundant, while along its eastern side, owing to its distance, it is with the cottiers, who have no means of conveying it, rather a scarce article.

Dress

The people, though comfortably clad, do not dress with nearly so much taste as in the southerly and northerly districts, and it is worthy of remark that the Roman Catholics do not dress either so well or so neatly as the members of the other persuasions. For instance, the women do not so generally wear bonnets and their clothes, as also those of the men, are neither so well made nor of so good a quality. On Sundays and at fairs and markets all the women wear shoes and stockings and the appearance of all classes is respectable.

Longevity and Marriage

The people are rather long lived than otherwise, and persons of from 70 to 80 are to be found in almost every townland. The family of McKeighan are remarkable for being long lived: one of them nearly 100 years of age is at present living in the grange. There are 2 women, one named McKenna and another, her sister, named Madden, who are each nearly 90 years old. There have not within memory been any instances of early marriage, nor do the people marry very early.

Amusements

Their amusements, which formerly consisted of cock-fighting and dancing, are now nearly given up. The former has not been practised for some years and the latter is now of rare occurrence. Attending one or two of the summer fairs may now be considered as their only amusement. Their traditions are fabulous and unworthy of notice, as they relate only to enchantments, fairies and banshees, in which most of the lower class have an implicit faith. They are as equally superstitious as the people of the surrounding districts.

Emigration and Migration

Emigration, as will be seen by reference to appendix, is carried to but a trifling extent, only 9 individuals having emigrated during the last 3 years. Of these, 6 went to New York and 3 to Glasgow. None have returned. 3 individuals, young unmarried men, annually go to the Scottish harvests and return in time for those in this country.

Remarkable Events

There is not any record or tradition of this grange having been the scene of any remarkable event, nor of its having given birth to any remarkable person.

ANCIENT TOPOGRAPHY

Ecclesiastical: Burial Ground

The grange of Shilvodan is said to have formed a portion of the mensal lands of the celebrated abbey of Connor in the adjacent parish of the same name. Connor was in early ages a city, the residence of the bishop of the see to which it gave its name, the site of the cathedral and also of several extensive religious houses and a castle, of which there are now but trifling remains; and the city has now dwindled into one of the most insignificant and uninteresting villages in the county.

The grange is episcopally united to the adjoining parish of Connor, the parish of Killagan and the granges of Killyglen and Solar, the two latter situated at a considerable distance, on the coast, and the parish of Killagan near the centre of the county. They form the prebend of Connor. There is not the slightest trace of any ecclesiastical building or burial ground in the grange.

In the townland of Tavnaghmore there is a circular vault 75 feet in diameter and but slightly raised, in which unbaptised children and "desolate persons" had, until within a few years, been interred. There are not any gravestones and but a few graves. This place as a burial ground has no pretensions to antiquity.

Military: O'Neill Mansion

There are not any military remains in the grange. The ruins of an ancient and spacious mansion of one of the families of the O'Neills are still to be seen in the townland of Tavnaghmore. This edifice was nothing more than a spacious family mansion consisting of 3 floors with a cellar, rather massively constructed, but without any pretensions to being termed military. It is now almost in total ruin and is inhabited by a few indigent individuals.

Pagan: Forts

The only remains of pagan antiquities in the grange are forts and coves. There are 15 forts or raths and 1 circular mound or tumulus. 12 of the forts are quite circular, 2 of them are nearly so and 1 of them is square. They are also constructed of earth. They generally, though not invariably, occupy elevated positions, but more frequently so than in any of the neighbouring districts. There is not anything relating to them worthy of further notice, and their dimensions and forms will perhaps be more clearly understood by referring to the plans in the appendix.

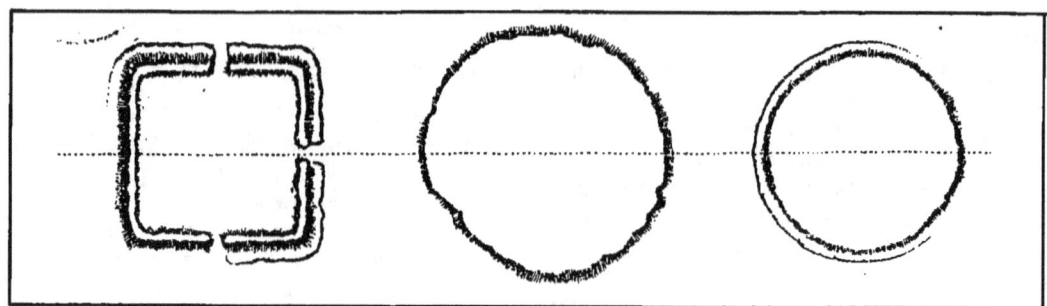

Forts from Lisnevenagh

The mound (see appendix) appears to be constructed solely of earth. Its form is hemispherical and its dimensions 9 feet high and 78 feet in diameter at the base. It is encompassed by a ditch 10 feet wide and 4 feet deep. Its position, in the townland of Eskylane near the north east side of the grange, 492 feet above the sea, is elevated and one of the most conspicuous in the grange. Most of these structures have been more or less mutilated and a superstitious dread of the usual consequences alone prevents the destruction or cultivation of many of them.

Coves

There are 7 coves in the grange, the sites of which are precisely known, either from their being partly open or from their having been recently closed, owing to their having interfered with the operations of the farmer, but none of them are in their present state accessible. There are coves in the townland of Eskylane which are open, but their entrances are obstructed by the lodgement of a quantity of water. There is one in the townland of Tavnaghmore which might with some trouble be entered, but the others could not without some considerable difficulty be entered. No discoveries of any kind have been made in any of these forts, though have all at some period within memory be[en] entered.

Coins

Silver coins of various reigns and copper coins of the reign of Charles II (bearing the thistle) are frequently picked up in the fields throughout the grange. The most prevalent silver coins are those of the reign of Elizabeth. Those of the Henrys and Edward III are also sometimes found. It is said that a great many silver coins have from time to time been found about the old residence of the O'Neills before alluded to, but of these not one is now in the country, as they all found their way into the hands of the watchmakers in the country towns and, by them, are sold as old silver in Belfast.

Weapons

The weapons shown in the appendix have, with many similar, been found in the grange, as have also flint arrow[s] of several stages or varieties of workmanship, stone hatchets, brass pins and fibulae, but none of these are now forthcoming.

Appendix to Memoir

SOCIAL ECONOMY

Names

The following are the names most commonly to [be met with ?] in the grange of Shilvodan: McKeighan, McKenna, McKeown, Madigan (commonly pronounced Madden), McQuillan, Hannan, O'Neill and Gorman, which seem to be of Irish descent; and Redmond, Brownlees, Orr, Cameron, Marshall, McNeely, Forbes, Ward and Canning, which are apparently of Scottish descent. There are not any peculiar Christian names nor any which are not [to] be commonly met with in the neighbouring districts.

Education

[Table contains the following headings: name, situation and description, when established, income and expenditure, physical, intellectual and moral instruction, number of pupils subdivided by age, sex and religion, name and religion of master or mistress, date on which visited].

National school, in a suitable and excellent

Grange of Shilvodan

house measuring 34 by 28 feet, built for the purpose partly by the Board of National Education and partly at the expense of the Reverend Daniel Curoe P.P., the total being 120 pounds; situated in the townland of Tavnaghmore, established 1832; income: from the Board of National Education 10 pounds annually, 20 pounds from pupils; expenditure on salaries 30 pounds; intellectual instruction: books and cards of the Board of National Education, reading and writing, English grammar, mensuration, book-keeping, geography; moral instruction: visited by the parish priest, all versions of the Scriptures read at stated hours, catechism taught on Saturdays; number of pupils: males, 19 under 10 years of age, 15 from 10 to 15, 6 over 15, total 40; females, 14 under 10 years of age, 11 from 10 to 15, 5 over 15, total 30; total number of pupils 70, 2 Established Church, 15 Presbyterians, 53 Roman Catholics; master James Ward, Roman Catholic; visited 10th August 1838.

Sunday Schools

[Table contains the following headings: situation and description, when established, number of teachers, superintendence, number of scholars subdivided by religion and sex, instruction, hours of attendance, remarks].

Held in the national schoolhouse in the townland of Tavnaghmore, established 1832; 5 male and 6 female teachers, total 11; under the patronage of the Reverend Daniel Curoe; James Ward, teacher of the day school, superintends; number of scholars: 46 Presbyterians, 138 Roman Catholics, 91 males, 93 females, total 184, 53 exclusively Sunday school scholars; instruction: spelling and reading in the books of the Board of National Education, their respective catechisms; hours of attendance from 3 until 5 o'clock p.m.; this school is increasing.

Emigration

[Table contains the following headings: age, capital, occupation, religion and sex].

1835: 1 under 10 years, 1 under 20 and over 10 years, 2 under 40 and over 20 years; 1 with over 50 pounds capital, 1 with over 10 and under 20 pounds capital, 2 with under 10 pounds capital; 2 labourers, 2 others, 2 Protestants, 2 Roman Catholics, 4 males, total 4.

1836: 1 under 40 and over 20 years, labourer, with less than 10 pounds capital, Protestant, male, total 1.

1837: 2 under 10 years, 2 over 40 years; 4 with less than 10 pounds capital; 2 labourers, 2 others, 4 Roman Catholics, 2 males, 2 females, total 4.

ANCIENT TOPOGRAPHY

Drawings by James Boyle

Plans and section of 5 forts in townland of Eskylane and 4 in townland of Tavnaghmore, scale 1 inch to 80 feet.

Plans and sections of 7 forts in townland of Lisnevenagh.

Brazen instruments: decorated pin brooch [fibula], decorated pin, pin, spearhead and axehead.

Fair Sheets by John Bleakly, May 1838

MEMOIR WRITING

Memoir Writing

Commenced 1st May 1838, completed 2nd May 1838, 12 hours employed [signed] John Bleakly. Forwarded to Lieutenant Bennett, Royal Engineers, 26th August 1838 [signed] James Boyle.

SOCIAL ECONOMY

Emigration and Migration

List of persons who have emigrated from the grange of Shilvodan during the years 1835, 1836 and 1837. [Table gives name, age, religion, townland, port of destination].

1835: Thomas Duff, 15, Presbyterian, from Tannaghmore to New York.

John Redmond, 30, Presbyterian, from Lisnevanagh to New York.

1837: Patrick Smith, 40, Martha Smith, 40, Michael Smith, 4, Ellen Jane Smith, 2, Roman Catholics, from Tannaghmore to Glasgow.

Charles Kelly, 26, Roman Catholic, from Tannaghmore to New York.

Migration: John McKenna, 25, James McKenna, 28, Patrick McKenna, 38, Roman Catholics, from Tannaghmore to Glasgow.

MODERN TOPOGRAPHY

Roman Catholic Chapel

The Roman Catholic chapel in the grange of

Shilvodan, and townland of Tannaghmore, measures externally 61 and a half feet by 32 feet, no gallery or pews but a few temporary seats. Built 1830 and cost 300 pounds, contains 300 persons. The average collection at the above chapel on each Sunday amounts to 3s per [week].

Schoolhouse

The national schoolhouse at the chapel measures externally 34 by 28 feet, slated. Information obtained from Revd Daniel Curoe, parish priest.

ANCIENT TOPOGRAPHY

Burial Ground

There is an old keille or burial ground like a fort, 75 feet in diameter, but part destroyed, on the farm John Heron. It is on the road leading from Randalstown to the Roman Catholic chapel. No gravestones; nothing but stillborn children or desolate persons are buried here.

Coves

There is a cove on Betty Rodman's farm, townland Eskylane, but water at the mouth, i.e. a spring well; also a cove on Widow <Widdow> Cromie's farm, same townland; cove on Paul McKenna's farm, closed up. [Signed] J. Bleakly, 2nd May 1838.

Description of Church at Rattass

Name

This is the place called Rath-muighe-deiscirt by the ancient Irish writers. Its ancient name signifies the "fort of the southern plain"; deiscirt "southern" having been added to distinguish this from Rath-muighe-tuaiscirt, now Rattoo, on the River Casan. Their names are now corrupted or rather shortened to [blank] "the southern rath" and "the northern rath."

Church

This church consists of a nave and choir, the nave measuring on the inside 31 feet 6 inches in length and 19 feet 6 inches in width, and the choir 17 feet 6 inches by 14 feet 10 inches; and the walls of the nave are 3 feet 1 inch in thickness and about 12 feet in greatest height and built of large blocks of red freestone laid in regular courses. The stones of the walls of the choir are not so large as those of the walls of the nave, but they are remarkably large and well laid. The quoin-stones are all chiselled. The east and west gables and the greater part of the north wall remains in good preservation, but there is a breach of 10 feet on the south wall of the nave and the south wall of the choir is destroyed except 3 feet of its height, and the middle gable and choir arch (which was no doubt a very beautiful one) are entirely destroyed.

The east window is nearly destroyed on the outside and its top is destroyed on the inside, where it measures 6 feet to the springing of the arch and 4 feet 3 inches in width. It was 3 feet 6 inches in height on the outside, where its width cannot be determined as its sides are destroyed. It was formed of chiselled freestone, each block extending the entire thickness of the wall. The doorway, as usual in churches of this antiquity, is in the middle of the west gable and now stopped up on the inside with rude mason work. It is of quadrangular form and its sides slope in a remarkable manner.

This doorway is formed of large blocks of cut freestone. It is 5 feet 3 inches from the present level of the ground to the lintel and in width 2 feet 8 inches at top and 3 feet 1 inch at the bottom. The lowest stone on the north side is 2 feet 5 inches high, 1 foot 7 inches wide, and enters the wall 2 feet. The next over this is 2 feet 1 inch high, 1 foot 10 inch wide and enters the wall 2 feet 2 inches. The third is 7 inches high, 5 and a half inches wide and enters the wall 1 foot 4 inches. The lintel is 7 feet 6 inches long, 2 feet high at the north end and 1 foot 10 inch at the south, and extends, I think, through the entire thickness of the wall.

What an immense block! The lowest stone on the south side is 1 foot 9 inches high, 1 foot 9 inches wide and enters the wall 1 foot 3 inches. The next is 1 foot 3 inches high, 1 foot 2 inches wide and enters the wall 2 feet. The next over this is 1 foot high, 1 foot 8 inches wide and enters the wall 2 feet 4 inches. The one next the lintel is 1 foot 1 inch high, 1 foot 5 inches wide and enters the wall 2 feet 3 inches. There are 2 small pillars 1 foot 8 inches in depth at the 2 corners of the gable, like those in the cathedral of Glendalough.

This is undoubtedly an erection of the primitive age of the Irish church, though Dr Smith does not say a word as to its antiquity. It stands in a graveyard in which there are many respectable tombs of modern date, but none worth description for age or magnificence.

www.ingramcontent.com/pod-product-compliance
Lightning Source LLC
Chambersburg PA
CBHW051212290426
44109CB00021B/2423